*Introduction
to the art of the*
MOVIES

INTRODUCTION TO THE ART OF

THE

MOVIES

An anthology

of ideas on the nature of movie art

selected, arranged and introduced

by

LEWIS JACOBS

The Noonday Press

New York

Acknowledgment

1097449

I wish to thank the following authors and publishers for their kind permission to reprint the selections included in this anthology: Hollis Alpert, Alexander Bakshy, Le Comte E. de Beaumont, Cedric Belfrage, Ralph Block, Kirk Bond, James E. Davis, Maya Deren, Sergei Eisenstein, Evelyn Gerstein, Mrs. Marcus Goldman, Paul Goodman, Henry Hart, Dorothy Jones, Siegfried Kracauer, Fernand Leger, Meyer Levin, Andre Levinson, Jay Leyda, Mrs. Vachel Lindsay, Dwight Macdonald, Kenneth MacGowan, Henry MacMahon, Dudley Nichols, Hans Richter, Herman G. Scheffauer, Gilbert Seldes, Andre Sennwald, Seymour Stern, James Johnson Sweeney, Slavko Vorkapich, Richard Watts Jr., Herman Weinberg, Amkino Corp., Dial Publishers, *Film Culture, Films in Review* (National Board of Review), *The Freeman, Little Review*, Macmillan Co., Museum of Modern Art Film Library, *National Board of Review Magazine*, New Directions, *The New York Herald Tribune, The New York Times, The Quarterly of Film, Radio and Television* (*Film Quarterly*), *The Saturday Review*, Theatre Arts Monthly, and the *Theatre Guild Magazine*.

I am especially grateful to my wife.

CONTENTS

PREFACE xi

INTRODUCTION/MOVIES: THE DIRECTOR'S ART/*Lewis Jacobs* 3

1 9 1 0 - 1 9 2 0

THE DRAMA OF THE PEOPLE/*The New York Independent* 41

THE BIRTH OF A NEW ART/*The Independent* 44

THE ART OF THE MOVIES/*Henry MacMahon* 47

THE PICTURE OF CROWD SPLENDOR/*Vachel Lindsay* 51

THE CINEMATOGRAPH AS ART/*Alexander Bakshy* 57

ON THE SCREEN/*Kenneth MacGowan* 70

THE VIVIFYING OF SPACE/*Herman G. Scheffauer* 76

1 9 2 0 - 1 9 3 0

ERICH VON STROHEIM/*Herman G. Weinberg* 89

A NEW REALISM—THE OBJECT/*Fernand Léger* 96

OF WHAT ARE THE YOUNG FILMS DREAMING?/*Le Comte
    E. de Beaumont* 99

NOT THEATER, NOT LITERATURE, NOT PAINTING/*Ralph Block* 101

SUNRISE: A MURNAU MASTERPIECE/*Dorothy B. Jones* 107

A DYING ART OFFERS A MASTERPIECE/*Richard Watts, Jr.* 130

RUSSIA'S FILM WIZARD/*Evelyn Gerstein* 134

THE WORK OF PUDOVKIN/*Jay Leyda* 140

THE NATURE OF THE CINEMA/*Andre Levinson* 145

GRIFFITH: PIONEER OF THE FILM ART/*Seymour Stern* 153

1 9 3 0 - 1 9 4 0

EISENSTEIN ON SOUND/*Sergei Eisenstein* 163

THE FUTURE CINEMA: NOTES FOR A STUDY/*Harry Alan Potamkin* 165

DISNEY AND OTHERS/*Gilbert Seldes* 170

LÉGER AND CINESTHETIC/*James Johnson Sweeney* 173

NOTES ON HOLLYWOOD DIRECTORS/*Dwight Macdonald* 177

FORMAL CINEMA/*Kirk Bond* 209

WHAT IS A MOTION PICTURE?/*James Shelley Hamilton* 217

JEAN VIGO/*Siegfried Kracauer* 223

PRELIMINARY TOPICS IN DEFINING CINEMA/*Paul Goodman* 227

THE FUTURE OF COLOR/*Andre Sennwald* 232

1 9 4 0 - 1 9 6 0

TUESDAY BROWN/*Meyer Levin* 239

ORSON WELLES' CITIZEN KANE/*Cedric Belfrage* 247

CINEMA AS AN ART FORM/*Maya Deren* 253

DEATH OF A CRITIC/*Dudley Nichols* 266

RASHOMON/*Henry Hart* 273

THE ONLY DYNAMIC ART/*James E. Davis* 277

THE FILM AS AN ORIGINAL ART FORM/*Hans Richter* 282

TOWARD TRUE CINEMA/*Slavko Vorkapich* 288

THE OTHER BERGMAN/*Hollis Alpert* 296

NOTES ON THE CONTRIBUTORS 301

PREFACE

The central idea of this book is to explore the nature of motion picture art through a series of essays written over the past fifty years. All the material is of a formalist bias in that it calls attention to the different ways in which film expression can be creative. There is also a persistent reiteration, not accidental, of the differences in technique and structure between movies and theater, and a stress upon movie values, principles and doctrines.

In selecting the articles, I have limited myself to material in American publications. Much of it was scattered in magazines of passing interest, in the main neglected by periodical indexes. Many originated in fugitive, obscure and out of print journals no longer available, some had to be borrowed from the files of individuals. The majority are entirely unknown to the present day generation of film enthusiasts. Together in a permanent book form, they serve to clarify moot artistic issues.

Because this is a retrospective collection, many of the essays were chosen aside from their intrinsic value for their suitability to a broad survey of the movies' creative growth. For this reason they are presented in a chronological format from 1910 to the present day. This arrangement in depth, so to speak, sets the essays in a more meaningful context. In looking back the historical interest is satisfied and in such a way as to seemingly set the course for the progress of film art itself. The arrangement further reveals what was significant in its own period and so provides a dimension of relationship and experience not obtainable otherwise.

It is my hope that this book will provide some answers to the many questions of film goers interested in the art of movies, and, more important, provoke new ones.

New York N.Y., October 1959   LEWIS JACOBS

Introduction
to the art of the
MOVIES

INTRODUCTION
MOVIES: *THE DIRECTOR'S ART*

Lewis Jacobs

Out of thousands of directors who have made tens of thousands of motion pictures in the past sixty years, a relatively small number stand out for their contributions to the development and progress of film art. These men in their efforts to become more expressive, discovered the special characteristics of their medium, extended the limits of technique and propelled the movies into deeper and more original forms of composition. The constant stimulus to treat material more fully heightened their techniques, deepened their compositions. The additions of technological improvements and new inventions which extended the medium's boundaries and powers, enabled them to further refine cinematic expression and achieve a synthesis of psychological depth and polished style. Given a crude novelty, they forged it into a vital medium of esthetic power with its own idiom, canons and standards, and a body of indigenous creative traditions.

Viewing the work of these men as a whole, one is struck by their uniqueness and freshness, their superior technical and formal excellences. Their pictures represent a variety of styles, techniques and philosophies, yet they reflect one constant aim: to present a world governed by the laws of their own personality in terms of the motion picture medium. Each director, in his own way and in his own day, created the best that movies had so far produced. Collectively their work helped create the art of movies, contributed to its esthetic heritage and turned world attention to the importance of movies as a cultural force.

I: *DECADES OF DISCOVERY*

During the first two decades of its existence, movies advanced from a scientific curiosity to an art with its own character and personality through the pioneering efforts of three men, George Melies, Edwin S. Porter, and D. W. Griffith. These directors introduced innovations which widened the movies' range, extended its resources, sharpened its tools and techniques and established a form of composition indigenous to film expression. Within twenty years their contributions came to a dazzling climax in the production of two extraordinary movies by D. W. Griffith that marked a milestone in screen creativity and still remain unsurpassed achievements of American film art.

In 1900 when the movies were still a commercial novelty limited to a minute or two in length, they were suddenly given a fresh direction in France by George Melies. As a former magician he was greatly excited by the camera's ability to create "supernatural" effects. He turned the lens away from mere recording of "true-life-action" to fantasy and introduced elements from the theater: costuming, setting, professional actors, and used literature as subject matter. In doing this he discovered numerous visual effects based on the camera's devices that had never been seen before. In his hands the camera became a magical instrument capable of astounding trickery.

The prime aim of Melies was to mystify. *The Vanishing Lady, The Haunted Castle, The Laboratory of Mephistopheles, Cagliostro's Mirror, The Bewitched Inn, The Devil in the Convent,* and many other pictures made by 1902, showed people disappearing, cut in half, flying through the air, apparitions taking horrible shapes, animals turned into humans and humans turned into animals. They were achieved by camera effects that only Melies had mastered: double exposures, masks, stop motion, reverse shooting, fast and slow motion, animation, fades and dissolves. These effects were not to become absorbed into general film technique until years later.

As Melies' skill with the camera developed, he undertook more ambitious enterprises. From single scene pictures, he progressed to movies of many scenes. Obvious as this seems today, no one had thought or dared it before. Melies staged scenes and photographed them in a continuity that related a story with a beginning, a middle and an end. He christened his new method, "artificially arranged scenes." *Cinderella, Joan of Arc, A Trip to the Moon, Gulliver's Travels, The Impossible Voyage* and hundreds of others made between 1902 and 1905, were full of theatrical tableaux, lavish costuming, spectacular settings, and elaborate camera effects, sometimes containing as many as thirty scenes selected and staged especially for the camera, and lasting for what was then a long time—eight to twelve minutes.

"Artificially arranged scenes," in addition to increasing the scope of movies, introduced a fresh concept: that of composition or film continuity. Heretofore movies had been an unselective process. They now became a creative enterprise involving planning, selection, direction, organization and the fusing of raw material and medium to produce a desired effect. A vast world of new subject-matter in stories, either taken from literature or "originals," readily came within the movies' reach.

But within a short time Melies' innovations were overshadowed by another, more revolutionary technique. Not content with the Frenchman's method of "artificially arranged scenes" which divided a movie into a series of completed scenes, Edwin S. Porter, in America, broke down the scenes into smaller components of shots. Each shot was an incomplete unit which had to be combined with other shots and arranged in a specific order for the scene's idea or action to be fully understood. The shot served as the smallest significant unit of composition. This process of selecting, combining and arranging shots, now known as editing, set the movies upon a new course fundamental to its own structure.

The Life of an American Fireman and *The Great Train Robbery* (1903-1904) were Porter's first dramatic story films utilizing his unique editing technique. One told of a last minute rescue of a woman and child from a burning building; the other, of a daring holdup, chase, and last minute capture of train robbers. Primitive classics for which Porter is remembered today, these pictures were the most successful and influential of their day. They initiated a vigorous style of movement and melodrama that captivated the American people and set into motion the industry's first boom.

In these pictures Porter showed that motion picture expression grew out of the relationship of shots and that the shot was a more basic organizational element of film structure than the scene. This discovery immediately distinguished movie technique from stage technique and introduced editing as the most important structural concept of movie making.

In the pictures that followed, Porter extended the editing technique from a straightforward application to one of comparison. The *Ex Convict* (1905) used editing to contrast the poverty stricken home of his protagonist with the luxurious household of a millionaire who refused him work. *The Kleptomaniac*, a later film and one of his more interesting achievements employed parallelism to relate two stories and provide a final ironic comment. Two women, one poor, the other rich, are caught shoplifting and arrested. The rich woman is freed, the other jailed. The movie ends with a figure of Justice, blindfolded, holding a scale on one side of which is a bag of gold, on the other a loaf of bread. The balance slowly tilts in favor of the gold. Then the bandage over the eyes of Justice is removed, revealing only one glittering eye fixed on the gold. The story's effectiveness depended on the paralleling of the two stories.

Although Porter continued to make movies for many years, he never developed nor deepened his editing concepts. Today acknowledged as the father of the story film, his contributions were more than narrative. His discovery of the film's ability to be cut and joined for narrative and dramatic purposes introduced editing as the form of composition peculiar to the screen medium. Editing pointed the way by which the latent powers of the movie could be released and appeal to the minds of an audience as well as to its emotions. Now a series of pictures or shots could communicate ideas, arouse and guide feelings and become esthetically meaningful. This concept of editing is still fundamental to screen art and has not been essentially altered to this day.

By 1908, the story film predominated movie making. It was at this time that David Wark Griffith emerged. He brought to bear an energy, ambition, imagination, boldness and inventiveness that made him a major figure in the development of the movies as an art.

A former actor and playwright, Griffith saw from the beginning the need to develop a body of technique that would permit a movie maker a fuller means of expression so that he could render a story more adroitly, develop the characters more fully, and handle deeper subject matter. Boldly he stepped into many new experiments in composition and structure and within six years almost single handedly opened up a rich reservoir of movie rhetoric. Working continuously, he made hundreds of short pictures, progressing from one and two reelers to four reelers and finally to those two feature productions for which he is renowned today and which marked his heights as a creative artist.

Griffith was the first to change the camera position in the middle of a scene and move it closer to the actors for greater clarity, and so established the medium and close shot. The close-up particularly proved to be one of the most valuable attributes of motion picture technique. By making it the natural complement of the full and medium shots, he created a new means of screen emphasis that had never existed before.

He also steadily increased the capacity of the camera for psychological, dramatic and poetic effects; developed a number of ways to make shots more expressive by panning, tilting, vignetting, by using a soft focus or the moving camera. Such narrative devices as the cut, dissolve, the fade and iris, he sharpened and deepened into potent connectives for structural relationships.

But even more important than these devices which enriched technique, was his contribution to structure through innovations in editing. He was the first to control the duration and length of a shot—its screen time—for dramatic effect. Until now, the duration of a shot had been governed by the time its action took in real life. Griffith established the idea that the duration of a shot need not depend upon its natural action at all, but could be shortened or lengthened at will to heighten or lessen the dramatic impact. Utilizing this principle he was able to create excitement and build suspense by deliberately prolonging the action of scenes, and cutting from one to another in ever shortening intervals, the effect of which heightened the climax so that when it was finally reached, the relief was all the more pronounced. He saw too, that in the manipulation of a shot's length, lay its power to generate tempo and movement, two powerful forces in the dynamics of a movie's rhythm.

Another contribution of Griffith, "the switch-back," freed the movie from its dependence upon a rigid chronology of time and space. Heretofore, two actions happening at different places, at the same time or at different times, had to be rendered by resorting to the primitive method of double exposure, using "dream balloons." The switch-back enabled the director to disregard strict temporal and spacial requirements and cut freely from scene to scene before either was completed.

The switch-back so greatly extended the director's editing power, it was immediately seized upon by the industry as a whole and became one of the screen's most potent structural devices.

The climax of Griffith's creative efforts were two masterworks, *The Birth of a Nation* (1915), and *Intolerance* (1916). High points in the progress of motion picture art, they far surpassed any others of their day in structure, imaginative power and depth of content. They foreshadowed the best that was to come in movies and earned for the medium its right to the status of an art.

The Birth of a Nation was based on two books, *The Clansman* and *The Leopard's Spots*, by Thomas Dixon, supplemented by material from the recollections of Griffith's father, a former Confederate Colonel. The film told the story of two friendly families, the Stoneman from Pennsylvania and the Cameron of South Carolina, who fight on opposite sides during the Civil War. In the aftermath of Reconstruction, however, they unite to oust the carpetbaggers from political power in the South.

The film's production was the most ambitious in scale and size of its day and, even compared to current standards, was a gigantic enterprise. Everything Griffith possessed—his reputation, his personal fortune, whatever money he could raise from friends—was poured into it. He was besieged by mounting debts, hounded by creditors, and discouraged by associates—an unbroken series of desperate financial difficulties and day-to-day borrowings, marked the making of this picture. The result was the longest American movie yet made—twelve reels, two hours in length, "a frightful waste and audacious monstrosity."

The Birth of a Nation opened in New York on March 3rd 1915, to phenomenal acclaim. It was the first movie to be honored by a showing at the White House. President Wilson is said to have remarked, "It is like writing history with lightning." Critics hailed the picture as a new milestone in film artistry that challenged the theater's supremacy.

Rich in imagery, deeply meaningful in social content, and powerful in construction, all Griffith's earlier creative efforts were here consolidated—magnificent camera devices, and highly calculated editing schemes—in a brilliant variety and emotional range.

The film pulsated with life. From the very beginning, shots were merged into a flux. Either the action within the shots had some kind of movement or the duration of the shots were so timed that the effect was one of continuous motion. This motion created a "beat," an internal pulse which underlay the relationships of the separate sequences of the film and produced a powerful rhythmic effect.

This undercurrent of movement had a remarkable variety, partly because of the nature of the material and partly because of the extensive and resourceful use of the motion picture's plastic elements. The battle scenes, basically all action, were broken down by Griffith into juxtaposed long, medium, close, and detailed shots, varied in duration and contrasting in composition, to provoke the excitement of battle itself. A group of soldiers swarming across the left side of the screen was followed by a group crossing at the right, so that the feeling of conflict was intensified. Often the contrast of numbers was brought into play; shots of individual soldiers were opposed to shots of many soldiers. There was also opposition of space relationships, as in scenes in which an extreme vista shot was followed by a cameo-like close-up. Finally, there was the expressive opposition of a still shot of a dead soldier to the moving shot of a live one climbing the ramparts to place a flag in position. Throughout these scenes, Griffith ingeniously employed structural and dramatic oppositions to aid the picture's dynamic quality and to endow the picture with its rhythmic sweep.

The Reconstruction sequences rose to a masterly climax in the ride of the Clansmen. Here tension was heightened by staccato cutting, night photography, acute angles, juxtaposition of extreme long and close shots, sweeping pans, and the moving camera. The rhythm was cunningly interwoven by a brilliant cutting pattern made more effective by fast and uneven tempo which imparted a rising tide of excitement and created an acute sense of dramatic suspense.

The film's impressive structural devices were supplemented by one that has since become celebrated: the iris, used strikingly in the sequence of Sherman's march to the sea and the burning of Atlanta. In the upper left-hand corner of a black screen, a small iris disclosed the pitiful detail of a mother and three children huddled together in fear. Gradually the iris opened to reveal more of the scene, and when it was fully opened, we saw the reason for their fear: in the valley below an army of Northern invaders was marching through the town from which the woman had just fled. The scene was startling in its implications, the dramatic effect gripping, another instance of Griffith's sensitivity.

The Birth of a Nation propelled the film into a new artistic level. So rich and profound in organization was this picture that for years thereafter, it directly and indirectly influenced movie makers everywhere and became the wellspring of much subsequent artistic progress. However, its extreme Southern bias aroused a storm of protest. Negroes and whites united in attacking it. In Boston and other "abolitionist" cities, race riots broke out. President Charles E. Eliot of Harvard charged the movie "with a tendency to perversion of white ideals." Oswald Garrison Villard condemned it as "a deliberate attempt to humiliate ten million American citizens." The raging controversy awakened the nation to the social import of movies and propelled Griffith into the subject for his next enterprise.

Griffith displayed more ambition and desire for a greater work of art in *Intolerance*. This picture was thirteen reels long and contained four stories of intolerance in the history of man: the fall of Babylon, The Christ legend of Judea, the massacre of the Huguenots on St. Bartholomew's eve, and a modern story, originally called, *The Mother and the Law*. The whole was as Griffith himself stated, "a protest against despotism and injustice in every form."

Declared Griffith: "The stories will begin like four currents looked at from a hilltop. At first the four currents will flow apart, slowly and quietly. But as they flow, they grow nearer and nearer together, and faster and faster, until in the end, in the last act, they mingle in one mighty river of expressed emotion." To tie the stories together, Griffith resorted to a thematic symbol: the recurring image of a mother rocking a cradle, suggested by Walt Whitman's lines ". . . endlessly rocks the cradle, uniter of Here and Hereafter."

Of the four stories, the modern was the most carefully developed and dramatically motivated. It had the most meaning and, despite minor absurdities, is as telling today in its ironic denunciation of reformers and profiteers, as it was then.

The four stories culminated in a plea for tolerance: symbolic double exposures of angels, prison walls dissolving into open fields, children playing and kissing each other were shown, and as a finale, after a vast multiple exposure, there was a close shot of the recurrent symbolic image, the Mother rocking the Cradle of Humanity.

The commanding feature of *Intolerance* was its internal structure. The scheme of editing in *The Birth of a Nation* was simple compared to the complexity of *Intolerance*. The multiple stories were rendered in four major movements, all progressing simultaneously. The film cut freely from period to period as the theme of intolerance in each was developed. Every structural means at Griffith's disposal was employed. The moving camera paralleled and reinforced a movement within a shot, iris and masks were used to emphasize significant details or eloquently effect a transition, extreme detail close ups and extreme long shots produced effects of intensity and vastness. All these camera devices were brought into play to create a rich mosaic which flowed in unbroken and mounting suspense until the very end.

In the climactic sequences, particularly, Griffith's artistry was supreme. Here all the opulent details of the lavish scenes were subjected to an unceasing movement, action followed action, and with none terminating, the rhythm swept along, increasing in frequency as the four stories approached their climaxes. There was not an image, not a shot, that was not controlled, paced, and organically related. The screen became a visual symphony, swelling steadily until the final moment when all the movements were brought together in a grand finale.

As in its form, so in its details, *Intolerance* had impressive originality. Huge close-ups of faces, hands, objects, were used imaginatively and eloquently to comment, interpret, and deepen the import of a scene. Typical was the celebrated instance of the close-up of the anguished hands of Mae Marsh during the trial of her husband. In another scene the industrialist was shown alone in his office, composed to suggest the Lord of his domain, in an extreme long shot—an effect later imitated by Soviet directors to caricature a capitalist. The handling of the crowds as units in movement, for example in the firing of the militia, and in the notable Babylonian sequences, heightened the dramatic intensity of such episodes. The use of a painted, foreboding sky above the onrushing charioteers which introduced to film making the technique of the "process shot," not only gave these vast panoramic shots depth and massiveness but reinforced the sense of impending doom.

With admirable daring, Griffith altered the conventional screen shape to heighten the effect of his compositions. Sometimes he blacked out entire sections, leaving them blacked out for the duration of an entire scene played as a vignette on only one portion of the screen. Sometimes he would single out a significant action on a darkened screen by means of lighting, an iris or a mask, and then as the action progressed, the shot would open up into full frame size and shape. Rarely did he use the same shape twice in succession but contrasted them so that the eye of the spectator was kept moving.

This dramatic "framing" of the image throughout the picture was done with a variety and skill that has rarely been equalled. The screen was sliced down the center revealing only the middle (the great wall of Babylon), then opened out. The screen was cut across diagonally, sometimes from upper left to lower right, sometimes from upper right to lower left. Details were brought to our attention and yet kept part of the larger scene itself in a more precise way than the use of close-up insertions could afford. This movement and variety of screen shapes kept the image ever fresh and vital and heightened the momentum of the whole.

If the "framing" of the screen was remarkable, no less so was the fluid and active participation of the camera. Its physical capacities for movement and dramatic angle—generally conceded to be the original contributions of the post-war German craftsmen—must have been strained to the breaking point. Yet there was never a sense of striving for sheer mechanical wonder, but always a subordination of such capabilities to the subject and the point to be made. The unceasing use of the camera to drain everything that was significant out of the scene, was reinforced in no small measure by the overwhelming sense of lavishness and opulence of the settings. Spectacular was the remarkable "trucking" shot which travelled hundreds of feet without a pause or a cut, moving from an extreme distant view of ancient Babylon to a large close-up of the scene itself in all its grandeur. This shot, embracing immense sets, thousands of people and animals, was unprecedented and is still an amazing piece of camera bravura.

Shown publicly September 5th, 1916, *Intolerance* evoked mixed criticism. Many of the critics of the day could not follow the four stories from period to period, and were confused by the "interminable battle scenes" and the recurring "mother rocking her baby." They found the idea obtuse and the effects exhausting. Subsequent criticism has been increasingly favorable. The film has been called "a timeless masterpiece," "the end and justification of that whole school of American cinematography," (Richard Watts, Jr.).

Intolerance has thus been placed in its rightful position as an apex of American movie making, the consummation of everything that preceded it and a profound work, unique and in its own way still unsurpassed. Its influence has travelled around the world, touched directors deeply everywhere—a remarkable testament to Griffith's outstanding artistry, the source of inspiration and study for many of the great film works that were to follow.

Griffith himself was to continue making films in Hollywood for years to come but none that ever equalled these two major works. His contributions struck so closely at the essence of the medium that many correlative aspects were also deeply affected. Acting, setting, lighting, writing, these are some of the other fields where practitioners had to examine anew their craft in its role as an ally in motion pictures; and had to adapt and modify its means to express the will of the motion picture medium.

II: *EUROPEAN INFLUENCES*

The introduction of new refinements in technique and form were to come after World War I, largely from European directors in Germany, France and Russia. With Griffith, movies had acquired not only all the main fundamentals of technique and structure, but an artistic status that was now to be consciously cultivated. From 1920 to 1930, gifted new men set off in individual directions to gain a bolder, surer grasp of the medium. The movies of this era reflected strong, artistically ambitious personalities for whom creative expression, the problems of movie rendition, movie form, and in some cases, social criticism, were of paramount importance. The result was a body of films that displayed a new range and variety of original styles and brought in some of the most valuable contributions in the history of film art.

The dominant personality in American movies at this time—the immediate post-war years—was Erich von Stroheim. A former Viennese, he had been trained in Hollywood, where he had worked as an actor, as an assistant director, and as a writer. His movies, in contrast to Griffith's—his mentor—displayed such a penchant for uncompromising characterization and detail that he quickly won recognition as America's first motion picture realist. Actually he was the culmination of a line of realists that went back to Porter.

All of von Stroheim's pictures, with one exception, were concerned with amorous intrigue. A most serious director with a creative passion for movies, he treated his subjects with the utmost integrity, in a highly sophisticated, objective and ironic manner. *Blind Husbands* (1919), *The Devil's Passkey* (1919), *Foolish Wives* (1922), *Merry Go Round* (1923), *The Merry Widow* (1928), and *The Wedding March* (1928), were handled with a hard, unrelenting psychological honesty which was blunt, mocking and penetrating. Essentially European in outlook, these movies had a glamorous surface which concealed their serious tone and made them even more effective indictments.

The exception to this group was Stroheim's most significant achievement and the high watermark of American realism in its day: *Greed* (1923). This picture was characterized by a biting criticism and a deep antagonism for material values that more closely approximated his American influences and experience.

Greed was based on a highly realistic novel of American life, *McTeague*, by Frank Norris. Like the novel, the picture attempted to portray the banalities of lower class life and to condemn the hypocrisy that stemmed from Puritanism.

As an achievement of motion picture art, *Greed* was not as profound in structure as Griffith's *Birth of a Nation* or *Intolerance*.

Nevertheless it deserves a place beside these as a cinematic landmark. Stroheim's intense honesty and deep insight into human behavior was expressed in a style so objective in its imagery and meticulous in its detail that it can be regarded as the forerunner of the documentary form that typified Italian neo-realism at its best after World War II.

While making *Greed*, von Stroheim had announced his artistic credo: "It is possible to tell a great story in motion pictures in such a way that the spectator will come to believe that what he looks at is real."

The picture's realism carried out Stroheim's intentions. Its naturalism and objectivity was so pronounced that it had the effect of an actual newsreel. The dingy wallpaper, the dirty dishes, the unmade bed, the prominent player piano, the full sink, built up the sordid atmosphere. The mining sequences, and the marriage ceremony and feast were documentary in their realistic re-creation of a cross section of life in that particular milieu.

That Stroheim had been a careful student of Griffith was evidenced throughout the film in the use of close ups, detail shots, camera angles, dramatic lighting, compositions, the use of the iris and mask. He also had qualities of his own as a profound observer of external action and in his flair for the pertinent detail to make an ironic comment. During the wedding of Trina and Mac, a funeral procession was seen through the window while the bride murmured, "I do." Later when Mac murdered Trina, a piece of Christmas tinsel hanging in the room provided a sardonic comment. The final sequence in the desert with the two men handcuffed to each other, dying of thirst under a blazing sun, tiny and insignificant in the vast space which encompassed them, was not only a superb visual finale but an eloquent comment on the picture's theme of avarice.

In its original form, *Greed* was said to have been forty-two reels long, lasting almost eight hours. It was cut to ten reels by the studio without Stroheim's agreement. "When I saw how the censors mutilated my picture, *Greed*," said von Stroheim in an interview, "I abandoned all my ideals to create real art pictures . . ."

Greed left in its wake fabulous tales of Stroheim's personality and his method of work, his strong will power, his steadfastness, his thoroughness, all of which suggested his urgent sincerity and his intense desire to make pictures as he believed they should be. Von Stroheim's was an original talent, undisciplined in some ways, but uncompromising, genuine, and penetrating. *Greed* was unique, a vital high point, valid to this day.

Meanwhile, new directors with new ideas, in Germany, France, and Russia, were making pictures that introduced dazzling new developments in technical refinements, camera craft, and editing concepts. They marked a period, so brilliant in the history of the screen, it became known as the "golden era."

One of the pictures of this group, and the first to appear in the United States, was *The Cabinet of Dr. Caligari*, which was produced in Germany in 1919, directed by Robert Wiene. Distributed here in 1921, this film was actually seen by comparatively few, but it was so unusual that it provoked more discussion than any other picture of its day.

In *Caligari* Wiene presented a new kind of fantasy, the first of its kind in motion pictures, a subjective fantasy of the mind. With the collaboration of two artists, Walter Reimann and Herman Warm who, like Wiene, were interested in "expressionism" and the Freudian concepts then firing the imagination of the art world, he applied these new ideas to the movie. The result was a picture which showed the adventures of a madman, seen entirely through his own eyes. In this way the film utilized "expressionism" to prove that sanity and insanity were purely relative states.

Wiene made *Caligari* into a fantasy of terror. Without explanation it immediately thrust the spectator into a world of weird images and maladjustments, holding him there with a growing sense of horror until the very end. Only in the final scene did the director disclose that all that had happened had occurred only in the mind of an insane person.

Wiene's style called attention to the importance of distortion and stylization for creating mood, using lighting, composition, setting, costuming and acting. His characters moved in constricted circular movements or leaned with the chimney to cause uneasiness. To accent the feeling of chaos and emphasize the mood, curves and dark tones were contrasted with straight lines and light tones. Compositions were carefully arranged to converge to focal points of interest. The stylized black tights and mask-like make up of the somnambulist contributed enormously to the ominous and tragic atmosphere, and emphasized the frailty and helplessness of the white-chiffon-draped victim whom he carried off. Never before had there been a movie so neurotic in tone.

Though *The Cabinet of Dr. Caligari* had no noticeable influence on other American directors, its effect in attracting the attention of intellectuals and artists in other media who had heretofore been indifferent to the movies cannot be underestimated. In its structural cohesion of design, lighting and psychological expression, it stands unique in film art for it opened the way to new directions movies could take.

More influential, actually, were the efforts of two other German directors, E. A. Dupont and Fred Murnau, whose work helped raise a white heat of enthusiasm over film art. Their pictures *Variety* and *The Last Laugh* (1925), introduced radical departures in the use of the camera which immediately brought many new adherents to the new art form; and which was to have a tremendous impact on American directors in Hollywood, working in the great industry movies had by now become.

Both directors displayed a brilliant flair for photography and camera virtuosity. Dupont and Murnau showed that the camera could be put to many versatile and astounding new uses to add to the language of film expression, particularly in the presentation of a subjective point of view. By means of multiple exposures, the use of negative, arresting angles and fluid camera transitions, the camera could reveal, without resorting to explanatory titles or even actors' pantomime, psychological insight. It could reveal a person's thoughts, dreams and desires. These directors lifted the camera from the passive role of an observer to the active one of a participant with a probing power. They endowed the camera with a fluidity and mobility it had never had before. The results were remarkable visual compositions and a flowing rhythmic unity that made for a new eloquence in screen art.

In *Variety*, Dupont moved the camera like a piercing eye that could see inside the characters. He swung the camera from the trapeze with the performer so that the spectator experienced what the character saw and felt. In another sequence, a man waited for a girl to come down the hallway past his door. As he listened for her footsteps, the camera moved swiftly into an extreme close-up of his ear, then superimposed over it came the feet of the girl moving past the door and down the stairs. The effect was as though the spectator too had heard and was following the girl's departure.

Murnau also told his story in *The Last Laugh* entirely in camera terms. From the opening scene the camera travelled without a letup, up and down streets, in and out of houses, through corridors, doors, and windows, like a participant in the movie's action. Windows opening on a courtyard showed the city awakening; bedding put out to air, sunlight moving across dark walls suggested the passage of time. Even the actor became subordinated to the camera lens. When Murnau's doorman got drunk, the camera did it for him by reeling and swaying so that the spectator saw everything through his eyes. It was a highly indigenous technique in which images alone unfolded the story.

Murnau's first American picture, *Sunrise* (1927), made in Hollywood, again told its story by a camera that roved everywhere: through the forest, into the city, over the lake—the camera often taking the place of a character so that the spectator became identified with the performer.

Both Murnau and Dupont were essentially interested in depicting the mind and feelings of the people in their films. Their glittering use of dissolves, gliding camera technique and subjective point of view was a radically new concept in film construction. The blending of shots through a moving camera produced a distinctive flowing rhythm that could not be achieved any other way, making for a rare style.

Utilizing this approach, Carl Dreyer, a Dane working in France, made one of the most unique pictures in the history of motion picture art, *The Passion of Joan of Arc* (1927). This film depicted—entirely from Joan's point of view—both physically and mentally—the last hours of her life: her inquisition, her trial, and her burning at the stake. The almost exclusive use of extreme close-ups in this picture made it a tour de force.

With a superb sense of rhythm, close-ups of groups, faces, eyes, mouths, hands, flowed across the screen revealing with tremendous force the thoughts and feelings of the characters. Joan is always seen looking up; the judges looking down at her. The contrast between the tortured, marvelously mobile face of Joan and the granite immobile faces of her accusers gave the spectator the sense of her overwhelming ordeal. Beautifully composed, balanced in design, striking in tone and shape, each shot individually had the eloquence of abstract art.

Like his German contemporaries, Dreyer paid scrupulous regard to the moving camera. His major departure lay in his photographic approach. Rejecting their glossy surface polish, he sought for the utmost photographic realism. His photography was stark and simple. The wrinkled faces of the actors with their dark skin textures, devoid of any make up or concession to glamor, stood out from the white backgrounds with startling reality.

Like his photography, Dreyer's settings were of the simplest kind. They were plain white with only an occasional dark shape of a window or door to convey the sense of place or environment. He strove for psychological truth rather than historical accuracy. The juxtaposition of the bare backgrounds and the photographic detail of the characters not only made for impressive and sometimes startling imagery, but more sharply focussed the complete concentration of the spectator on the dramatic conflict. The mobile camera was thus better able to capture, with quick pulsating, back and forward movements, the subtlest reaction of the judges—the flicker of an eyelash, a sudden glance, a mouth suspended in surprise, the very instant of a lost or regained composure—or of Joan, herself—hesitating, perplexed, anguished, tortured.

The Passion of Joan of Arc was an original film that needed neither sound nor color, no cinemascope, to augment its extraordinary dimension. Even today, it is a beautiful, intense and remarkable work.

Meanwhile, a brilliant group of movies from Russia began to appear which marked a further peak in motion picture art. These newcomers displayed vigor, imagination and artistic insight. Acclaimed, with cheers of praise there were at the same time cries of propaganda. Their work aroused greater controversy than that of any predecessors.

These Russian directors, penetrating in research, aware of the medium's powers and resources, disciplined in their art, wrote at length about their methods. They produced a large body of literature of permanent value, defining and clarifying the nature of film expression.

The men who made these movies were former chemists, engineers, factory workers, theater technicians. They approached movie making with a long range program supported by the State. Students first, they examined what others had done, analyzed, theorized and experimented to discover the intrinsic values and basis of their medium. In the works that followed, they carried to fruition what Porter and Griffith had sensed many years before: that in movies the basis of expression was the shot, which in itself contained the elements of the larger forms. By editing, relationships could be created which gave their films clarity, effectiveness and style. This emphasis on editing was more profound than either the German or French emphasis upon the camera eye or camera mobility. Russian editing demanded the use of all the elements of film art. The sum of their research and experimentation was expressed in the esthetic doctrine they called "montage."

The leading theoretician and director was Sergei Eisenstein. "Montage," he said, was "ingenuity in its (the shot) combinations." Next to Griffith the greatest figure in the movie world, Eisenstein made three films that for cinematic impact and masterly form have never been surpassed: *Potemkin* (1926), *Ten Days That Shook the World* (1927) and *The Old and New* (1928). In them, movement, like color in a Cezanne painting, became the architectural basis, pervading the subject matter, the shots, the scene development and the sequences. There was motion within the frame, camera motion, cutting on motion, the whole given further mobility through tempo and pace in a tremendous variety of editing schemes. These films were unequalled for concentration and conciseness. All had a pulse and power that was the result of highly organized movement in complex rhythms.

In these pictures, Eisenstein displayed an original pictorial imagination and a dynamic sense of continuity that had a symphonic sweep. Shots were related to each other with great intuition for the precise image, the exact duration, the appropriate psychological angle, and with a diversity of editing patterns that offered endless examples of striking cinematic compositions. Like all fine works of art, they became sources for study for creative workers in the medium.

Potemkin told of a crew's mutiny on the Czarist cruiser, Prince Potemkin, during the 1905 uprising. It began with a gradual build-up of tension, gathered momentum, burst into action, then sub-sided. The introductory section opened with a moderate movement—with evenly paced shots of the flowing sea, the swaying hammocks of sailors' quarters, the sailors' morning activities, and the sailors' protest over wormy meat. The tempo of the shots, imperceptibly speeded up, gained force in the conflict between the sailors and officers, and reached a climax in the revolt, with a crescendo of fast close and angle shots used in the battle for the ship. From this high point, the movement receded to a sequence of calm—the burial of the dead sailor, presented in extreme long shots, curving panoramic shots, and pans, all set to a quiet, slow rhythm.

The second section was swift and vigorous. Gay groups on the harbor steps of Odessa acclaimed the battleship *Potemkin*, now in control of the sailors. The shots were full of motion: twirling parasols, laughing faces, hands waving, cheering, boats sailing out with food, happy sailors on deck. Then suddenly and without warning, this gay mood was broken by the introduction of the steady, methodical beat of the march of the oncoming impersonal Cossacks. The two contrasting rhythms burst into a powerful climax in the massacre on the steps.

Here the intensity, speed, and impact of the staccato close shots of firing soldiers, screaming victims, and a careening baby carriage, intercut with flashes of legs, steps, blood, made this sequence one of the great formal passages in the history of film art. The pitch increased, then stopped short, taut. In this way the horror of the event was implanted in the spectator's consciousness.

The third movement opened with a slow watchful awakening of the crew nervously awaiting attack; the cutting here created a sense of foreboding. Then as the crew learned of the approaching Czarist fleet, their preparations for defense involved quickening excitement. Shots of the Potemkin's sailors were rapidly intercut with the approaching Czarist Navy: huge close-ups of the ships' engines, men loading guns, shells moved into position, cannon rising—all the shots set to a rapid-fire tempo.

The climax was held back so that the ensuing suspense became unbearable. The cutting was slowed down to a crawling pace as the ships approached each other with guns trained. All movement seemed to stop during a prolonged pause as the sailors on the Potemkin awaited the first shots of their adversary. Finally the Czarist fleet hoisted peace signals and steamed past the Potemkin without firing a shot. The frenzied relief of its sailors was depicted in a swift movement of shots that imparted a kind of exuberance to their pent up emotions and left the spectator with a strong sense of victory and triumph.

Ten Days That Shook the World dramatized the ten days that followed the establishment of the Kerensky provisional government. So real seemed its photography that many critics claimed they were actual newsreels of that historic event. Like *Potemkin*, there was no individual hero, but unlike that picture, instead of dealing with a single episode, it dealt with a whole series of episodes.

The film was a brilliant example of Eisenstein's forceful cutting technique. There were striking instances time and again of a scheme of dynamic construction which Eisenstein called "the mounting of attractions," obtained by "evoking in the spectator a series of successive thrills": Kerensky's ascension to temporary power, the Cossack dance, and the sensational drawbridge episode. In this last people were running from Czarist soldiers. A machine gunner shot them down as they made for the drawbridge, which was opening to trap those who escaped the bullets. Men and women fell as they turned back in panic. A horseless carriage and a dead girl were both caught on either side of the drawbridge just at the place of opening. Detail shots of the scurrying populace and the firing soldiers were intercut furiously as the desperation and excitement increased. The movements of the running people were never shown completed; they were cut short, and the rhythm was continued with another shot of a similar or opposing movement and intercut with the dead girl and the horseless carriage, each time from another camera viewpoint (dependent upon the preceding shot) and in a more precarious position, to emphasize the plight of the fleeing victims. As the hair of the dead girl slipped bit by bit into the opening of the rising drawbridge, the carriage was also lifted higher and higher on the rising side of the drawbridge. Eisenstein, destroying all sense of real time, repeatedly (he cut back to the girl at least fourteen times and almost as many times to the carriage), prolonged the suspense unbearably. At last the dead girl fell into the river; the carriage, aloft on the upraised span, rolled furiously down to the bottom. It was a moment of horror.

Numerous instances in Eisenstein's films imposed on the audience an intellectual participation for full understanding and appreciation. In *Ten Days,* as Kerensky arrogantly walked up the grand staircase of the Winter Palace, there were shots intercut of nearby statues to make the ironic comment that he was ambitious for power. At the very top of the stairs, under a marble statue whose outstretched arm held a laurel leaf, Kerensky paused, a self-imagined Caesar. But Eisenstein photographed him from above to dwarf his figure and emphasize his weak, chinless head.

Inside the Czar's room, Kerensky toyed with the cap of a whiskey flask before him. Intercut were statues of Napoleon. When Kerensky leaned forward to place the cap on the flask, the spectator saw that the cap was a miniature coronet. At that very moment of realization, the picture cut to a screaming factory whistle, announcing the attack on Petrograd by Kornilov, another would-be ruler. The ambitions of the two were then symbolized by the statues of Napoleon which merged, then crashed, as the October Revolution burst.

The Old and New offered another brilliant example of the intellectual basis for many of Eisenstein's compositions. Religious peasants and their priests were in the drought stricken fields praying for rain which did not come. Eisenstein built this episode out of several inter-dependent forces or lines of continuity which advanced through the sequence simultaneously, yet maintained an independent compositional course, but came together at the end like a multi-colored ball of yarn. Clearly drawn from the structure of Griffith's *Intolerance,* Eisenstein's organization was made up of many more complex psychological and cinematic elements. Eisenstein himself listed them as: the line of increasing heat of the peasants from shot to shot; the line of changing close-ups increasing in plastic intensity; the line of mounting ecstasy; the line of women singers; of men singers; of those who kneel, the bearers of ikons, crosses and banners; and the line of grovelers. Handled with masterly control the sequence was an uninterrupted stream of brilliant images bearing a multiple responsibility—to contribute to the total flow of the structure, to carry on the movement within the tributaries themselves, and to build a devastating portrait of religious frenzy.

Though Eisenstein was to make a number of other pictures after these three, with sound, none ever surpassed them.

Of lesser stature than Eisenstein, Pudovkin perhaps enjoyed greater popularity. His pictures were more traditional in structure and less intellectually demanding. They had a story, a protagonist and a narrative form suggestive of Griffith's pictures. The End of St. Petersburg (1927) and Storm Over Asia (1928), were the two pictures that made Pudovkin famous in this country.

Both pictures had a simple protagonist, who in the confusion of events, became socially awakened and led his fellow men against their oppressors. Pictorially, these movies had a sweep and richness comparable to Eisenstein's, but structurally they were not as brilliant or complex. Pudovkin's feeling for the vastness and atmosphere of the countryside—a characteristic of all Soviet films—his innumerable satirical touches, such as the shrieking Kerensky in St. Petersburg and the pompous police commissioner in Storm over Asia, his portraits of the bewildered hero who emerged from perplexity to an understanding of the social and political upheaval, were rendered in a sharp staccato style that emphasized the intensity of the events and carried the spectator away by the sheer force of the execution.

Pudovkin's most compelling structural device was his use of cross cutting. The stock exchange sequence in The End of St. Petersburg became celebrated. Here Pudovkin portrayed in extreme close shot, the hysteria of the war profiteers, then cross cut to another kind of hysteria, to the men in the war zone being mowed down by bursting shells, killing and being killed, forcing the spectator to draw a specific conclusion from the contrast of cutting. In another sequence, a demagogue exhorting a crowd to join the army, smashed his own top hat, explaining that the enemy made it; then he broke his cane because that, too, was enemy made; then he aired his admiration for a passing soldier, and called upon the onlookers to join the army. But the crowd knew the soldier was a released convict who was forced to join the army. A further satirical touch was given the scene when the Soldier revealed that he carried, much against his will, a large portrait of the Czar.

In *Storm Over Asia* the hero, a Mongol, who through a series of circumstances was mistaken for the heir of Genghis Khan, was trained by British interests to be used as a dupe to control his people. But upon discovering the duplicity of the British, he turned against them.

In the middle of the film, Pudovkin used parallel and contrast cutting with telling effect. A small battle between the insurgents and British was going on in a distant valley while the English commander and his wife were dressing to attend a ceremony at a Mongolian lamasery. A witty analogy was created by intercutting shots of the dressing Britishers and the Mongolian dancers; both donned clothes, trinkets, headgear and masks (paint, powder, and a "best smile" for the commander and his wife). The rhythm of the sequence was deft and precise. But the episode was only the preparation for a more ironic touch. The commander, his wife, and the staff came to the temple for the ceremonies and paid their compliments to the priest: "My government," the commander murmured, "deeply regrets your recent demise"—here Pudovkin cut in a flash shot of a Mongolian infant (the new Lama playing with his toes)—"and hails with joy your new birth." This was followed by a shot of the British shooting down Mongols. As the General continued to mouth platitudes his soldiers were shown shooting down Mongolian insurgents. By such referential cross-cutting of contrasting ideas, Pudovkin achieved a bitter irony.

Pudovkin ended the film with a powerful example of what he called "implanting an abstract concept into the consciousness of the spectator." The Mongol youth had fiercely fought his way out of the British headquarters and was riding across the desert pursued by his former captors. A windstorm began. The Mongol raised his ancient sword and cried out: "Oh my People!" As if in answer to his cry, the desert became alive with hundreds of mounted followers. Again the Mongol called: "Rise in your ancient strength!"

The screen now filled with thousands of Mongolians riding furiously with him and when he once more called out: "and free yourselves!" the desert storm and the ancient warriors merged into the force of a hurricane that swept everything before them—the British army, trading posts, trees—in a tempestuous movement symbolical of their united strength and the imminent "storm over asia."

The differences that distinguished the work of Eisenstein and Pudovkin were reconciled in a third lesser known director, Dovzhenko. His pictures did not receive the widespread publicity and distribution that his colleagues enjoyed, but they were equally unique and valuable works of film artistry. Dovzhenko had a deep personal and poetic insight which made his films utterly unusual. *Arsenal* (1928), and *Soil* (1930), were the only two shown in America. Both were laconic in expression, with a strange wonderfully imaginative flavor. Both dealt with Soviet problems but stressed philosophical rather than social or political issues. So personalized were these films, so concentrated, rich and unexpected in their imagery and style, that they achieved the emotional intensity of fine lyric poetry. Perhaps more than anyone else, Dovzhenko could be called the first poet of the movies.

With these three giants, movie art took a great leap forward and reached new heights of creativity. The controlled rise and fall of tempo, sharp juxtapositions of sweeping action, significant pictorial symbolism, original and complex editing patterns, and vigorous content, introduced new power and artistry. The *montage* credo marked a great stride forward in the formulation and understanding of screen art and helped the recognition on a world-wide scale of the full acceptance of the movies as an art medium with its own structural forms.

These Russian directors made clear that the art of movie making need no longer flounder for a methodology or for its own standards. Thirty years of artistic development had evolved a body of creative work from which could be derived an intrinsic tradition that elucidated the movie's own esthetic roots and its singular process of expression which distinguished it from all other media. Movies seemed headed for a dazzling esthetic future.

III: *EXTENSIONS IN SOUND*

Then suddenly in 1930, this wave of progress was brought to an abrupt halt. The addition of sound, and the incorporation of spoken dialogue as an element in motion picture expression, produced a cataclysm. Overnight motion picture technique lost its sophistication and reverted to its primitive beginnings. In the chaos that the advent of sound produced, new ways of film expression were aborted and the art of film making was abandoned in a panic. Every phase of movie production was subjected to the domination of the microphone and reverted to its rudiments. It was literally a time of sound and fury.

The next years saw frenzied attempts to bring the expanded sound-picture medium to a completeness of expression equal to its physical development. By 1933, science had so improved the tools and techniques of sound recording and editing, that talking pictures had all their basic techniques ready-made. It became apparent that sound was a technological improvement that added an important force to movie expression. The problems of the movie creator were both multiplied and simplified. Esthetics now had to include aural as well as visual concepts.

As the creative potentialities of sound began to be explored, movie art entered a new phase. Directors introduced extensions in sound and picture which gradually enlarged the scope of movie technique and form, and enabled cinematic expression to achieve a richer maturity of style.

How richly and imaginatively sound could be manipulated and fused to intensify the image was first demonstrated by a man who worked in a branch not usually considered an important part of motion pictures, the animated cartoon field. Walt Disney, a technical innovator of great skill, almost from the outset exhibited a distinctive exploitation of the sound-picture medium. He made the short animated cartoon the finest expression of movie art at this time.

Whatever animal characters Disney created, *Mickey Mouse*, *Donald Duck*, *The Three Little Pigs*, *Pluto* the bloodhound, or the cast in the *Silly Symphonies*, the form of his pictures was always the same. On the surface comparatively simple, their structural design was of a high esthetic order. Fantasy, humor, satire, sentiment, violence were blended, one or another sometimes predominating. At all times their compositions were rich in visual and aural coordination. Images moved rapidly and blended smoothly without a wasted frame, arousing excitement, provoking laughter, building suspense, always advancing with remarkable cinematic fluidity to a last minute crescendo and a final hilarious and unexpected resolution.

Disney, like all gifted directors before him, employed movement as the basis of his structure. Sound was so integrated that it functioned as an additional mobile element. Sound was expanded or condensed to reinforce movement of the image from shot to shot; animals, birds, plants, machines, furniture, carry on an unbroken rhythm of sounds and music with as many aural as pictorial variations.

In the fantasy world, Disney fabricated an unreal world of sounds in unheard of combinations. Sometimes the effects were created by the junction of actual sounds, at other times by synthetic means, as in the use of light vibrations applied to a sound track to mechanically create intensities and tones otherwise impossible. Not bound to imitating sounds in nature, he distorted it at will—a piano became a grand opera singer, a daisy a chorus girl.

In the first days of sound, Disney was the virtuoso of the medium. Technical dexterity and a remarkable command of structural movement gave his pictures a brilliancy of rendition that made the least of them dazzling. His contributions at this time in the application of sound to visual movement added new concepts to the body of film knowledge and to the artistic progress of the expanded medium.

Another director who showed that motion pictures with the addition of sound need not forget everything they had learned about technique and form, was the Frenchman, Rene Clair. He had, originally, been opposed to sound, calling it: "An unnatural creation thanks to which the screen will become poor theater."

Clair began around 1923 as an avant-garde film maker. His silent pictures, the most outstanding of which were *En'tracte* and *The Italian Straw Hat* won him an enthusiastic following, though they were seen only by a small circle of cognoscenti. Within a few years of the advent of sound, he had developed into a highly original and distinctive director of sound movies. His work was inventive cinematically as well as highly styled, and Clair saw to it that sound, instead of restricting him, led him into even more interesting and expressive paths. He worked out an approach that was the opposite of that used by other sound film makers. Instead of making his sound more natural to go with realistic pictures, he made his pictures more unnatural so that the sound would appear more realistic. The result was a delightful series of satirical and social comedies, highly personal in form, charming and significant in style.

Under The Roofs Of Paris (1930), *Le Million* (1931), *A Nous La Liberte* (1932), *July The Fourteenth* (1932), and *The Last Millionaire* (1934), were Parisian in vernacular and idiom. But they revealed a Paris not to be found in actuality except as a product of Clair's own vision. It was a world, sustained in mood and atmosphere, of lower class Parisian life; here the problems of romantic love and human foibles were depicted with a light satirical humor among delicately artificial settings. These films had an urbanity, precision and elegance, the result of an individual touch that was always recognizable.

The essence of Clair's cinematic style, which was delicately shaded and suggested more than it said, can be described as choreographic. Treating his stories as fantasies, he solved the problems of dialogue and music by having his characters sing and dance at the slightest pretext. They moved like dancers to the rhythm of some inner music. By placing the camera on wheels and demanding that the microphone follow, he freed sound from its static and limited role and gave it flexibility, mobility and perspective. The range of sound was further extended by manipulating it to function for transitions, association and contrast. By blending all his technical resources, and creating sound-images, Clair gave his pictures a flow and rhythm that reinforced his humor and was a basic characteristic of his style.

Under the Roofs of Paris opened with a theme song which flowed through the film like a stream—a dominant part of its cinematic continuity. When the lovers quarreled the scene was staged in darkness so that we did not see the actors but only heard their angry voices—at that time an impressive bit of image-sound counterpoint. A fight scene near a railway yard showed the combatants struggling in silence. But an approaching freight train hissed steam as though to give voice to the men's struggle. At the very height of the conflict, the train set off a sudden blast of steam that obliterated the fighters, then moved on with a triumphant roar.

In *Le Million*, Clair created a new kind of screen musical. His characters were like delightful puppets. Their chase for a winning lottery ticket became a kind of ballet. Dialogue was replaced by music and by lyrics fitted to the action and related to the musical rhythm. A particularly witty touch was the scene at the opera where a stout tenor and a stouter prima donna sang a sentimental love duet; while in the wings, hiding from their pursuers, the young lovers acted out the singers' words in earnest. In another audacious and witty sound-image association, some characters were seen fighting over the coat which contained the winning lottery ticket. Suddenly on the sound track was heard a referee's whistle and the thud of a football. Immediately the fight took on the attributes of a football game, with the coat tossed from player to player as though it were an actual football.

Clair's *A Nous la Liberte* and *The Last Millionaire* stood apart from his other sound pictures. In these he displayed a more pointed use of his ballet-musical approach, for social comment. A factory assembly line and a prison are compared through a counterpoint of image and sound—a similar music and monotonous sound track underlay both. In another sequence high hatted officials were shown scrambling for bank notes blown about by the wind as they supposedly listened to the pompous oration of a magnate reciting platitudes about justice, liberty and the fatherland.

Rene Clair appeared at a time when the medium's expressive powers were being sorely tested, and pioneered in extending the medium's range and scope. He created pictures that stood out for their grace, wit and inventiveness. Though always strikingly disciplined and distinctive in flavor, his more recent works have not had the same importance or impact.

In America one of the few silent film directors who survived the upheaval caused by talking pictures was John Ford. A prolific worker, his career had extended over more than twenty years of silent film making during which time he had turned out innumerable productions, good, bad and indifferent. Then suddenly in 1935, in collaboration with the notable screen writer, Dudley Nichols, he made a picture which staked his claim to fame: *The Informer*.

In this picture, the tragedy of a stool pigeon was told in a sombre key; dark shadows, muffled voices and night sounds, mood, pace, character and sound were blended into a fluid unity from the first scenes of fluttering newspapers to the last scene of the shooting of Gypo. A slow restrained tempo, enforced by the dense Dublin fog and the night that enveloped the film, deepened the sense of tragedy and ominousness—the tension and suspense building a mental rather than physical excitement.

In addition to using sound to intensify the drama, Ford used it in new relationships for transitions, or in different ways for reflection, inner monologue or symbolism. After Gypo informed on his friend Frankie, there was suddenly heard the ticking of a clock; we had a prescience of evil. The ticking continued into the next shots—Frankie at home with his mother and sister where another clock continued the sound and fused the transition. Later the tapping of a blind man's stick when Gypo has escaped from the rebel's headquarters, once more took up the sound, in this way recalling the earlier scene of Frankie's betrayal.

In another sequence, Ford used sound subjectively in a striking counterpoint to image. Gypo was looking dreamily at a model of a steamship, and on the track Frankie's voice was heard warning him that he was lost, that without the aid of Frankie's brains, Gypo was helpless.

With sound, Ford did not forsake the use of images. Gypo stood outside a travel office studying an advertisement. The camera followed his eyes as they lowered to a drawing of a ship crossing the Atlantic. The drawing became a real one on which Gypo and his girl Katie were dressed as bridegroom and bride, revealing at once the secret dream of Gypo. At another time Gypo returned to the place where, from the poster on the wall, now bare, he first got the idea of betraying his friend. Suddenly as Gypo stared at the wall, the poster of Frankie took shape, but now accusing and angry. Later we saw into Gypo's mind when, drunk, he approached a strange girl whose features changed into those of his girl Kate.

The Informer was a high mark in American sound films and coming from a seasoned silent film director indicated that the death knell of cinematic form had not been sounded as many had been contending at the first flood of the stilted Hollywood stage-struck dialogue films.

In the years that followed, there were so many fine sound productions of high quality that the debate of silent vs. sound pictures lost its vehemence. Sound became an integral part of the enriched movie medium with numerous productions of a high order of excellence. Significantly enough, it was from a young talent, fresh from the theater and radio, that the most strikingly original American sound film was to come.

Few directors had been the subject of so much controversy in so short a lifetime as Orson Welles, when in 1940 he arrived in Hollywood to make his first movie. Before then his fame and notoriety had rested upon three factors—his youth; a sensational radio broadcast about an imagined invasion from Mars; and a remarkably successful theatrical career on Broadway as the director of The Mercury Players. The release of his first motion picture in 1941 burst dramatically onto the American film scene to cap his other accomplishments. He was hailed as the most brilliant screen director to appear since the introduction of sound.

Citizen Kane electrified the movie world. In it Welles displayed an inventiveness, a maturity of technique and form and a vitality of style that was completely unexpected, even from one with his extraordinary attainments in the other entertainment media. His command of the best devices which the movies had developed through the years, plus original innovations of his own, marked the debut of an important new creator in the American screen. Welles deserved the accolade.

Citizen Kane was supercharged with brilliant and original touches. From the moment the picture began with the camera moving through an almost totally black screen toward a small illuminated window in the distance, past barbed wire, cyclone fencing, through an enormous and elaborate grilled gateway to hold on a large initial "K," beyond which could be glimpsed the fairy tale castle of Xanadu—(the same shots were repeated in reverse at the end)—the spectator felt that he was in the presence of something genuine and fresh.

This impression was carried out by what followed. In one uncommon way after another Welles displayed a surprising technical virtuosity with the movies' plastic forces: exciting visual compositions, vivid symbolism, disregard for the strict chronology of time and space, striking transitions, ingenious settings. Outstanding was his inventive staging, his unconventional camera technique, and his use of sound for structural movement.

Welles' staging was contrived to compensate for his inexperience with movie technique, but he endowed it with such kinetic dexterity that it became a cinematic attribute. *Citizen Kane* was almost devoid of close-ups and medium shots. Instead, the staging was in depth with the entire playing area in sharp focus all the time and the actors placed in positions equivalent to close, medium or long shot. This was accomplished by a specially coated, extra wide angle lens which could take in the entire acting area.

In his effort to make the staging cinematically meaningful in terms of close, medium and long shots, Welles employed light in a new way. He shifted the actors in and out of light and from one staging area to another, often shooting against the light and blotting out the features of his players in order to emphasize the important incident, fix the significant gesture, underscore the emphatic speech, or counterpoint the vital reaction. This set up a kind of weaving movement within the scene and also from one scene to another, which in effect simulated cutting and provided the film with a sinuous rhythm and vitality.

In addition Welles displayed an unfettered and imaginative use of the camera. Without regard for Hollywood conventions, he shot from the floor, or two hundred feet away; he focussed his lens into spotlights, floodlights, or framed his compositions in dramatically new ways. Wherever it was possible, he used the camera to advance the story. When Kane's second wife made her disastrous operatic debut, the camera told the story by climbing high in the flies to focus on a stagehand pinching his nose in disgust. In another place, a large empty medicine bottle through which could be seen tiny figures hurrying forward, told the spectator that Susan had attempted suicide.

His background in radio as well as theater helped Welles bring to motion pictures a heightened awareness of the possibilities of sound. He adapted a device that became one of *Citizen Kane's* most vital features—a kind of aural montage in which sound, music or dialogue, begun in one scene, was completed in another, thus uniting two or more scenes separated in time and space, and at the same time advancing the continuity of the whole.

Kane had just met Susan. He went back to her room to hear her sing. As she started her song, the scene shifted to an elaborate apartment, with Susan at a grand piano and Kane luxuriously stretched out in a basket chair listening to her complete the song —thus, instantly, the change in their relationship was revealed.

In another part of the picture, Leland was addressing a small group of men in a small meeting room: "He entered this campaign . . ." Immediately Kane's voice continued—we see him in a huge auditorium addressing a much larger crowd: ". . . with one purpose only!" Without a break in dialogue, the story was carried forward both in time and in movement.

One of the highlights of *Citizen Kane's* sound was the telling of the gradual disintegration of a marriage through a series of conversations at the breakfast table. Kane's first wife began a conversation, Kane replied. Between each question and answer that followed there was a shift to a later and later time, always without a break in their dialogue and without a change in camera position. From a romantic and intimate start, the conversation changed to one of growing estrangement, and ended finally with the two reading rival newspapers, barely on speaking terms.

Welles used sound with equal effectiveness and originality for comment, contrast and characterization. Kane and Susan have quarreled in their tent during the Everglades picnic. Off screen a singer is heard: "It can't be love; there is no true love . . ." Later Susan's departure from Xanadu was preceded by the piercing scream of an angry cockatoo. At another time, after Kane's political defeat, while Leland, drunk, was returning to the newspaper office, we heard a hurdy-gurdy playing the song that Leland had written many years before: "This is a man . . . a certain man . . . you may be sure . . . will do all he can . . ." But this time the song instead of being played in a lively tempo as before, came across as a dirge, underscoring the pathos of Kane's defeat, and his growing estrangement with Leland.

Bold, arresting, *Citizen Kane* showed Welles a seasoned stylist with his first effort. His brilliant and facile use of the movies' resources and his own contributions in sound linkage and the plastic use of light and shade, gave the expanded film medium a new eloquence.

Welles' subsequent films, *The Magnificent Ambersons, The*

Lady from Shanghai, Journey into Fear, Macbeth, Othello, Mr. Arkadis and *Touch of Evil*, while exciting in parts, never matched the achievement of *Citizen Kane*. An innovator by nature, everything Welles undertakes has great interest. He may yet make further important contributions to film art.   1097449

IV: RECENT FILM MAKERS

From 1941 to 1945 the second World War concentrated all energies. The best films at this time in America were the *Why We Fight* series directed in the main by documentary film makers working together with Hollywood craftsmen. Generally these films were of high excellence in concept and form, reflecting how highly advanced and complex the motion picture medium had become.

In the immediate post-war years, there emerged a group of vigorous and important film makers in Italy—a group that later became known as the neo-realist movement. This school of film makers drew their material from life in post-war Italy and treated it with great vitality and humanity. By working almost entirely on location and often with non-professional actors, a high degree of realism was achieved. Fresh from the war, the Italian film makers were skeptical, ironical, anti-puritanical, unromantic, although not without traces of idealism. They treated people not as puppets, as statements of impersonal facts, but as human beings. With vividness and heart, their work faced up to dire social problems that needed solution.

In style, these directors worked in a naturalistic genre that was terse, vernacular, understated, with emphasis upon content and characterization. The most eminent men and the pictures they made were Roberto Rossellini—*Open City* (1944-5), *Paisan* (1946); Vittorio De Sica—*Shoeshine* (1945), *Bicycle Thief* (1948), *Miracle in Milan* (1951); Luigi Zampa—*We Live in Peace* (1947); Giuseppi de Santis—*Tragic Hunt* (1947); Frederico Fellini—*La Strada* (1956), *Cabiria* (1957). Each one of these, highly personal and deeply moving, deserves a place in the gallery of fine films.

Of the foreign pictures coming to America at this time, the most singular achievement, *Rashomon*, came not from Italy but from Japan. The director, Akira Kurosawa, was essentially Western in film style and subscribed basically to the film tenets of Eisenstein and Pudovkin, but with his own personal vision.

Although he had been directing pictures in Japan since 1943, Kurosawa was unknown outside his country until *Rashomon* captured the Grand Prize at Venice in 1951. This picture proved to be one of the most uncommon made since the end of the war, adventurous in idea, sophisticated in technique, artful in style and significant in humanistic values.

Rashomon inquired into the nature of truth. One observer and three participants in a killing related the events, each from his own point of view. Each version was different and contradictory. In one, the wife was raped against her will. In another, she lured the bandit and tried to make him kill her husband. In the third account, the husband bribed the bandit to attack his wife. The audience is confronted with the problem of determining which one was telling the truth.

In an epilogue there was a new revelation pointing out that there was no truth—that all men act out of selfishness. But then in a last minute reprieve for mankind, the audience was shown another kind of truth: that as long as there is compassion of man for his fellow men there is hope for the future of mankind. And this was the only truth that mattered.

Much of *Rashomon's* artistic power stemmed from its physical beauty. The brilliant photography and extraordinary compositions displayed a fine balance of realism and impressionism. The viewers' eyes and senses were overwhelmed with the loveliness of nature. This expressed itself in the very beginning in one of the most lyrical passages ever seen when the woodcutter moved warily through the forest between leaf and twig, while the dazzling sun burst through the branches in an explosion of light. Nothing had happened yet, but already there was a vague sense of foreboding, of mystery and of beauty.

In contrast, the later testimony of the participants, staged against a plain white wall, achieved a forcefulness that was highly dramatic. Light and shade also achieved a haunting beauty in the scene of evocation of the anguished face of the dead husband who found no peace even in death.

A daring use of violent camera movements created rhythm, pattern and intensity of feeling. The camera panned from characters, to details of leaves, rain on the surface of a lake, the sky. The striking juxtapositions of long and close shots, especially in the sequences of the woodcutter's journey through the forest, the duel between the Lord and the bandit, and the wife's idling beside a stream, built up a dynamic cohesiveness. Kurosawa's vivid treatment of the action scenes, the variety and movements of his camera angles with their wonderful imagery and precise rhythms, displayed a profound feeling for the film idiom that strikingly recalled the best of the silent Russian films.

Currently there is little question that the Swedish director, Ingmar Bergman, is among the leading film makers of the world. So far only five of his pictures have appeared in America: *Naked Night* (1955), *Smiles of a Summer Night* (1957), *The Seventh Seal* (1958), *Wild Strawberries* (1959), and *The Magician* (1959). These films are involved with the meaning of values in human relationships. In a statement in the French *Cahiers du Cinema* (Summer, 1956), Bergman said his purpose in making films was "to express in an entirely subjective manner, the ideas that are part of man's conscience."

In pursuit of this objective, he uses the protagonist's mind as the stage upon which all action centers. Without resorting to the usual narrative devices, dramatic situations, or actions, he conjures up an interior drama and attempts to penetrate the dark places of the mind in moral and social relationships. He explores in various degrees the mind's actual and dream experiences, records its memories and fantasies, and traces its subconscious flow, moving freely back and forth in time and space. What takes place is shown either from a first person or third person point of view, or both at will, as the director peers through an imaginary window in the protagonist's mind.

In his efforts to evoke "previously unknown worlds, realities beyond reality," Bergman uses broken chronology, intricate formal patterns, subtleties of speech and sound, suggestion, symbol, sudden changes of mood, differences in photographic style, stylization of setting, unusual camera placements and lighting, superimpositions, unconventional transitions, variety of rhythms. But most particularly he places great stress upon close-ups of the human face.

To Bergman, the face is the key to all those conditions and tensions of inner truth with which his films concern themselves. "Our work in films begins with the human face," he said in *Films and Filming* (July 1959); and continues: "We can certainly become completely absorbed in the esthetics of montage, we can bring together objects and still life into magnificent rhythms, we can make nature studies of astounding beauty, but the approach to the human face is without doubt the hallmark and distinguishing quality of the film."

Fascinating, baffling, a controversial figure, Bergman falls into none of the usual categories. There is no one else like him. He is original and technically intricate. His complex mental film journeys though sometimes obscure, often allegorical, are, at their best, deeply revealing; and they are frequently of great visual beauty. He stands today at the threshold of what may turn out to be a new artistic development of the medium, one as radical as Griffith's was in his day.

The directors I have discussed showed that the motion picture medium was a way of seeing, feeling, thinking. They broke away from the stereotyped standards of their day and helped shape screen art into an important esthetic medium. Any consideration of the art of movies must therefore take into account the work of these film makers. Their pictures represent the touchstone of value in the medium; in them can be found a screen rationale, a criteria and an esthetic heritage.

1910-1920

"The time is coming when we shall see the essential cinematographic artist—the man who thinks in moving images and transmits that to us in its most individual form, unmodified by the ideas of others—on the screen. That time is nearer than imagined."

ROBERT NICHOLS

THE DRAMA OF THE
PEOPLE

The cinematograph is doing for the drama what the printing press did for literature, bringing another form of art into the daily life of the people. Plays are now within the reach, literally, of the poorest, as are good books and good pictures. The secret of cheapness in art as in other things is mechanical multiplication. So long as a play required for each presentation the active cooperation of a considerable number of more or less talented persons it could never be cheap, and in its better forms it was necessarily accessible to a comparatively small part of the population. But once on a celluloid film a spectacle can be reproduced indefinitely, the good as cheaply as the poor, and superiority is no longer handicapped. The same effect is shown in the field of literature. Among the dollar and a half books published every year there is a large proportion of trash or worse, but the volumes sold for fifty cents or less comprise the world's best literature.

The moving picture shows are in general superior, both artistically and morally, to the vaudeville and melodrama that they have driven out of business. It is a mistake to suppose that their amazing popularity is due altogether to their low price of admission. On the contrary the cinematograph has some advantages, not only over the cheap shows which it at first rivaled, but over any previous form of dramatic art. The most conspicuous of these advantages is spaciousness, distance. The stage is at the best but a narrow platform. The characters must dodge out of the wings or pop out of a door at the back. They have their exits and their entrances, but all both necessarily sudden, more "dramatic" than lifelike.

But the moving picture show has a third dimension. The characters have a gradual approach and recession. The railroad train rushes toward the spectator; the horseman rides off through the woods or across the plain until he disappears in the distance. The scene of action is all outdoors. Rejoicing in this release from the limitations of the old drama, the moving picture plays at first were mostly routs. They gave their spectator a run for his money, a chase of comic or tragic character.

The abolition of the painted scenery of the backdrop gives to the drama a sense of reality, a solidity, that it never had before. The mountains and clouds do not now show spots of threadbare canvas. The tumbling waves do not throw up dust. The rocks and trees do not shiver at the touch of the actors. The sunshine is such as never came from calcium or carbon, and the wind that blows about loose hair and garments is not that of the electric fan.

In the al fresco performance of troupes of Summer players one corner of a lawn must serve as scene, helped out by a few potted shrubs and by trees with artificial limbs. The modern manager limits his playwrights to three or four changes of scenery on account of expense and the time it takes to set them. But for the cinematograph there are no such restrictions. There may be as many scenes as in an Elizabethan drama, for the setting may be changed in the twinkling of an eye, or it may be gradually shifted to follow the actors without jar or rumble. The moving scenery of Wagner's "Parsifal" and the treadmill of the race-course plays which aroused the admiration of our fathers, seem to us absurdly crude and clumsy.

The divided stage, with its broken partition end on to the spectator, may also be sent to the lumber room. The moving picture has it in its power by alternating scenes to show us what is going on simultaneously in two different places, inside and outside a house, for example, or in adjoining rooms. He can vary at will the distance of the stage, giving us a closer view at critical moments. When we would see more clearly what emotions the features of the heroine express or what is in the locket she takes from her bosom we have no need to pick up our opera glasses. The artist has foreseen our desire and suddenly the detail is enlarged for us until it fills the canvas.

On the ordinary stage there is no good way of showing what is being written or read, however essential this may be to the plot. The actor has to read aloud his letter as he writes it as though he was not sure of its grammar. This device is no longer necessary. The incriminating note, the long lost will, the visiting card, the portrait, and the newspaper paragraph are shown to us directly and we do not have to hear of them at second hand. We see instantly what the hero sees when he puts the spyglass to his eye and what the housemaid is looking at through the keyhole. Ghosts, visions and transformation scenes are accomplished in a manner truly magical, without the aid of the old stage contrivances, the steam curtain, the trap and the *deus ex machina*. Flying is as easy as walking. Acrobatic feats are unlimited. All miracles are possible, even that most marvelous of miracles, the reversal of the course of life.

The cinematograph theater is international. We do not have as formerly, translations, adaptations and misinterpretations. We have the real play, exactly as presented in Paris, London or Berlin. Villages in the Rocky and Carpathian Mountains look at the same scenes on the same day. Still, in spite of manifolding and syndicate management, some differences of national taste may be observed by one who visits the popular theaters of various European countries. Americans seem to prefer comic incidents corresponding to the usual short story; Germans, the sentimental novelette; English, the melodrama; French, passionate intrigue; and Italians, classical tales. But in any place one may often have the opportunity of comparing the acting of several different nationalities.

First night performances are no longer the privilege of the favored few. Every moving picture show is an original and unique presentation. The actors have had no time to become jaded and mechanical.

The replica of a painting, though by the same artist, is not esteemed so highly as the original. The three hundredth replica would be thought ridiculous. Yet of such repetitions our drama has hitherto consisted. The cinematograph actors, once their drama is satisfactorily played, are released from it and may go about their business of preparing another.

Their achievement has now the permanence of a painting or a statue. Dramatic art may have a true history and make real progress now that direct comparisons can be made with the past. The great actor will still have fame but his head will not be turned by constant personal adulation. It is not the least of the advantages that dead men cannot rise to receive the applause that follows their death-scene.

We expect to see some time a stereoscopic colored speaking moving picture drama and it will be well worth seeing. It will be a new form of fine art not unworthy to rank with the elder arts.

New York Independent, Oct. 8, 1910.

THE BIRTH OF A
NEW ART

It is interesting to live at a time when we can witness the birth of a new art. Such was the last quarter of the fifteenth century when the art of printing books was being developed. Such is the first quarter of the twentieth century when the art of depicting motion is being developed. In fact the moving picture has a better title to the term "a new art" than had printing to which it was applied so long ago. Printing was not so much "a new art" as a mechanical extension of an old art, one of the oldest and best developed of the fine arts, the art of calligraphy. The first printed books were but cheap and inferior imitations of the handsome hand-written volumes of that day. Even today with 450 years of progress it is in cheapness and convenience rather than beauty that the modern book surpasses the ancient manuscript.

Now in the same way the moving picture does for the drama what printing did for literature, that is, it brings it within reach of the multitude through a process of mechanical manifolding. But it does something vastly more important than this. It makes possible for the first time the unlimited reproduction of actual events. This world of ours is a moving world and no static art can adequately represent it. There is no such thing as still life, or still anything else in the whole universe. Everywhere and always there is motion and only motion and any representation of reality at rest is a barefaced humbug. The more realistic the painting or sculpture the more obvious the failure. Myron's "Discobolus" and Meissonier's "Friedland" are as unnatural and fictitious as a centaur or a hippogriff. The most beautiful painting ever put on canvas, the finest statue ever carved, is a ridiculous caricature of real life compared with the flickering shadow of a tattered film in a backwoods nickelodeon. We have now for the first time the possibility of representing, however crudely, the essence of reality, that is, motion.

Bergson has shown us what a paralyzing influence static conceptions of reality have had upon the history of philosophy and how futile have been all attempts to represent movement by rest. The scientist of today thinks in terms of motion. All modern thought is assuming kinetic forms and we are coming to see the absurdity of the old ideas of immutability and immobility. A similar revolution is impending in art. At least we glimpse the possibility of a new form of pictorial art which, if capable of development as it seems to be, will make our present pictures appear as grotesque as the reliefs carved on Egyptian tombs or the scrawls on the caverns of Altamira. What will our posterity, familiar with moving portraiture, think of our admiration of Mona Lisa's smile, frozen on her lips for four centuries? A smile is essentially a fleeting thing, an evanescent expression. A fixed smile is not a smile at all but a grimace. It is only by the most violent effort of the imagination that we can ignore the inherent artificiality and limitations of paintings sufficiently to get from them the illusion of reality.

But we need not speculate as to the future of the motion picture. Its present progress is sufficient for consideration. Its advance has been much more rapid than that of printing. It has reached more people in the first twenty years of its life than printing did in two hundred after its invention. It has in fact already overtaken the older art in some respects. There are very likely at this moment more people looking at moving pictures than there are reading books, if we except students and others who read books as a business.

But there is this important difference. One who wishes to read the best books can easily find out which they are by reading the reviews in reputable periodicals, but one who wishes to see or procure for exhibition the best motion films has no such guidance. The photo plays that are being turned out by the hundred every month are of the same general character as the short stories and novels of the cheap and popular fiction magazines, innocuous for the most part but also for the most part devoid of distinction and literary or dramatic value. The "movies" are on the whole the decentest form of popular amusement we have. Their most objectionable feature is not the films, but the vaudeville stunts interposed between them. The censorship has practically eliminated indecency and reduced vulgarity and vice to their lowest terms. To go further in the direction of restriction and prohibition would be to impose upon the new art limitations that have been found impolitic in regard to the older arts of literature, drama and painting.

What is needed now is work upon the other end of the business; that is, selection of the best rather than further suppression of the worst. It must in some way be made possible to pick out what is worth while from the mass of trash in which it is now submerged. The way to do it is doubtless the same as that which has been found most effective in the case of books, pictures and plays, that is, independent and conscientious criticism from the standpoint of the public.

The Independent, April 6, 1914.

THE ART OF THE
MOVIES

Henry MacMahon

The lack of adequate interpretation and criticism must astonish the Martian or other visitor coming to these shores and noting the predominant position rapidly being taken in the amusement world by the motion pictures. The cinema is a Topsy "dat jes' growed." There are no canons of the art, no rules of criticism, no intelligent body of opinion, and no agreement on anything except that D. W. Griffith as a producer is the "best ever" and his film *The Birth of a Nation* is by far the greatest motion picture work yet put forward.

My especial interest being in that film, I have taken pains to collate the expressions concerning it by such "old-line" critical leaders as Metcalfe, Eaton, and Hackett. Not one offers any comprehensive analysis of the new art. Not one offers any constructive suggestion as to the future. Walter Prichard Eaton, writing in *The Boston Transcript*, March 31, is singularly obtuse to the possibilities of the new art.

"The assumption," he says, "that we can go back to what

amounts to sign language at this stage of civilization is one of the most touchingly naive examples of motion-picture makers' credulity."

How about the "sign language" of pure music? The "sign language" of sculpture? The "sign language" of painting? Mr. Eaton's choice of a sneer at the motion-picture art seems singularly unfortunate. For the function of all art is to touch the emotions ideally, and it matters not whether the "signs" or media be words or tones or carvings or pigments or mere facial and bodily attitudes and expressions.

No one seems to have sensed the fact that the new art is symbolistic. Mr. Eaton ridicules the throw-back and the simultaneous action, while Mr. Metcalfe in *Life* objects to "the constant shifting of scenes, the intrusion of things that are not essential, the prolongation and repetition of the same actions." With all due respect to these eminent thinkers, the fact must be stated that they are talking in terms of their old art—the "indoor drama." The technique of the motion picture is closer kin to music; the frequent recurrence of parallel themes is both agreeable and necessary, and the "constant shifting of scenes," instead of being a blemish, is the very virtue of this new dramatic-musical-photographic form, which is best characterized as "art by lightning flash."

Every little series of pictures, continuing from four to fifteen seconds, symbolizes a sentiment, a passion, or an emotion. Each successive series, similar yet different, carries the emotion to the next higher power, till at last, when both of the parallel emotions have attained the n*th* power, so to speak, they meet in the final swift shock of victory and defeat.

A series of pictures has to be swiftly moving. The picturemaker has to use the rapier of suggestion rather than the bludgeon of logic. The environment often counts for more than the act. The fiction of the "removed fourth wall" of the staged drama is gone forever, and the position of the motion-picture spectator is that of one who looks out of doors from an open window upon the whole of life spread as on a panorama, seeing swiftly, understanding swiftly, because the eye is so much swifter and more understanding than the ear.

Suggestions for the improvement of a new artistic vehicle are always welcome. Mr. Eaton, in his *Transcript* article, complains of "amateur kodakery." Alas! There is too much of that every-where. But so there is likewise too much of amateur English and amateur drama. There is ugly sculpture and badly botched paint-ing; discordant, unharmonious music; and (whisper it in the pres-ence of the High Priest of the Older Art!) "legitimate" staging galore that grossly offends both eye and ear. Where in the Older Art is there the selective reverence for beauty that is exhibited in the making of a great film? For example, *The Birth of a Nation*, wherein Mr. Griffith took 140,000 feet of pictures to cull out 12,000 feet (less than one-tenth) for public use. Would David Belasco build and rebuild ten times as many stage scenes as he wanted?

My point is that the efforts at criticism are neither truly analy-tical nor constructive. They do not lead anywhere, nor show the direction the next great step forward will take. Often they be-little the New Art or deliberately ignore its finest phrases. Thus we are told by one prominent New York reviewer that youth, beauty, and facial expressiveness are the sole requisites of a great motion-picture actress—in other words, it's not art at all, but merely a trick imparted to a bright girl by a clever director. I wonder if that reviewer ever studied the career and achievements of Mae Marsh? If he had, he would have found genius in the film as well as in his Old Art.

In general, the most learned critics of the pictures seem to be as far behind the art-form they are criticizing as the Edinburgh Reviewers were hopelessly to the rear of Wordsworth, Shelley, Keats, Coleridge, and Byron, whom they vainly attempted to ex-tinguish whilst upholding the time-worn art of Dryden and Pope. There are honorable exceptions, however. Let me quote from two of them. James Shelley Hamilton in the current *Everybody's* says:

"People who call movies a cheap and inferior substitute for the spoken play base their opinion on pictures that are made in imitation of the spoken plan. Griffith . . . saw that the story must be told wholly by action, that the introduction of long, explanatory substitutes was just as awkward a method of construc-tion as it would be in a spoken play if each character were to ad-vance to the footlights and explain to the audience who he was and how he came to be there. He saw that past action had to be presented visually, and that often it had to be recalled to the audience to give point to the present action: so he invented the 'flash-back,' which is a view of a past or distant scene, inserted almost as an illustration is inserted in a story. To give emphasis to a particular character, a face, or an important bit of stage property, he invented the 'close-up.' . . . He introduced, too, the device of simultaneous action, the method by which the last part of *The Birth of a Nation*, is made so exciting. . . . All of Griffith's pictures have excelled in some particular respect, and they have all been different. But Griffith is not the only man who is doing good things in motion pictures. Directors who make artistic productions are multiplying rapidly."

Lastly, as to the position and future of the film art, let us hear from *The New York Independent* reviewer, Dr. E. E. Slosson, whose technical insight is entirely and rightly unswayed by the fact that he is a bitter opponent of *The Birth of a Nation* on social grounds:

"The film play, compared with its rival, the stage play, has certain serious defects, notably the absence of sound and color. But on the other hand it has certain compensating qualities of its own and producers are very wisely laying more stress on these instead of imitating what the stage can always do better. For instance, the film playwright can use all outdoors for the background instead of a painted and rumpled back drop. He can change the scene oftener than the Elizabethan dramatist. He can dip into the future or the past as though he were in Wells time-machine. He can use literally an army of supernumeraries in place of a dozen attendants with spears. He can reveal the mind of his characters in two ways, neither of them possible on the stage, first by bringing the actor so close that the spectator can read his facial expression, and second, by visualizing his memories or imaginings. He can, if he so desires, wreck a train, burn a house, sink a ship, or blow up a fort, since he does not have to repeat the expense every night. It is natural that the new art should tend to run to excess in those things which it can do best. The film artist is so tickled at the idea that he can portray motion that he is apt to put in too much motion. . . . But these are the inevitable extravagances of youth and are already being eliminated in the best of the feature films. The motion picture has established itself, and in some form or other will become a permanent part of the intellectual and aesthetic life of the nation."

The New York Times, June 6, 1915.

THE PICTURE OF CROWD SPLENDOR

Vachel Lindsay

The shoddiest silent drama may contain noble views of the sea. This part is almost sure to be good. It is a fundamental resource.

A special development of this aptitude in the hands of an expert gives the sea of humanity, not metaphorically but literally: the whirling of dancers in ballrooms, handkerchief-waving masses of people in balconies, hat-waving political ratification meetings, ragged glowering strikers, and gossiping, dickering people in the market-place. Only Griffith and his close disciples can do these as well as almost any producer can reproduce the ocean. Yet the sea of humanity is dramatically blood-brother to the Pacific, Atlantic, or Mediterranean. It takes this new invention, the kinetoscope, to bring us these panoramic drama-elements. By the law of compensation, while the motion picture is shallow in showing private passion, it is powerful in conveying the passions of masses of men. Bernard Shaw, in a recent number of the Metropolitan, answered several questions in regard to the photoplay. Here are two bits from his discourse:

"Strike the dialogue from Molière's Tartuffe, and what audience

would bear its mere stage-business? Imagine the scene in which
Iago poisons Othello's mind against Desdemona, conveyed in a
dumb show. What becomes of the difference between Shakespeare and Sheridan Knowles in the film? Or between Shake-
spare's Lear and any one else's Lear? No, it seems to me that all
the interest lies in the new opening for the mass of dramatic talent
formerly disabled by incidental deficiencies of one sort or another
that do not matter in the picture-theatre . . ."

"Failures of the spoken drama may become the stars of the picture palace. And there are the authors with imagination, visualiza-
tion and first-rate verbal gifts who can write novels and epics,
but cannot for the life of them write plays. Well, the film lends
itself admirably to the succession of events proper to narrative
and epic, but physically impracticable on the stage. *Paradise Lost*
would make a far better film than Ibsen's *John Gabriel Borkman*,
though Borkman is a dramatic masterpiece, and Milton could not
write an effective play."

Note what Shaw says about narrative, epic, and *Paradise Lost*.
He has in mind, no doubt, the pouring hosts of demons and
angels. This is one kind of Crowd Picture.

There is another sort to be seen where George Beban imperson-
ates *The Italian* in a film of that title by Thomas H. Ince and
G. Gardener Sullivan. The first part, taken ostensibly in Venice,
delineates the festival spirit of the people on the bridges and in
gondolas. It gives out the atmosphere of town-crowd happiness.
Then comes the vineyard, the crowd sentiment of a merry grape-
harvest, then the massed emotion of many people embarking on
an Atlantic liner telling good-by to their kindred on the piers,
then the drama of arrival in New York. The wonder of the steer-
age people pouring down their proper gangway is contrasted
with the conventional at-home-ness of the first-class passengers
above. Then we behold the seething human cauldron of the East
Side, then the jolly little wedding-dance, then the life of the East
Side, from the policeman to the peanut-man, and including the
bartender, for the crowd is treated on two separate occasions.

It is hot weather. The mobs of children follow the ice-wagon
for chips of ice. They besiege the fountain-end of the street sprin-
kling wagon quite closely, rejoicing to have their clothes soaked.

They gather round the fire-plug that is turned on for their benefit, and again become wet as drowned rats.

Passing through these crowds are George Beban and Clara Williams as *The Italian* and his sweetheart. They owe the force of their acting to the fact that they express each mass of humanity in turn. Their child is born. It does not flourish. It represents in an acuter way another phase of the same child-struggle with the heat that the gamins indicate in their pursuit of the water-cart.

Then a deeper matter. The hero represents in a fashion the adventures of the whole Italian race coming to America; its natural southern gaiety set in contrast to the drab East Side. The gondolier becomes boot-black. The grape-gathering peasant girl becomes the suffering slum mother. They are not specialized characters like Pendennis or Becky Sharp in the novels of Thackeray.

Omitting the last episode, the entrance into the house of Corrigan, *The Italian* is a strong piece of work.

Another kind of crowd picture is *The Battle*, an old Griffith Biograph, first issued in 1911, before Griffith's name or that of any actor in films was advertised. Blanche Sweet is the leading lady, and Charles H. West the leading man. The psychology of a bevy of village lovers is conveyed in a lively sweethearting dance. Then the boys and his comrades go forth to war. The lines pass between hand-waving crowds of friends from the entire neighborhood. These friends give the sense of patriotism in mass. Then as the consequence of this feeling, as the special agents to express it, the soldiers are in battle. By the fortunes of war the onset is unexpectedly near to the house where once was the dance.

The boy is at first a coward. He enters the old familiar door. He appeals to the girl to hide him, and for the time breaks her heart. He goes forth a fugitive not only from battle, but from her terrible girlish anger. But later he rallies. He brings a train of powder wagons through fires built in his path by the enemy's scouts. He loses every one of his men, and all but the last wagon, which he drives himself. His return with that ammunition saves the hard-fought day.

And through all this, glimpses of the battle are given with a splendor that only Griffith has attained.

Blanche Sweet stands as the representative of the bevy of girls
in the house of the dance, and the whole body social of the village. How the costumes flash and the handkerchiefs wave around
her! In the battle the hero represents the cowardice that all the
men are resisting within themselves. When he returns, he is
the incarnation of the hardihood they have all hoped to display.
Only the girl knows he was first a failure. The wounded general
honors him as the hero above all. Now she is radiant, she cannot
help but be triumphant, though the side of the house is blown
out by a shell and the dying are everywhere.

This one-reel work of art has been reissued of late by the Biograph Company. It should be kept in the libraries of the uni-
versities as a standard. One-reel films are unfortunate in this
sense that in order to see a favorite the student must wait
through five other reels of a mixed program that usually is bad.
That is the reason one-reel masterpieces seldom appear now. The
producer in a mood to make a special effort wants to feel that he
has the entire evening, and that nothing before or after is going
to be a bore or destroy the impression. So at present the pains-
taking films are apt to be five or six reels of twenty minutes each.
These have the advantage that if they please at all, one can see
them again at once without sitting through irrelevant slap-stick
work put there to fill out the time. But now, having the whole
evening to work in, the producer takes too much time for his good
ideas. I shall reiterate throughout this work the necessity for restraint. A one hour program is long enough for any one. If the
observer is pleased, he will sit it through again and take another
hour. There is not a good film in the world but is the better for
being seen in immediate succession to itself. Six-reel programs
are a weariness to the flesh. The best of the old one-reel Bio-
graphs of Griffith contained more in twenty minutes than these
ambitious, incontinent, six-reel displays give us in two hours. It
would pay a manager to hang out a sign: "This show is only
twenty minutes long, but it is Griffith's great film *The Battle*.

But I am digressing. To continue the contrast between private passion in the theater and crowd-passion in the photoplay,
let us turn to Shaw again. Consider his illustration of Iago,
Othello, and Lear. These parts, as he implies, would fall flat in

motion pictures. The minor situations of dramatic intensity might in many cases be built up. The crisis would inevitably fail. Iago and Othello and Lear, whatever their offices in their governments, are essentially private persons, individuals *in extremis*. If you go to a motion picture and feel yourself suddenly gripped by the highest dramatic tension, as on the old stage, and reflect afterward that it was a fight between only two or three men in a room otherwise empty, stop to analyze what they stood for. They were probably representatives of groups or races that had been pursuing each other earlier in the film. Otherwise the conflict, however violent, appealed mainly to the sense of speed.

So, in *The Birth of a Nation*, the Ku Klux Klan dashes down the road as powerfully as Niagara pours over the cliff. Finally the white girl, Elsie Stoneman (impersonated by Lillian Gish), is rescued by the Ku Klux Klan from the mulatto politician, Silas Lynch (impersonated by George Seigmann). The lady is brought forward as a typical helpless white maiden. The white leader, Col. Ben Cameron (impersonated by Henry B. Walthall), enters not as an individual, but as representing the whole Anglo-Saxon Niagara. He has the mask of the Ku Klux Klan on his face till the crisis has passed. The wrath of the Southerner against the blacks and their Northern organizers has been piled up through many previous scenes. As a result this rescue is a real climax, something the photoplays that trace strictly personal hatreds cannot achieve.

The Birth of a Nation is a crowd picture in a triple sense. On the films, as in the audience, it turns the crowd into a mob that is either for or against the Reverend Thomas Dixon's poisonous hatred of the Negro.

Griffith is a chameleon in interpreting his authors. Wherever the scenario shows traces of *The Clansman*, the original book by Thomas Dixon, it is bad. Wherever it is unadulterated Griffith, which is half the time, it is good. The Reverend Thomas Dixon is a rather stagy Simon Legree: in his avowed views a deal like the gentleman with the spiritual hydrophobia in the latter end of *Uncle Tom's Cabin*. Unconsciously, Mr. Dixon has done his best to prove that Legree was not a fictitious character.

Joel Chandler Harris, Harry Stillwell Edwards, George W. Cable, Thomas Nelson Page, James Lane Allen, and Mark Twain are Southern men in Mr. Griffith's class. I recommend their works to him as a better basis for future Southern scenarios.

The Birth of a Nation has been very properly denounced for its Simon Legree qualities by Francis Hackett, Jane Addams, and others. But it is still true that it is a wonder in its Griffith sections. In its handling of masses of men it further illustrates the principles that made notable the old one-reel *Battle* film described in the beginning of this chapter. *The Battle* in the end is greater, because of its self-possession and concentration all packed into twenty minutes.

When, in *The Birth of a Nation*, Lincoln (impersonated by Joseph Henabery) goes down before the assassin, it is a masterscene. He falls as the representative of the government and a thousand high and noble crowd aspirations. The mimic audience in the restored Ford's Theatre rises in panic. This crowd is interpreted in especial for us by the two young people in the seats nearest, and the freezing horror of the treason sweeps from the Ford's Theatre audience to the real audience beyond them. The real crowd touched with terror beholds its natural face in the glass.

Later come the pictures of the rioting Negroes in the streets of the Southern town, mobs splendidly handled, tossing wildly and rhythmically like the sea. Then is delineated the rise of the Ku Klux Klan, of which we have already spoken.

In the future development of motion pictures mob movements of anger and joy will go through fanatical and provincial whirlwinds into great national movements of anger and joy.

A book by Gerald Stanley Lee that has a score of future scenarios in it, a book that might well be dipped into by the reader before he goes to such a play as *The Italian* or *The Battle*, is the work which bears the title *Crowds*.

Mr. Lee is far from infallible in his remedies for factory and industrial relations. But in sensitiveness to the flowing street of humanity he is indeed a man. Listen to the names of some of the divisions of his book: "Crowds and Machines; Letting the Crowds be Good; Letting the Crowds be Beautiful; Crowds and Heroes; Where are We Going? The Crowd Scare; The Strike, an Invention for Making Crowds Think; The Crowd's Imagination about People; Speaking as One of the Crowd; Touching the Imagination of Crowds." Films in the spirit of these titles would help to make world-voters of us all.

The World State is indeed far away. But as we peer into the Mirror Screen some of us dare to look forward to the time when the pouring streets of men will become sacred in each other's eyes, in pictures and in fact.

The Art of the Moving Picture, 1915.

THE CINEMATOGRAPH
AS ART

Alexander Bakshy

The wonderful popularity enjoyed by the cinematograph during the last decade has been for a long time a subject of eager discussion in those circles which have the interests of the theater at heart. The various groups of art-workers connected with the theater—the dramatists, the actors, and the artists—are directly involved in the problem, and it is interesting to note how different has been the attitude revealed toward it by each of these groups. The artists, perhaps the most cultured of these three groups from the standpoint of art, have simply ignored the cinematograph, regarding it as something so crude and inartistic as to be unworthy of serious notice. It is true that a few genuine experiments have been made in this direction, but for several reasons, chiefly because the artists failed to comprehend the real nature of their medium, they have all proved a complete failure.

The attitude of most actors has been much more condescending. Those actors who have generally concerned themselves very little with matters of art, accepted the cinematograph with the docile humility accorded to all things in the natural order. They transferred to the new invention whatever knowledge of drama they had gained on the legitimate stage, and supplied only one new feature: extreme exaggeration in mimicry and action, which they held to be the chief peculiarity of moving pictures. On the other hand, the more advanced members of the theatrical profession, who have been really anxious to establish on the stage the principles of vital art, however much they may have differed in their interpretation of them, at once realized the danger which threatened the drama from the encroachment of the modern cinematograph theaters, and did not hesitate to proclaim a most resolute opposition in an endeavor to protect their art from being contaminated by the vulgar "mechanical" device. Thus we see large sections of the community, for whom art is an object of vital faith, rejecting the cinematograph as a medium devoid of any artistic qualities. But it would be wrong to infer that it has always lacked faithful champions. Strange as it may seem, these have come from the group which is furthest removed from the actual problems of the theater—the dramatists. As might be expected, the only fault that the litterateurs were able to detect in moving pictures was in the plot, and so they set themselves the task of remedying it. With enviable ease, they began to pour out elaborate philosophical dramas, mystery plays, tragedies, "literary" melodramas, and what not, in order to demonstrate what artistic possibilities have been lying dormant in the neglected and abused cinematograph. Once they found that the theater was no longer held in popular esteem, they had no compunction in erecting their rostrum on the picture-screen, the more so as they perceived in it the fulfillment of two objects: the popularization of the drama and the elevation of moving pictures to a higher artistic level. We need only mention such names as Gabriele D'Annunzio and Leonid Andreyev to show what resolute and self-confident arch-priests of literature have undertaken in the task of reforming the moving-picture play. But though their attempts have raised a host of arguments and controversies among all who are interested in the theater, there can be little doubt that failure must be the inevitable result of their efforts. Their defense of the pictures is as inherently fallacious as the opposition of artists and actors, since both are the outcome of a complete failure to understand the peculiar nature of the cinematograph as a medium of art. If the dramatists' defense leaves us entirely unmoved, since it comes from virtual outsiders, we cannot but deplore the opposition of those who should be the first and foremost exponents of the new art. For there is an artistic future for the cinematograph, a future as great as any form of artistic drama can hope to attain. We may ignore the criticisms of those who condemn as utterly vulgar all moving pictures, photographs, and gramophones, as well as most other products of our resourceful mechanical genius. These well-intentioned dilettantes are only victims of prevailing artistic conventions, and have no standard of their own by which they may discriminate between what is art and what is not. The future of the cinematograph does not rest with them. It depends upon those enlightened and liberal lovers of art who can see beyond the conventions of the moment, who possess a range of sympathies which is already wide enough to embrace such divergent revelations as we find in the static art of Egypt, the decorativeness of Eastern art, and the rudimentary work of Cezanne and Matisse, or to refer strictly to the domain of drama, the medieval booth, the puppet show, and the productions of Mr. E. Gordon Craig. Theirs is the task of creating the canons and standards, of shaping the conventions of cinematographic art, and of building up a tradition which will pass, in due course, through the period when it is merely fashionable, and attain finally the position of an acknowledged medium for artistic expression.

It is with the object of securing a more sympathetic attitude for this discredited medium that I venture, however conscious of the heresy, to advance a plea for the cinematograph as a vehicle of genuine art-expression.

Much has been said in the press about the issues involved in the problem of moving pictures: their special appeal to the masses; their competition with the theater; whether they are to supersede the latter, or whether they are doomed to be merely a transient fashion and eventually disappear; their artistic crudity; that is to say, whether they are a reversal to the methods of the booth, and whether they indicate the birth of a new democratic art; and many other similar questions. With these issues we shall not concern ourselves at present. Without underrating their interest and importance, we hold that they overlook the most essential factor of the problem: the peculiar nature of the medium which alone should form the basis of its possible artistic application. Before we are able to enter upon a discussion of this problem, a number of deep-rooted popular misconceptions must be cleared away. I almost despair of my task, for in the sphere of ideas, as in that of biology, the lowest forms are the most tenacious of life.

One of the critic's first duties is discrimination. Yet the criticisms hurled so liberally from all sides at the cinematograph have been little distinguished by this character. Two things which are entirely distinct have been persistently confused by all critics: the cinematograph as a medium, and the cinematograph theater as we know it at the present time. That the second is below criticism—indeed, something coarse, crude, and altogether ugly —can be easily and unreservedly admitted. But to deduce from this fact the impossibility of an artistic cinematograph betrays a lack of logic and imagination. It is evident, in the first place, that many drawbacks of the modern moving-picture play are in no way connected with the cinematograph as a peculiar medium of dramatic expression. For example, take the vulgar realism of moving pictures about which we hear so many complaints. Is it a peculiar feature of the cinematograph? The students of the theater will agree that naturalism as vulgar as this ruled the legitimate stage long before the cinematograph became a competitor. The pictures simply followed along the beaten track, bringing to logical absurdity what the legitimate drama, not endowed with the infinite resourcefulness of its competitor, could only pursue half way. It is unnecessary to dwell upon the many similar drawbacks of the cinematograph. We are not so much concerned with what it actually is as with what it might be. The problem that really matters may be stated in the following words: Is the cinematograph a medium capable of artistic achievement in the two fields that make up the art of the stage—the dramatic field and the pictorial field? The answer to this question necessarily involves discussing the vexed question of mechanical art. However reluctant I may be to touch upon this controversy, I am unable to avoid it altogether. So I bow before the inevitable, and shall try to dispose of it in the briefest possible manner.

It is often contended that automatic mechanism can never attain to anything like artistic perfection, and that consequently there is no artistic future for the cinematograph.

It is obvious that the whole argument stands or falls with the definition of "mechanism." But this definition is never stated in anything like exact terms. That there are no absolutely automatic mechanisms hardly needs to be pointed out. All mechanisms must be controlled by human power at one moment or another, and, what is still more important, they are all products of human intelligence. Whatever forces may be involved in their operation are brought together by the action of human thought compressed and wound up like a spring, their actual prime mover throughout the whole process of their operation. Thus the problem is reduced to defining the degree of independence from immediate human control and power which mechanism can possess. This is so indeterminate that we see similar kinds of action styled mechanical in one case, and highly individual in another. Who will doubt, for instance, that the action of an organ played at a concert is individual, and that of a locomotive engine mechanical? Yet it cannot be disputed that the second requires as much skill and personal control as the first. The point is not whether these operations are art or are not art, but whether they are mechanical or nonmechanical. I maintain that there is no real distinction between the one and the other, and that both may serve artistic ends if properly utilized.

One more example of the prevailing confusion of thought on this subject: the gramophone is admittedly a mechanical contrivance and so is the telephone; yet no one listening to the opera through the telephone ever says that the music he hears is a mechanical production. The sole difference, however, that exists between this music and its record on the gramophone, is that the gramophone fixes only one stage of the process—the vibrations of the telephone membrane—and allows one to "switch on" the flow of sound at will, while the telephone receives and transmits the sound in one continuous process.

These two illustrations not only show the vague popular use of the term "mechanical," but also the elements that go to make up the significance of this term. They are three: complexity of mechanism, the number of intermediate stages, and the extent of time between the application of human power and the appearance of the effect. It is only necessary to rid the mind of the prejudice for a moment to be able to see that not a single one of these elements is in any way incompatible with artistic work and achievement. And if at the present time mechanical methods of production under the capitalistic system have served to destroy whatever artistic feeling the producer may have had, this does not militate against the mechanical methods as such, but rather against the way they are used in our time.

Now let us examine the problem itself. First of all, let us endeavor to realize the peculiar nature of the cinema drama, and then we shall be able to see how far this "mechanical" medium lends itself to artistic expression.

One of the most startling facts about cinematograph productions is that the actors who play for these pictures are all members of the legitimate dramatic profession. Their attainments on the theater stage need not be discussed in this instance, but it seems quite apparent that of cinema acting they understand very little indeed. The cinema drama raises some of the most fundamental problems of art. But what do they know about them? Are they aware that the cinematograph play is the most abstract form of the pantomime? Do they realize that if there is any stage on which the laws of movement should reign supreme, it is the cinematographic stage? If they did, they would not have monopolized the cinematograph play, but would have left it to dancers, clowns, and acrobats who do know something about the laws of movement. By no means do I presume to say that dancers and clowns are necessarily artists. But movement is their natural element, and it is also movement that constitutes the real nature of the cinematograph. The patrons and devotees of present-day pictures may boast of their "wonderful realistic effects," but this popular conception only betrays a complete failure to grasp one salient fact: viewed from the standpoint of the drama, just as from many other standpoints of which more will be said later on, the cinematograph is essentially and preeminently dynamic. It is necessary at this point to realize the effect of picture plays if this principle of pure movement were recognized throughout. Rolling eyes and wild gesticulation would be abolished. Sham "natural" talking would give place to mimicry and gesture, free and eloquent. The movements of the actors would no longer imitate actual life, but would synthetically express it in the peculiar laws of rhythmic motion. Pantomimes, harlequinades, ballets, would take the place of the present melodramas and comical pictures, thus giving adequate expression to the wordless nature of the medium. Would it be possible, then, to argue that there is no art in the cinematograph? So far as the dramatic aspect is concerned, this at any rate would constitute a most decisive step in the direction of art. And other advances would immediately follow, once the fundamental principle was firmly established.

It is often contended that the presence in bodily form of the actor in the play is the *sine qua non* of artistic drama. This view is held alike by those who believe in realism on the stage and by those who do not. The attitude of the latter is particularly droll. After disposing of all the realistic mummery, they cling to the last citadel of the "true-to-nature" gospel of art, the bodily shell of the actor. Why, is it not his personality that really matters? And is that expressed only in the frail physical body of the actor? To the spectator of some artistic culture it is in a sense irrelevant whether the acting on the stage is performed by living persons, by dolls, or by cinematograph shadows. The effect in each case must necessarily be different, but only in so far as the artistic properties of each of these media of drama differ from one another. Their absolute artistic value remains unaffected by their being animate or inanimate. In fact, it is open to argument, whether man is at all suitable as a medium of dramatic art, as readers of Mr. E. Gordon Craig already know. But we need not go so far. In the case of cinema drama, we do not dispense with the actor. We dispense only with his body. Perhaps those who cannot reconcile themselves to this fact will find comfort in reflecting upon the time when poets were gradually led to recognize that singing a poem in person is not the only way of rendering the artistic beauties of the composition. In our age of reduplication, to the list of arts which already resort to this process (poetry, music, lithography, etching), we now add the sacred art of the theater. It is a process of natural development, and it would be sheer stupidity on our part if we continued to ignore it or to notice only its outward features. Just as it did not degrade the profession of the painter when he realized the artistic possibilities of lithography, so it will not degrade the modern actor if he makes full use of the new medium which human ingenuity has placed at his command. The real and the only problem for him is to find out what actually constituted the peculiar properties of the medium and how these properties should be managed to achieve the highest artistic effect. The fact that the problem can be solved only by practice and experiment and that present-day cinematograph practice has produced in the artistic sense some appalling results, must not be taken as proof of the inartistic nature of the medium itself. The truth of this statement has been shown above as applied to the playing of actors. It will be seen that it is equally true applied to the pictorial element of stage production.

The peculiar optical effects of the cinematograph are a resultant of two processes: the photographic process of making the film, and the process of projecting the film on the screen.

What artistic possibilities do these processes possess?

There is no need to enter in this instance upon a discussion of photography as art. Its shortcomings as a medium and the triteness of the average photographic work can hardly be disputed. But only narrow prejudice can deny it any artistic quality whatever. The magnificent work so often found at various photographic exhibitions proves most conclusively that photography and art are not so incompatible as some of our purists would like us to believe.

The same is the case with cinema photography. So long as it remains in the hands of mere operators and chemists, so long will its pictorial value be on a par with the artistic conceptions held by these craftsmen. And this can hardly be wondered at, seeing that the nature of the new medium, to be properly understood, requires such a culture of mind as is seldom met with even amongst professional exponents of art.

The greatest question it raises is that of the psychological significance pertaining to its various dramatic and pictorial forms.

One important fact must be stated at the outset. The cinematograph has at its command two distinct ways of producing plays: the two-dimensional production on the ordinary screen, and the three-dimensional production by means of different stereoscopic devices and of the kineplastikon. Too much stress cannot be laid upon this distinction. Its importance is enormous, since in the two forms of space—of two, and of three dimensions— we obtain two aspects of the world which are opposed to each other in their very elements. Without going deeply into the philosophical and psychological nature of these forms of space, it may be said that the first symbolized and incarnates the principles of continuity, cosmic unity, spontaneity, pure sentiment and kindred psychic experiences, whilst the second stands for differentiation, individuality, clear-consciousness, and the like, thus forming two distinct worlds: one monistic, fused into one integral whole, and the other atomistic, broken into numberless mutually opposed units. The same two principles obtain in the theater. The staging in one plane produces an effect of dissolving the world, when reproduced in the mind of the audience.It destroys the barrier between the stage and the spectator, turning the play from a mere spectacle into an actual incident in the life of the audience, an incident which, though experienced passively, enters into the soul of the spectator as an integral element of his being. Such, for instance, is the effect of some of Maurice Maeterlinck's religious plays when staged in one plane. This method may be called subjective-monistic. Its counterpart is the objective-monistic method, which again destroys the barrier between the stage and the audience, but this time by transporting the spectator onto the stage and making him actively participate in the play. The early forms of the Greek drama and the medieval mystery plays may be quoted here as examples of this method, though the first also contains considerable elements of the subjectivity.

The other way of apprehending the universe is based on the consciousness of all its component parts or atoms—on the opposition of self and non-self. The world acquires an atomistic aspect. The self-affirming personality always feels its aloofness from the ambience. By a process of active contemplation it may embrace and absorb this encompassing world, but it never fuses into it. In the theater this sovereignty of self-affirming personality finds its expression, on the one hand, in the abstractly sculpturesque stagings of Mr. E. Gordon Craig, which we may rightly call subjective-atomistic. These definitions may appear somewhat obscure, but they show the problems of staging which obtrude in the cinematograph, determining the pictorial represen- tation. The cinematograph possesses a greater command of space than the legitimate stage, or than painting on flat surfaces. It is able, and therefore obliged, to discriminate between the different methods of pictorial presentment. Unlike the others, it can afford to be logical. But it would only gain in effect and would reveal the inner monistic nature of the two-dimensional space if it were more consistent and eliminated every atom of natural relief. Play of lines and colors is all that is required on the flat screen, and if properties of the medium have, as everybody believes nowadays, any importance in the achievement of artistic effect, then it is ob- vious that the cinematograph can only gain by consistent ap- plication of the principle of two-dimensional space to pictures on the ordinary screen.

On the other and, to represent the atomistic world as distinct from the self-conscious personality, the method of three-dimen- sional staging affords both the actor and the pictorial artist un- limited scope for new and altogether artistic achievements.

The stagings of Mr. E. Gordon Craig, for instance, unfetter and expand the stage. They are not theatrical in the narrow sense of the word. They purport to create on the boards a world of their own, one entirely distinct from the stage world, however far it may be removed from the realistic world. But the stage is only a stage, and the space on it has its well-known limitations. The case with the stereoscopic cinematograph is different. Its command of space is practically boundless. It can create another world and place it before the eyes of the audience to watch it with admiration, sympathy, or disdain. The stereoscopic cinemato- graph in the hands of real artists could raise even realistic drama (in its wordless form, of course) to its proper position, representing the world stated objectively and watched from out- side.

As to the pictorial artist, both the plane and the stereoscopic moving picture open before him a new field for artistic develop- ment. It would be impossible at the present stage of the cine- matograph's development to discuss in detail the multifarious problems arising out of the application of this new process.

Only practical experience could give satisfactory answers to many of these questions. But there are some general features of the cinema-pictorial process, which already allow of analysis and discussion.

The most important of them is the dynamic character of the cinematograph. In addition to the third dimension which the cinematograph provides by stereoscopic projection, it possesses yet another co-ordinate—time. How does this element enter into the pictorial and plastic arts? We know the Egyptians answered this question by discarding the notion itself. Instead of transient time they imparted to their immovable, frigid productions a spirit of eternity. The Greeks, the artists of the Renaissance, and most modern artists try to give the impression of movement by arranging the elements of a picture or a statue in such a way that the eye must travel over the production.

Now the cinematograph is the first medium by which one can deal with time fairly and squarely without recourse to the tricks of the cubist or futurist. Is that not in itself a sufficient reason why artists should seize this unique opportunity?

Following the distinction stated above, we shall have two branches of this mobile art: the flat-screen cinematograph (the realm of the flat-surface artist), and the stereoscopic cinematograph (the realm of the sculptor who thinks in form and color). At present, the only indications of this future mobile art are found in the best theatrical productions. I may point out as examples the exquisite stagings of Russian ballets by Bakst, Anisfeld, and Golovin, and their designs for costumes in particular, since in the varying combinations of lines and colors on the background of the scenery the basis of the mobile art is present implicitly.

It is necessary at this point, in the light of the foregoing theories, to consider what position the artist will occupy in future cinematograph productions. In the stereoscopic cinematograph he has already at his command nearly all that he can desire. It is true that the colors of life are yet wanting, but an artist can obtain a real color-tone from black and white. Moreover he can tone the film just as he pleases, so that after all he is not entirely deprived of color. Otherwise the stereoscopic cinema photography leaves hardly anything to be desired. It gives a facsimile reproduction, color excepted, of the actual scene. If the legitimate stage affords scope for the application of artistic talents, the stereoscopic cinematograph has the additional advantage of a much greater command of space than the stage.

The problems of photography in the one-plane cinematograph are somewhat different. They are akin to those met with in other arts dealing with the flat surface; on the other hand, they are naturally distinguished from them in so far as they all depend on the mobile conditions of the cinematograph. The influence of these conditions on other artistic effects can be judged from the fact that in moving pictures, we are seldom able to fix our attention on one given position for any considerable length of time. This being so, the criteria of art applied to moving pictures must be obviously different from those applied to paintings or lithographs. The laws of composition cannot possibly be the same. What they are I shall not here attempt to define, but an artist who took up the cinematograph would find that such laws do exist and, gradually, by experiment and practice, he would subject them to his control. At present, our ideas on mobile composition are so undeveloped and so crude that posterity will hardly be able to believe that they were ever held. It is only necessary to remind ourselves of the revolution started in this field by Jacques-Dalcroze with his rhythmic gymnastics. It is still open to an artist to give it a worthy counterpart in fixing it on the film. In this connection the attempts made by Mr. A. Wallace Rimington in England and by A. Scriabin, the well-known composer, in Russia, to create a new art of color-music are of interest. Mr. Rimington has already given us a detailed exposition of his theory and a description of the color-organ, the instrument he specially invented for this purpose. There can be little doubt that this new form of art will have a great future, and that in one way or another it will become one of the most essential components of the artistic cinematograph.

The second cinema photographic problem is akin to the question of ordinary photographic prints. Line drawing being excluded by the nature of photography as we at present know it, the problem is how to achieve the best results with a medium similar in character to the wash. The problem lies not so much with the lighting of models as with the production of the film and projection on the screen. Greater artistic effect would probably be achieved on screens of more solid consistency than those now in vogue, on screens of a grained surface, such as a white plastered wall would provide. Then the lights and shades on the film should give more concentrated, solid, and flat masses, thus obviating unnecessary details, which are often annoyingly conspicuous. The silhouette picture film, which is practically unknown, possesses wonderful possibilities. For fairy-tales or grotesque and sentimental stories, hardly any medium could be more fitting.

In conclusion, let me recapitulate the principal points. The artistic failure of the modern cinematograph is due solely to lack of understanding of this medium's peculiar properties. It is dynamic throughout. Expression of the rhythmically moving body must be the only law of the actor, expression of rhythmically moving form and color the only law of the pictorial artist.

The actor must cease ignoring the dumb nature of the cinematograph in performing "realistic" plays. Pantomime and ballet are the only forms open to him. He can achieve greatly varying psychological effects by staging his plays in two or three dimensions. The silhouette is the form of acting where the one-plane principle of staging finds its most complete expression.

The pictorial artist must discriminate between the flat-screen and the stereoscopic cinematograph projection. With the first, he must try to eliminate all relief, to evolve the color value of light and shade, and to make the screen as good an artistic medium as paper is. With the second, he must solve the complicated problems of planes and volumes which this stereoscopic form of projection places before him. In application to both methods he must evolve the formulae of mobile composition and mobile color.

So much for the actor and for the artist.

Above all, however, the cinematograph needs men of genius, of deep insight, and of great spiritual culture. More than the theater it is a synthetic form of art, as both the dramatic and the pictorial arts constitute the basic elements of its nature. To be raised from its present state of degradation it requires men who combine a genius for dramatic and pictorial presentation with the deep wisdom of sages. It requires that clear-consciousness without which there is no real personality and no individual feeling of the world.

Art is the revelation of the human spirit in everything capable of expressing it, conditioned only by the nature of the medium used. So the cinematograph will rise to the level of art when men of great intelligence and insight express themselves in forms determined by the natural properties of this new medium. Everything seems to indicate that we shall not have long to wait for this fulfillment.

Drama Magazine, May, 1946.

ON THE SCREEN

Kenneth MacGowan

Two things I find that give the movies a promise of art. Both are imponderable. One is light, the creation of an expressive atmosphere. The other is sequence, the assembling of innumerable pictorial impressions in an order which not alone tells a story but reinforces it with a mental, almost a subconscious, gathering of details. It is manner, not matter, that makes a day of even the most routine of weekly "features" in some degree profitable. The stories may be no better than the traffic of stage and popular magazine. The technique of camera and scenario brings keen pleasure and keener promise into ten hours of such habitual screen-gazing as has been my bi-weekly duty as photoplay editor of a daily newspaper.

The first impression of the theatergoer at the movies used to be that, amid scores of flat, almost footlighted, scenes, the camera showed every now and then a lighting effect such as the American theater had never risked and probably could not achieve. Generally it was the illuminating of an interior from a single point, as, for instance, a lantern or a candle. Thousands of striking lights and shadows filled the scene. They created an atmosphere of vivid life. Faces became more expressive, more beautiful or more hideous. Of course, it was not often that the action of a film gave excuse for this effect; only once in Morosco's *Peer Gynt*, for example, in the cabin scene, was the director who exploited this effect able to use it. But presently a producer, Cecil De Mille, and his art director, Wilfred Buckland, began to try something of the kind on almost all interior scenes. Instead of utilizing the filtered sunlight of open air studios, or the even glare of banks of Cooper Hewitts from top and sides, they threw their illumination in a great strong sheet from one or at the most two angles. The result was the brilliant "Lasky lighting" that the movie fan began to note in Farrar's *Carmen*.

Beginning at first as an effect on the level with prints in sepia, it has developed in the Lasky company's productions into something that heightens atmosphere. In Mary Pickford's film, *A Romance of the Red Woods*, the variations in this lighting within a single room are most interesting. Under a small, single source of light, the walls of the cabin and the faces of the actors are filled with staring shadows to match the terror of the episode enacted. Under ordinary clear studio lighting, the same scene takes on the cold grayness of the morning that follows. When comparative peace and security reign again, the cabin is warmed into mellow evening lamplight by the use of two or three brilliant sources of illumination.

Still further refinements of this matter of lighting come to me in this day at the movies. In the Thomas H. Ince production, *Chicken Casey*, as in virtually all his films, the possibilities of half illumination have been wonderfully realized by his art director, Robert Brunton. Light becomes atmosphere instead of illumination. Coming naturally from some window, lamp, or doorway, it illumines the center of the picture and the people standing there, with a glow that in intensity, in volume, or in variety of sources has some quality expressive of the emotion of the scene. Moreover, it illumines only the human figures and the things with which they are concerned. Behind them is a great, solid, realistic room, far more complete in every detail than any stage setting yet absolutely unobtrusive. In the ordinary screen production it is lit up within an inch of its life. Care is taken to make us see the sculptured reality of its every molding, each sure-enough wrinkle of its hangings. The result, of course, is that we don't see the drama. The tawdry human figures jump about and distract us; that is all. In an Ince production all that massive detail fades into the dimness of shadowed corners. We know reality is there, rich reality, but we have something more important in hand. It is the human drama that Ince is presenting. He centers our attention on the one thing we need to understand, the people and the things they do and feel. There is something of Rembrandt in the Ince method.

Another type of production tries to do the same thing by a trick of the camera. It is well represented by *The Americano*, a film made by another and now departed element of the Triangle Film Corporation, the Fine Arts Studio, once dominated by Griffith. Here we watch the actors, too, and nothing but the actors. In a clear and mellow light, we see a man at his desk; behind him the details of his office fade off into the shadows of the theater outside the screen. Out of the shadows steps Douglas Fairbanks, and into the spot of light where we have been watching the older man. The same general effect of concentration of acting and atmosphere is gained in almost all the other interior scenes of the film.

But it is gained, as you may observe, by hardly any genuine use of light. The margins of the picture outside the central portion given to the figures are masked in by an iris which makes a vignette of the center. As the background is always of dark wood or canvas, the effect is almost the same as in the Ince method; for the edge of the iris fades into the dark hue of the setting. The usefulness and necessity of a dark background are easily apparent by comparison with pictures where this iris effect is used in out-of-doors scenes, as in *The Barrier*. There the edge of the iris cuts sharply across the light sky or landscape. And the instant that line is visible, you not only become aware of the trick, but you grow camera-conscious. The mood of belief is lost; you are thinking of the director and the actors and the camera and all the make-believe, instead of feeling the story as a reality.

Aside from the fact that the Fine Arts method is a trick that keen observation can penetrate, it lacks pictorial virtues which the Ince enjoys. By the Ince method, the light is not only concentrated on the actors' figures; it may be composed in designs other than the rough circle of the iris. In the club scene from *Chicken Casey*, for instance, the light strikes across a group of men in evening dress from a tall window, throwing shadows that suggest in the angle and the lines of the panes the height and magnificence of the room. In the dramatist's library, the daylight is shaped and tempered by simple but handsome hangings at the windows. It enters his bedroom by both window and door, accomplishing the necessary job of illumination yet suggesting too the more Spartan arrangement of the room and the proximity of the library, from which the action flows.

Naturally, other directors have learned these tricks, and some use them extremely well. There is Alan Dwan, for instance, a keen-minded student of the screen since the early days. In *Panthea* he builds up amazingly effective prisons with nothing but inky shadows, and constructs a palatial dining room out of a great space of floor and table and a very large chandelier above. He knows how to control his light even in exteriors where he must depend on the sun. For this Russian photoplay he has built up Vermeer-like walls and shadowed commons that are full of the quality of Russian historical painters. His opening scene is as genuine a work of art as any composition by Steichen. Out of the darkness of the theater comes a gray room, with three patches of photographic color. One is a small window high at the left. Under its light a young woman is just distinguishable above the corner of a grand piano. To the left is the door of a dimly lighted passage in which stands her old teacher. Then the camera picks out for us other features of this room, composed with the simplicity and dignity that reside in the piano itself. They are three men sitting apart from one another in the half light, listening. Music and the occasion—a private recital before connoisseurs—are the very breath of the scene.

But what is all this atmosphere alone? True, it is nothing unless it is spent on stories by a method that makes of them something filled with the completeness of life as our minds roam over it. And that the American movie has learned to do. It is our contribution. We have gone by experiment, by trial and error, by instinct, straight to the intricate, submental nature of the photoplay which Munsterberg recognized in his valuable analytical volume. We throw on the screen in half a minute a dozen aspects, great and small, immediate and remote, obvious and inferential, actual and reminiscent, of the thing that is to be told.

It is a quality which resides first in the scenario and which the director must realize as he works. Alan Dwan, who makes his own scenarios, uses this thoroughgoing, Griffithian technique with sure effect in *Panthea*. He gathers that music room into our vision with undeniable sureness. He gives us Russian through a dozen small touches, crisp "flash-backs," intimate and pungent "close-ups." When he gets to the swiftest part of his story, he drives us through it unerringly by following physical actions to the minutest details. When, for instance, the police raid a dwelling, he shows not only the approach, the groups on both sides of the door, the violence of the entry and the scattering of the dwellers, but as the police charge upstairs after the hero, he smashes it home to us with a sudden flash of feet pounding the steps. Again he uses that same "close-up" expedient—and with an even greater, because characterizing, effect—when, after the officer has shot the hero, he kicks him over with his spurred boot to make sure he is harmless. Dwan catches in his "close-up" of the kicking boot not only the beastliness of the act, but a curve in the boot itself and in the direction of the blow which is amazingly characteristic of the hard, perky, Prussian-like little officer. Such a detail serves no purpose in the tale. Eliminate it and every necessary step of the action would be there. But, when not dwelt on at such lengths as to seem to have a plot importance which it lacks, such a means builds up conviction and atmosphere to an astounding degree. It is things of this sort—intuitions of writer and director—which will give photoplays some of the quality of observation and character that make literature.

Occasionally these technical means of light and of sequence and observation get themselves used in an episode that grows big with imagination. Such a moment occurs in the last photo-play of this blissful day, *The Golem*. It is a German film, which though using the Ince type of lighting with fine effect through-out, realizes the possibilities of the true movie technique only at rare moments when the story calls imperatively for this Ameri-can-made device. One of these is unforgettable. The Monster is an old stone figure which comes to life when a scroll of magic has been inserted in a sort of hollow button on his chest. After many centuries of solitude in an abandoned well, the stone figure comes into the possession of an antiquarian who possesses also the secret of the scroll. He brings the stone giant to life and uses him for various picturesque purposes, including the guard-ing of a daughter who prefers to frisk with a young nobleman. The woman arouses the curiosity of the Monster, and ultimately a sort of passion, and when she escapes from the house, he fol-lows her. Then comes the discovery of the world, still more wonderful than the finding of passion. The giant lumbers across the square of the German village staring at its Gothic buildings. He reaches a brook and with a grin of amazed pleasure wades and splashes across. On the other side he finds a flowering bush. He takes a blossom in his great hand. Staring at it, he brings it close enough to his nose accidentally to smell the odor. Another of life's simplest and grandest things is caught on the broad, ele-mentally stupid countenance of the creature. All, of course, in varied "long-shots" and "close-ups."

And now the best and most perfect moment, as we, and the camera follow the *Golem* across country. We climb a slight rise of ground to a wooden crest. Out of that wood we stare, through a fine arts circle of shadowed boughs, towards a cathedral city, raising its spires to God. Suddenly, up from the foreground, rears the bulk of the *Golem*. His head is turned to gaze at the sight which, if it has arrested us, must strike him dumb. We watch with an amazingly personal interest. The body rises higher and higher, the head tilts back, the shoulders lift, the arms spread from the sides in a gesture of astounded wonder which encircles our vision of the miraculous city. Light and shadow, composition, selection and arrangement of pictures, drive home that miracle-laden pilgrimage of the *Golem* as few arts could do. Through them it realizes every quality of the imagination that word or paint can summon. It is the foreshadowing of such things in even the most commonplace of pictures that makes the routine of the movies in some degree a glorious venture.

The New Republic, Sept. 15, 1917.

THE VIVIFYING OF
SPACE

Herman G. Scheffauer

Ever since the camera learned the trick of manifolding in swift succession, the picture-film has been a mechanical product, full of artificiality and even artfulness, but denied the breath and pulse of true art. It has been a mere medium of reproduction of the external photography, however sumptuous some of its theatrical or scenic effects, however fantastic and ingenious some of its mechanical and optical possibilities. But Art fled the lens which only the concrete reality or the constructed sham would enter. Moving-pictures—movies—the populace pierced instinctively through all pretenses and named them for what they were.

A true art-form for the film had not yet been invented or evolved. It had not yet found its true expression or convention.

It was still the lively daughter of dead photography. A mock-world, the phantasm of the actual, projected itself upon the screen in all the tones of black and white and seared itself upon our aching retinae. It mimicked the photograph, the stage, the painted picture, the formal tableau.

But at last the revolution of this world of light and shadow has begun. The creative element has entered it. The smug phantoms, the gorgeous settings, the smirking dolls with bared teeth and ox-like eyes, the creased cavaliers, prettified puppies and exotic sirens are threatened in their easy monopoly of this domain. The background which to them had been a mere foil for their mouthings, oglings and struttings, has become alive. The artist has slipped into this crude phantasmagoria and begun to create. He has seized upon unconjectured, aesthetic, dramatic and optical possibilities. Space—hitherto considered and treated as something dead and static, a mere inert screen or frame, often of no more significance than the painted balustrade-background at the village photographer's—has been smitten into life, into movement and conscious expression. A fourth dimension has begun to evolve out of this photographic cosmos.

The sixth sense of man, his feeling for space or room—his Raumgefühl—has been awakened and given a new incentive. Space has been given a voice. It has become a presence. It moves and operates by its distances and by its masses, static yet intinct with the expression of motion; it speaks with forms and with color-value. It has taken on something dynamic and daemonic, demanding not only attention but tribute from the soul. It has become an obedient genius in league with the moods and dreams and emotions of the artist bent on forcing his will upon the audience.

This art, as I have already implied, is not a reflection of reality but a transformation of it: it may even be a distortion of it. The film is not to be a mere reproduction of life and the outer world, but a sublimation and adumbration of it. The frozen and rigid forms and values of the outer and apparent world to which the lens and the sensitized celluloid-strip are so relentlessly faithful, are broken up, dissolved and endowed with a new role. They are no longer a dead, two-dimensional background for the animate walking, kissing, dancing, murdering pantomimes and automata, but expressive presences, immanent forces that act not, but react and enact.

They claim and exercise the right to share in the dumb action of the living. The frown of a tower, the scowl of a sinister alley, the pride and serenity of a white peak, the hypnotic draught of a straight road vanishing to a point—these exert their influences and express their natures; their essences flow over the scene and blend with the action. A symphony arises between the organic and the inorganic worlds and the lens peers behind inscrutable veils. The human imagination is fructified and begins to react, willingly or unwillingly. A new magic ensues, a new mystery possesses us.

This new treatment of the sense of space and feeling for room was first given expression in a film entitled *The Cabinet of Dr. Caligari*. It was described as the first expressionistic film and embodied many original and instructive ideas. The creators were Walther Reimann, Walther Rohrig and Hermann Warm. These men did not wish to produce a series of new and startling pictures. What they undertook was a scientific and aesthetic experiment in a new treatment of space. The sculpturesque, plastic treatment of space, that is, the three-dimensional, opposes itself to the two-dimensional world of the painted picture. Yet paint and color are liberally made use of. It is as if the third dimension—depth—had actually been added to the picture and had begun to develop itself—unto infinity, if you will. From this it would develop into the fourth dimension which may be conceived as time. Pictures are condition: space is existence. Space overrides a poster or a signboard.

The adaptation of these laws and theories to the film was not mystic or esoteric but very practical. A new instrument or medium is given us for playing upon the souls and imaginations of the Earth-dwellers. The film undergoes a kind of spiritual metamorphosis. The creative artist works in mass and matter like a god, reshaping the outer world or creating new worlds. The scenic architect comes into his own: he broods upon and dominates furniture, room, house, street, city, landscape, universe!

Exaggeration and distortion of realistic or idealistic forms, the dissolving of the petrified Existent into other worldliness or arbitrary forms, are part of the expressionistic creed. We need not be discouraged nor have our respect for a new and vital principle lessened by the bizarre expressionistic form it has been given. In this the film is but part of this subversive period. Its creativeness is at the same time dynamically destructive—a solvent of the old. It is partly chaos but only the chaos of the old, familiar and outworn which reappear as disorganization; as suggestion or survival—matter retains its memory—the abstraction would equal annihilation.

The creators of *Dr. Caligari* as a film spectacle have used an audacious freedom in their exploitation of space. The plastic is amalgamated with the painted, bulk and form with the simulacra of bulk and form, false perspective and violent foreshadowing are introduced, real light and shadow combat or reinforce painted shadow and light. Einstein's invasion of the law of gravity is made visible in the treatment of walls and supports.

Trees are resolved into conventionalized, constructed forms; foliage becomes a mass of light, dark and shaded crescents, rounds and silhouettes—brilliantly colored in the original scene. Floors and pavements are streaked, splashed and spotted, divided and decorated in bars, crosses, diagonals, serpentines and arrows. The walls become as banners or as transparencies, space fissured by age, or as slates upon which the lightning blazes strange hieroglyphs; or they become veils and vanish in a mosaic of scrambled forms and surfaces, like a liner in camouflage. A grim effort is made to extend perspective not only in flight from the spectator, that is, towards the background, but into and beyond the foreground, to overwhelm the spectator with it, to draw him into the trammels, the vortex of the action.

The first effect that strikes the eye in this film *Dr. Caligari* is the plastic richness and accentuation of all masses. We are plunged into a cubistic world of intense relief and depth, a stereoscopic universe. The modeling of the scenery is emphasized by painted high-lights, by artificial shadows, by bands of color outlining masses and contours. It will, perhaps, prove interesting if I describe a few of these scenes:

A corridor in an office building: Walls veering outward from the floor, traversed by sharply-defined parallel strips, emphasizing the perspective and broken violently by pyramidal openings, streaming with light, marking the doors; the shadows between them vibrating as dark cones of contrast, the further end of the corridor murky, giving vast distance. In the foreground a section of wall violently tilted over the heads of the audience, as it were. The floor cryptically painted with errant lines of direction, the floor in front of the doors shows crosslines, indicating a going to and fro, in and out. The impression is one of formal coldness, of bureaucratic regularity, of semipublic traffic. Life is given to this architectural energy, human life, by the wizard-like shape of Dr. Caligari himself, white-haired, spectacled, in a bulky cloak and tall hat. His cane touches, and seems like an extension of one of the floor-lines. The actor fits himself into the composition in costume, gesture and attitude.

A street at night: Yawning blackness in the background— empty, starless, abstract space, against it a square, lopsided lantern hung between lurching walls. Doors and windows constructed or painted in wrenched perspective. Dark segments on the pavement accentuate diminishing effect. The slinking of a brutal figure pressed against the walls and evil spots and shadings on the pavement give a sinister expression to the street. Adroit diagonals lead and rivet the eye.

An attic: It speaks of sordidness, want and crime. The whole composition a vivid intersection of cones light and dark, of rooflines, shafts of light and slanting walls. A projection of white and black patterns on the floor, the whole geometrically felt, cubistically conceived. This attic is out of time, but in space. The roof chimneys of another world arise and scowl through the splintered window-pane.

A room; or rather a room that has precipitated itself, enclosed itself in cavern-like lines, in inverted hollows of frozen waves. Here space becomes cloistral and encompasses the human—a man reads at a desk. A triangular window glares and permits the living day a voice in this composition.

A prison-cell: A criminal, ironed to a huge chain attached to an immense trapezoidal "ball." The posture of the prisoner sitting on his folded legs is almost Buddha-like. Here space turns upon itself, encloses and focuses a human destiny. A small window high up and crazily-barred, is like an eye. The walls, sloping like a tent's to an invisible point, are blazoned with black and white wedge-shaped rays. These bend when they reach the floor and unite in a kind of huge cross, in the center of which the prisoner sits, scowling, unshaven. The tragedy of the repression of the human in space—in trinity of space, fate and man.

A white and spectral bridge yawning and rushing out of the foreground: It is an erratic, irregular causeway, such as blind ghouls might have built. It climbs and struggles upward almost out of the picture. In the middle distance it rises into a hump and reveals arches staggering over nothingness. The perspective pierces into vacuity. This bridge is the scene of a wild pursuit. Shafts of bifurcated cacti or skeleton-shrubs lean at all angles along the parapet-walls, expressing excitement and tumult. Lanterns at all angles point to nowhere, battered out of the perpendicular as long grass is driven obliquely by the suction of an express.

Several aspects of the market place of a small town: An imposing and exposing play and interplay of masses, perspectives, lines, outlines, light and shadow, foreshortening of walls and arches. A lantern askew under an arch—the old lamplighter as the black core of an enormous star of light that is splashed upon the ground and eats into the shadows. A crisscross play of light from doors and windows down the vistas of crooked streets in which the houses move and stretch, attract and repel one another. Channels full of latent human destinies. The town cries out its will through its mouth, this market place, its fears and hopes assemble here, its century-old soul is laid bare. The spots and lines of travel on the cobblestones people it with the specters of generations of passers-by. They are the symbols of the town's life and traffic.

Another scene: Climax—catastrophe. A vision of lurching roofs and pitching walls—the setting for another pursuit. The top of one wall is marked by a broad and tapering trail, shooting forward like an arrow, like a beam of flight or light, and at the arrow's head a group—the tragic hero in his black, skin-tight garment, carrying a white-clad woman in his arms, looming above vacuity, standing on the watershed between life and death. Gaunt chimneys rear and slant like masts in this city storm. Cunning lines of composition and the adroit use of diagonals drive the perspective into an invisible "vanishing-point." Two bright windows, trapezium-shaped, glow beneath in the world of men, directly under the roof. Here the outer husks, slopes and ridges of human habitations, man's formal, architectonic division of space, above the universal ocean of space and time. Human destinies in sharp contrast with naked annihilation. Space as the eternal, the all-embracing, the all-absorbing.

Another interpretation of space may be seen in the film-play *From Morning Unto Midnight*. Here space is not treated, as in the *Caligari* film, as something concrete and plastic, but as something abstract, diffused, immaterial. Light and shadow are not massed, but broken and dissolved. The original settings are not constructed in the round and in color, but are suggested in the flat in different tones of black and white. Space does not obtrude; the world becomes a background, vague, inchoate, nebulous. Against this obliterating firmament, this sponge of darkness, the players move, merge into it, emerge out of it. In order that they may not be visually lost, their hands, faces and the outlines of their clothing are relieved by means of high lights carefully applied.

In such surroundings the actor no longer feels the support of active space and a living environment, but is flung back upon his own resources. He is stripped naked of accessories. He even loses much of his own corporeality and relief and becomes two-dimensional, an actual picture. The universe is flat, a plane; beneath and above it, before it and behind, primeval darkness rules, perspective is engulfed, life and action transpire in a world of breadth and height.

A pawnshop: A rudimentary door in white lighting out of walls that are simply black emptiness. Steps, the relief of which is destroyed by streaks and spots passing athwart both treads and risers. To left and right a jungle-like mass of amorphous odds and ends, pawnshop paraphernalia, things that are material but half obliterated and negatived to ghostliness, to mere hints of themselves. The long-haired youth and the long-bearded pawnbroker take on almost the appearance of phantoms.

A staircase hall: Walls, as before of night and nothingness. The balusters, rail, and steps in ghostly contours and semi-relief.

A luminous clock like a moon in a sky of ink. An electric light like a ragged giant bullrush or gourd, glows on one wall, in the center of a burst of painted rays. The corners of the inleaning invisible walls are demarcated by white hatchings. A youth and a girl in strange attitudes, like figures in a dream. The whole phantasmal and limbo-like—like the spookish banquet-hall in Strindberg's *Nach Damaskus*.

The two-dimensional conception was forced to make compromises in several scenes, but even in these the third dimension was effaced and masked as much as possible. Thus in a Salvation Army Hall, the foreground it curtained off in dead black, the middle ground is dazzling white, like plane contrasted with plane. The focus: a cross shining upon a platform, crippled chairs in disarray, crying of a world of want and moral decrepitude.

When depth and distance are rendered necessary in this world of flatness, as on a country road, this too is indicated partly in relief, spectral and infernal trees, a serpentine path, winding amongst these solitary guardians and losing itself in infinity—a path shadowy and without goal.

The action in *From Morning Unto Midnight* the settings of which strive to dissolve and negate reality and the outer world, is as harmonious in its way as that in the *Caligari* film which strives to intensify and animate the fabric of the outer world.

Another film-play, *Algol*, the scene of which is laid on the star of that name—a vision of Paul Scheerbart, the poet-architect—has also been "staged" by Walther Reimann. Here the forms are not broken up expressionistically, but space acts and speaks geometrically, in great vistas, in grandiose architectural culminations. Space or room is divided into formal diapers, patterns, squares, spots and circles, of cube imposed upon cube, of apartment opening into apartment.

One scene represents a stellar landscape of abrupt and fantastic contours, a convulsed, volcanic world, revealing matter in a struggle with space and time. There are surfaces of snow and silver, spines and crevasses, rounded tumuli of primeval stuff, sharp crags rising like outstretched arms to the stars. A female figure, like a triumphing spirit, and invested with veils of different darknesses, lifts out of the stone. Above her, there is spanned arch upon arch

of a borealis and swarm upon swarm of stars. What a Dantesque
vision is here, the marriage of space and matter. Space in its
ultimate juxtaposition with eternity.

Another interesting treatment of space in the world of the
cinema, is that devised by Professor Poelzig and Miss Moeschke,
the designer and the sculptress of Reinhardt's *Grosses Schauspiel-
haus*. The theme was *Der Golem*, a fantastic, cabalistic Jewish
romance of ancient Prague by Gustav Meyrink, one of the most
imaginative of German writers. Professor Poelzig conceives of
space in plastic terms, in solid concretions congealing under the
artist's hand to expressive and organic forms. He works, therefore, in the solid masses of the sculptor and not with the planes
of the painter. Under his caressing hands a weird but spontaneous
internal architecture, shell-like, cavernous, somber, has been
evolved in simple, flowing lines, instinct with the bizarre spirit of
the tale. These vaults and groins are hoary with an evil age, the
mildew of the breath of suffering, hunger and prayer cries out of
them. The gray soul of medieval Prague has been molded into
these eccentric and errant crypts. They suggest a kind of Jewish
Gothic—a blending of the flame-like letters of the Jewish alphabet
with the leaf-like flame of Gothic tracery.

Poelzig seeks to give an eerie and grotesque suggestiveness to
the flights of houses and streets that are to furnish the external
setting of this film-play. The will of this master-architect animating façades into faces, insists that these houses are to speak in
jargon—and gesticulate!

The shadowy ribbon of the light-play, hitherto overladen with
photographic fetters, theatrical trumpery and mob-idolatries, has
freed itself from the iron reel and begun to soar upwards towards a higher purpose and a nobler expression. It has spun
through the brains of true artists and vitalized itself with an element of creative art. From this beginning may arise something
which will enrich not only art but life. If alone our feeling for
space be developed aesthetically by the possibilities of the airplane, if alone this sixth sense grow subtler and sharper, we shall
achieve a finer adjustment of man to his environment, a closer
contact with the abstract and concrete worlds, a new harmony
with nature, and the universe. Man shall not only know by
hypothesis that the earth is not flat and still, but shall feel by

sense and instinct that it is round and in flight. He shall come to know the earth as his own house, though he may never have escaped the narrow confines of his hamlet. The blurred, narrow windows of his imagination may then become doorways—wide and always open.

Freeman, Nov. 24-Dec. 1, 1920.

1920-1930

"*The camera is the director's sketching pencil. It should be as mobile as possible to catch every passing mood, and it is important that the camera should not be interposed between the spectator and the picture.*"

FRED W. MURNAU

ERICH VON STROHEIM

Herman G. Weinberg

When Eisenstein visited America he was asked what, in the American cinema, he admired most. He replied: "Chaplin, von Stroheim and Walt Disney."

As for Chaplin and Disney, they have had accolade enough showered upon them, by native and visiting celebrity alike. Our concern is with Stroheim, whose unhappy art flowered for a decade, then withered and died, plucked by the hands of the money-grubbers and the fake morality tutored by the Haysian regime in Hollywood. Stroheim's uncompromising realism struck a sympathetic chord with Eisenstein and it is natural that the two should have admired each other's work. But whereas Eisenstein was working in a Socialistic state, where the movie was regarded as something more than an innocuous diversion, Stroheim worked in the hot-house atmosphere of that great citadel of reaction—Hollywood. Eisenstein shelled a decadent capitalistic society from the vast plains of the USSR, which served as a stand from which he could hurl those projectiles—*Potemkin* and *Ten Days*—shattering the hypocritical complacency of a Europe which confused its death rattle with the crunch of tanks, the thud of regimented

hordes and the megalomaniacal screeching of dictators. Stroheim
bored from within, and while Eisenstein knocked off Europe's
armor plate, he dissected an aristocracy in its last stages of sophisticated decay with the precision and effectiveness of a surgeon's
scalpel.

Stroheim revealed the great festering wound which was eating
away the heart of this society. *Foolish Wives*, *The Merry Widow*
and *The Wedding March*—not projectiles, surely, but subtle and
insinuating cups of poison. Kings, queens, princes, great barons,
wealthy industrialists, the glittering haut-monde—locomotor-
ataxia, haemophilia, nymphomania, satyriasis, perversions, glut-
tony, rape. This was Stroheim's "High-world." His brief war
scenes in the lamentably unfinished *Merry-Go-Round* had all the
terrible indictment of those in *The End of St. Petersburg*. In
Greed he ripped the last shreds of respectability off the body of
man as an animal and cried: "For shame!". The spectacle he
revealed was shameful enough, but the disclosure only made him
enemies and his eventual social ostracism was sealed with the
mutilation of this film—a mutilation that endeavored to lessen
the shock of this whining, pitiful creature that God was supposed
to have created in His own image, and which Stroheim revealed
so mercilessly under his microscope. But Stroheim disowned the
adulterated version of his masterpiece (as he had disowned every
one of his preceding and succeeding works, all of which were
similarly mutilated) just as Eisenstein, years later, was to disown
the adulterated and perverted version of his great epic of the
Mexican people, *Que Viva Mexico!*

In truth, both men had much in common.

But Eisenstein's art persists in its growth, fostered by a new
society. Stroheim's was ferreted out and uprooted, by a vicious
clique that answered all guarantees of "freedom of expression,"
"democracy," "integrity of the artist," etc., with a sardonic smile.

Once, a rumor penetrated that Stroheim wished to go to Russia.
What happened about this, no one seems to know. But now,
thanks to an unexpected inheritance and the help of several
friends, word comes that we will once again hear from von Stroheim. Perhaps he will film his novel, *Paprika*, a gypsy prose rhap-
sody published here last Fall. Let us hope it is true.

Yet, what strange destiny for a man!

Is his name really Erich von Stroheim? Is he really a former lieutenant of the old Imperial Austrian Guard, the son of a great Bohemian nobleman? Is he not, rather, a creature from another world, marvelously possessed of a mysterious spirit, a monster caparisoned to mystify the throng?

This much we know: He lived in Vienna at the height of its dying imperial splendor, before the hounds of Europe brought her to bay, a graceful, wounded stag. Stroheim lived in the Vienna of dainty carriages with their rigid lackeys, trotting along on their light springs, making their carefree way to Schönbrunn; the Vienna of a thousand glistening lights flickering in the Prater, lighting up the gaiety at Sacher's, reflecting its sparkling brandy in the saucer-like eyes of its gypsy demi-mondaines . . .

Saber-scarred and monocled . . . Hearts filled with chivalry, souls filled with poetry, the young Uhlan officers lived, danced and loved. When the war came, they left, forgetting to pay their tailor bills—but they did not hesitate to fight and die brilliantly at Piave. One could see them near the Cathedral of St. Stephen in 1922, asking for alms in the courtyard. Black glasses covered their burning eyes, and in the hot swirling dust they dragged their poor tattered military rags, still clinging to their withered frames, from which dangled torn epaulets . . .

Others, more fortunate, or—maybe—less fortunate, became gigolos, confidence men, or forgers . . . and then, when the artificial years of inflation collapsed, they, too, collapsed, and wound up in prisons . . .

Only one among them knew how to turn defeat into glory—into millions. Only one among them knew how to, phoenix-like, re-create the Imperial Court of Vienna out of the ashes left by the awful years of holocaust.

The Imperial Austria of old! Shattered by defeat, it returned more brilliant, gayer and more glittering than ever—in the films made by Erich von Stroheim in Hollywood.

Into the heavy, wholesome diet that the American movie public consumed before his advent, he subtly poured a few drops of venom.

First came *The Pinnacle*, then *Foolish Wives*, that subtle and perverse sexual comedy which was exploited by Universal as "The First Million Dollar Picture," with an electric sign on Times Square

changed daily as the production cost sheet mounted—which she-
nanigans was subsequently to react as a boomerang to von Stroheim and gain him an unwarranted reputation for insane ex-
travagance.

In *The Pinnacle* Stroheim, himself, portrayed a little weasel of
an Austrian officer on a holiday in the Alps, with just enough energy to attempt to seduce every woman he met. Eventually, he
gets himself thrown from a high cliff by a jealous husband. The
title was a symbolic one—nor did the symbolism run to an esoteric deck of cards somewhere in the film. In *Foolish Wives*,
Stroheim again played a similar officer on a holiday, this time in
post-war Monte Carlo. For his seductions he winds up with a knife
in his back and his body thrown with that of a dead cat into a
sewer. Retribution has always run riot in the Stroheim films.
They were the most moral things imaginable. The villain invariably got his in his end, in the most unsavory manner Stroheim
could devise.

Thanks to him, the women and young girls of America learned
to prefer the slick, insolent archdukes, whose kisses burned like the
lash of a whip, to the bucolic American heroes. Stroheim was the
true creator of a "sophisticated" cinema.

But the art of the "sophisticated" cinema was degraded, corrupted and commercialized by others.

Dilettantes appeared, with all the surface polish and superficial
tricks which Stroheim could not or would not have. Let us be
generous and name no names. It is true, Stroheim's technique was
frequently distressingly static, for a motion picture, but his individual scenes were so heavy-laden with thought, so beautifully
prepared, lighted and composed, that one easily forgave him a lack
of movement, pace and camera angles. Stroheim had always something to say, and knew how to say it, which was more important.

And then Stroheim did the thing that suddenly made him
great—he broke the rules of an art which he created.

When he had gained all that he wanted, when he had lost all
taste and feeling for money, he suddenly began to know anguish
and despair. Torment followed.

He made *Greed* (from Frank Norris' *McTeague*) into which he
poured all his soul. Flying in the face of the box office, he made a

film that was the negation of what the entire motion-picture industry in America had been built upon. He not only flew in the face of the box office—he spat in its eye. For once the screen would tell a measure of truth, even if it killed von Stroheim to do it (which it did—the mutilation of Greed snuffed out the spark that kindled in the artist and left a broken and bitter man).

Greed was the apotheosis of the ugly, the sordid, in human beings. The film opened with a quatrain:

"Gold, gold, gold,
Molten, yellow, hard and rolled,
Hard to get and hard to hold—
Gold, gold, gold. . . ."

From that opening title to the last shot in the desert of Death Valley, with the bewildered McTeague, handcuffed to the body of the dead Marcus, going insane from thirst, and a few yards off a bag of gold coins spilled out futilely on the scorched terrain, Stroheim told a story of greed that struck home so deep in the hearts of all who saw it that many hated the film (in Berlin they hissed it off the screen), and it was the biggest failure at the box office of its time.

It was dedicated: "To my mother."

The very photography stank of the squalor it sought to depict. But Greed was beautiful, as truth is beautiful.

The fake morality tutored by Hollywood would not let Stroheim have his masterpiece. They cut it. From seventy reels it had been reduced, grudgingly, by its creator, to forty reels—beyond that Stroheim would not cut it. They called in a hack who brought it down to a regulation ten. Its elements of greatness were but partially discernible in the version released to the public. Whole episodes, upon which he had labored for weeks and months, were lopped off, and swept away on the cutting room floor. Stroheim disowned it, just as he was to subsequently disown the milk-sop version of his sly comedy, The Merry Widow, in which he sought to depict the decadence in the old royal family of Vienna. Those who saw the original version of Stroheim's Merry Widow said it was a shrewd and sardonic thing. The version shown was but a step better than the usual Ruritanian operetta stuff—but it had infinitely more verve than Lubitsch's version which was so Americanized that all the glamor and mystery of the original was lost.

In *The Wedding March* (and its sequel, *Marriage of the Prince*) Stroheim strove to become the Goya of the films. Necromancer of the spirit, he liberated the instincts which he had repressed so long. . . .

It was these instincts that gave us those twisted, tortured candelabras (from which Sternberg was later to borrow for *The Scarlet Empress*) whose translucid flames were agitated by the wind; those nightmarish lights from behind which emerged an ebony crucifix; the weather-beaten faces of soldiers; the horrible, grimacing, laughing faces; the exotic foods, chaotic visions mixed with orgies and cemeteries . . . the rape in the butcher's shop with thick blood oozing all around and a pale little girl struggling on the stone floor . . . and another girl, the pathetic little cripple in a wedding gown, with horror stricken eyes, prostrating herself on the stones in a deserted chapel before the Madonna. . . .

Then America got angry.

It pronounced Stroheim a madman.

You cannot defy a young and healthy nation with impunity—its people are not interested in lecherous, demented worlds.

The Wedding March, cut by alien hands again, and again disowned by its creator, was released without benefit of its sequel, which carried the story to its logical conclusion. Paramount was through with Stroheim. So was MGM, Universal and Pat Powers (who backed *The Wedding March*). No one would have anything to do with a director who could not discipline himself to tell a film story as everyone else did, in the regulation eight or ten reels and in such a form as would not require the inevitable wholesale censorial deletions which characterized every Stroheim film to date.

But the winning personality of the man was not to be downed even yet. He persuaded Joseph P. Kennedy, the Wall Street financier, to give him financial backing for an original story, *Queen Kelly*, set in Africa and Berlin. It was to serve as a starring vehicle for Gloria Swanson. After a reputed 850,000 dollars had been spent on it and three months had elapsed and Stroheim was just getting started, La Swanson objected to the character she was playing (the Madame of a bordello) and stormed off.

This was the end of von Stroheim. The dizzy decline of the idol followed. He was reproached for his megalomania, his arrogance—his wanton spending, brought about chiefly through an almost fanatical insistence on realism and fidelity of detail. The producers resented his insolent demeanor, the eternal monocle stuck in his eye. They tore up his contracts. They ruined him financially. Alone, without even a servant, he lived in thirty immense, cold rooms, from which his creditors had removed furniture, rugs, sculpture, books. He sought refuge in a hotel—he drank heavily. To make a living, he accepted bit parts in absurd films. One felt ashamed and squirmed in one's seat while watching Stroheim, broken and defeated, playing a ham actor's part in so ridiculous and cheap a film as *The Great Gabbo*, directed by a man who had not a tenth of Stroheim's talent.

A spring had snapped—he did not recover.

His own son, a youth of 18, brought him a summons for nonpayment of his wife's alimony. At a hearing before the judge, Stroheim confessed that his worldly goods consisted of but eight dollars.

America turns a cold shoulder to those who dare to frighten her. . . .

But here he is again. He returns!

To say what? To do what?

He will film his novel, *Paprika*, they say. *Paprika* is purposely scandalous, exaggerated, heavily erotic; "slang" mixed with Germanisms becomes uncouth; but occasionally from its depths there comes a cry, bursting like a flash of lightning—a flash behind which we see the old Stroheim.

Will he succeed? We can doubt it or not. The world of 1936 is a different world from the one that witnessed the birth and development of Stroheim's inspired art.

He no longer seeks death. It is life he now seeks.

But this phantom who returns among us, dressed in an old cashmere dressing robe, burned full of cigarette holes; this phantom who comes back with his blase, tired look—still wearing his monocle; is he not a more touching, more vital figure than those happy men before whom the road of life passes straight and clear?

Little Magazine, March, 1936.

A NEW REALISM—
THE OBJECT

(its plastic and cinematic graphic value)

F. Léger

Every effort in the line of spectacle or moving picture, should be concentrated on bringing out the values of the object—even at the expense of the subject and of every other so called photographic element of interpretation, whatever it may be.

All current cinema is romantic, literary, historical expressionist, etc.

Let us forget all this and consider, if you please:

A pipe—a chair—a hand—an eye—a typewriter—a hat—a foot, etc., etc.

Let us consider these things for what they can contribute to the screen just as they are—in isolation—their value enhanced by every known means.

In this enumeration I have purposedly [sic] included parts of the human body in order to emphasize the fact that in the new realism the human being, the personality, is very interesting only in these fragments and that these fragments should not be considered of any more importance than any of the other objects, listed.

The technique emphasized is to isolate the object or the fragment of an object and to present it on the screen in close-ups of the largest possible scale. Enormous enlargement of an object or a fragment gives it a personality it never had before and in this way it can become a vehicle of entirely new lyric and plastic power.

I maintain that before the invention of the moving picture no one knew the possibilities latent in a foot—a hand—a hat.

These objects were, of course, known to be useful—they were seen, but never looked at. On the screen they can be looked at—they can be discovered—and they are found to possess plastic and dramatic beauty when properly presented. We are in an epoch of specialization—of specialties. If manufactured objects are on the whole well realized, remarkably well finished—it is because they have been made and checked by specialists.

I propose to apply this formula to the screen and to study the plastic possibilities latent in the enlarged fragment, projected (as a close-up) on the screen, specialized, seen and studied from every point of view both in movement and immobile.

Here is a whole new world of cinematographic methods.

These objects, these fragments, these methods are innumerable—limitless. Life is full of them. Let us see them on the screen.

The point is to know how to "exploit" them—the point is to find out the right way of using them. It is more difficult than it seems.

To get the right plastic effect, the usual cinematographic methods must be entirely forgotten. The question of light and shade becomes of prime importance. The different degrees of mobility must be regulated by the rhythms controlling the different speeds of projection—*la muniterie*—the timing of projections must be calculated mathematically.

New men are needed—men who have acquired a new sensitiveness toward the object and its image. An object for instance if projected 20 seconds is given its full value—projected 30 seconds it becomes negative.

A transparent object can remain immobile, and light will give it movement. An opaque object can then be moved in rhythm with the tempo of the transparent object. In this way an enormous variety of effects can be achieved by the use of totally different objects having in themselves absolutely no expression, but handled with understanding and knowledge. Light is everything. It transforms an object completely. It becomes an independent personality.

Take an aluminum saucepan. Let shafts of light play upon it from all angles—penetrating and transforming it. Present it on the screen in a close-up—it will interest the public for a time, yet to be determined. The public need never even know that this fairy-like effect of light in many forms, that so delights it, is nothing but an aluminum saucepan.

I repeat—for the whole point of this article is in this: the powerful—the spectacular effect of the object is entirely ignored at present.

Light animates the most inanimate object and gives it cinematographic value.

This new point of view is the exact opposite of everything that has been done in the cinema up to the present. The possibilities of the fragment or element have always been neglected in order to present vague moving masses in the active rhythm of daily life. Everything has been sacrificed for an effect which bears no relation to the true reality. The realism of the cinema is still to be created— It will be the work of the future.

Little Review, Winter, 1926.

OF WHAT ARE THE YOUNG
FILMS DREAMING?

Le Comte Étienne de Beaumont

In 1900 a Swede found a block of magnetic steel which retained the invisible vibrations of sound and retranslated them for the human ear. The steel, when demagnetized, became deaf and dumb.

If matter hears and speaks, do not objects see? Do not lines adjust themselves to one another? A process not yet accessible to the human consciousness.

Similarly, do not the vibrations of the cinema have speech, thought, will? Scientific investigators may track down the evidences of this life; Egyptian hieroglyphists may interpret its system of logic; but is not the imagination to be permitted its faith in an arrangement of living lines which, going beyond pretext and scenery, play the leading role?

Of what are the young films dreaming? This title is not a program. I am not proposing a new art. I lay no claim to the sublime. I simply desire the satisfaction of working with these living lines which arise in such profusion from the objects about us, whether hard and sharp like crystals, reflections, prisms; or curved and liquid as in clouds, mists, smoke, the very life of form. I have enjoyed imagining things in motion; I have stirred up atoms of all kinds and compared them with forms grown human: a face, a landscape, speed, immobility, the infinite gradations of black and white.

The art of the cinema offers us a new expression of thought; it allows us to attempt the translation of our dreams.

I say "attempt," because the eye of the camera functions differently from our own—and what a difference there is between the thought and its realization! There is the same diversity in the way we see things. The gulf separating one mind from another is wide. Things have a different meaning for each of us. What I see, I alone see. We are always in isolation. When something enters our consciousness, it has a color and a significance peculiar to the individual. Alas! and yet fortunately, we are not made in series! Communication is only approximate, which is at once a virtue and a defect.

I am reminded of a passage in Marcel Proust, the second chapter of *Albertine Disparue:* "I cannot realize that each person on opening his eyes will fail to see the images which I see, believing that the thought of the author is perceived directly by the reader, whereas it is another thought that takes shape in his mind."

All humanity joins in the attempt to provide the materials for such distortion. And it would be a great satisfaction to me should I succeed here, in this country whose cinema productions have given the whole world fresh emotional experiences to an extent which no other art has rivaled for some time.

Little Review, Winter, 1926.

NOT THEATER, NOT LITERATURE, NOT PAINTING

Ralph Block

An art may have a large body of aesthetic tradition and be moribund. It may have none to speak of and be very much alive. The movies are this kind of art. It is not possible to understand them, much less truthfully see them, within the limitations, judgements, and discriminations of the aesthetic viewpoint. The movies are implicit in modern life; they are in their very exaggerations—as a living art often may be—an essentialization of that which they reflect. To accurately size them up, they should be seen functionally, phenomenalistically, in relation to their audience.

Like music, painting, and the drama in their primitive stages, the movies are manifestations in some kind of aesthetic form of a social will and even of a mass religion. They are in effect a powerful psychic magnet, an educing force which draws submerged dreams from hidden places to the surface of the common life. By releasing wishes which are on the margin of accepted behavior, they partake of the social function of art. In a transitional civilization the *mores* of the people no longer reflect their real social and tribal requirements, nor to any appreciable extent their individual and social hungers. The movies help to disintegrate that which is socially traditional, and to clear the field for that which, if not forbidden, has been at least close to the shade of the tabooed.

Primitive art is usually recognized as art only after it has become classical. In the manner of all primitive expression, the movies violate accepted contemporary canons of taste. Even as they arouse the sentinels of moral tradition, so they draw the attack of aestheticians, who are unconsciously measuring expressive works by the standards of those arts that have completed their cycle, especially painting and sculpture. But it is absurd to praise or blame the movies in their present state, or do any more than try to understand them. Whether the movies or what they reflect represent the Good Life depends on whose Good Life is being selected. They exist—massively, ubiquitous. It will be time enough to judge them as an art when they become a historical method of presenting selected truth, mellowed and tested by time, and captured by an audience saturated with tradition—acclimated by use to an understanding of the laws, intentions, and refinements of the medium. The movies by that time will have lost their excitement, but at least they will be aesthetically correct.

The movie is a primitive art, equally as the machine age is a new primitive period in time. But being a machine, the motion camera is not a simple instrument. Like the pianoforte, it is an evolved instrument, predicated on the existence and development of other forms. It is itself still in an evolving state. Indeed those who make use of it and those who appreciate it without empirical knowledge of its use, have failed to grasp, except in a loose intuitive sense, a full understanding of the complicated laws that govern it. Here and there in its past performance are startling bits of technical excellence, discoveries of how the instrument may be properly used in its own field. Bound together these form a rude body of technique, already complicated, but not yet pushed to any important limits by personal genius, nor classified significantly in use by any development of important schools.

It is fashionable to say that the camera is impersonal, but those who use the camera know this is untrue. Indeed, even abstractly, it is no more impersonal than a steel chisel, or a camel's hair brush. The camera is on the one hand as intimate as the imagination of those who direct it; on the other hand it has a peculiar selective power of its own. Its mechanism is governed by an arbitrary set of rhythms—sixteen images to each foot of celluloid—and reality is seized by the camera according to a mathematical ratio, established between the tempo of what is in front of the lens and the tempo of the machine itself. The camera is also governed by another set of relations, which have to do with light and its refraction through lenses. These are no less arbitrary in a physical sense, but within their limits they are open to a large number of gradations and variations, according to the human will behind them. Far from being impersonal, the camera may be said to have pronounced prejudices of rhythm.

Most critical discussion of pantomime in the movies is vapor. Screen pantomime is not pantomime in the conventional Punch and Judy sense. In the theater, pantomime is in the large, a matter of long curves of movement. On the screen the lens intervenes between the eye and its objective. The camera not only magnifies movement but it also analyzes action, showing its incompletions. It is indeed more prejudiced than the human eye itself, helping the eye to detect false rhythms in the utterance of action, or an absence of relationship between sequences of movement, where the eye alone might fail. The intervention of the camera necessitates not only a modification of what might be called the wave length of pantomime for the screen, but also a more closely knitted flow of movement. Traditional pantomime on the stage is a highly schematized and rigid organization of units of movement in which every motion has a definite traditional meaning. But for the camera, movement must be living, warm, vital, and flowing rather than set and defined in an alphabet of traditional interpretation. Like Bergsonian time, it must seem to renew and recreate itself out of the crest of each present moment. It is in this sense that it resembles music. It is also because of this necessity that the stage actor who essays the screen is often exposed at the outset in all the barrenness of habitual gesture and stock phrasing of movement.

Experience rather than theory has taught many actors on the screen the need of plasticity, composure, modulation of gesture, and an understanding of how to space movement—a sense of timing. The screen actor at his best—the Beerys, Menjous, and Negris

—tries to give fluency to pantomime, so that action may melt out of repose into repose again, even in those moments when an illusion of arrested action is intended. He recognizes that against his own movement as a living organic action is the cross movement of the celluloid. It is only by long experience that the motion-picture actor discovers a timing which is properly related to the machine; but that experience has already produced screen pantomimists whose rhythmic freshness and vitality the modern stage can rarely match.

The actor is the living punctuation of reality. He is conscious and has the power to make his action valid in an imaginative sense. But Appearance—the face of Nature—is itself sprawling and only vaguely connotative. Words are packed with the reverberations of human history; Appearance on the other hand, must be selected, organized, and related to ideas that conform to the limitations and possibilities of the camera, before it can be robbed of inanity and made significant.

All this is the function of the director. The movies are full of mediocre directors. But, comparatively, there are not as many poor motion picture directors as there are poor musicians, painters, and creative writers in the world; it is easier to go to school and become any of these than it is to direct a motion picture. In its present state of development, motion picture direction demands not only logic, tact, sensibility, the ability to organize and control human beings and multifarious materials, and the power to tell a story dramatically, but it also requires a gift which cannot be learned in any school. This is a richness, even grossness, in the director's feeling for Life, and abundance of perception, a copius emotional reflex to the ill-assorted procession of existence.

Good motion picture direction has little to do with literacy or cultivation in its conventional sense. Several of the most cultivated and literate gentlemen in the movies are among the most prosaic directors. They have brought with them a knowledge of other arts, which has blinded them to the essential quality of the camera. They think of the movies as a form of the theater, of literature, or of painting. It is none of these things. It demands at best a unique kind of imagination which parallels these arts but does not stem from them. It is true that the rigid economic organization of the modern studio demands the same kind of prevision and preparation on the part of the director as on the part of any other creator. Even aside from urgencies of this kind, the St. Clairs, Lubitschs, Duponts, Einsteins, are under the same imaginative necessity to organize their material as a Cézanne or Beethoven. But there the similarity ceases. Directors of this kind know that their greatest need is the power to seize reality—in its widest sense—and make it significant in forms of motion. This power, this understanding, is a gift by itself. It requires a special kind of eye, a special kind of feeling about the relationship between things and things, events and events, and an intuitive as well as empirical knowledge of how to make the camera catch what that eye sees and that imagination feels. It has nothing to do with words, as such, nor with history or politics or any of the traditional matters which are politely assumed to represent cultivation, and which so often debase the metal of the imagination.

The movie is in other words a new way in which to see life. It is a way born to meet the needs of a new life. It is a way of using the machine to see what the machine has done to human beings. It is for this reason that the best motion picture directors arise from strange backgrounds, with a secure grasp on techniques of living rather than on academic attitudes. They are not always preoccupied with proving that life is so small that it can be caught in the net of art. It is the pragmatic sanction hovering over them which offends academicians.

Here and there are indications that the movie is arising out of its phenomenalistic background into the level now occupied by the novel and the theater, touched by the same spirit of light irony, and predicating the orientation of a special audience. But there are no signs at the moment that it can rise higher than this point. Pictures such as *The Cabinet of Dr. Caligari* are interesting laboratory results in experimental psychology, but they have as little to do with the direct succession of the motion picture as Madame Tussaud's has to do with Rodin. *The Last Laugh* and *The Battleship Potemkin* are technical explosions, important only in their power to destroy old procedures and light the path ahead.

American directors have always mistaken cruelty on the one hand and sentimental realism on the other, for irony. Satisfaction for the sadistic hunger of the crowd is present in almost all popular entertainment. Griffith early understood this crowd desire, and his technique in exploiting it has filtered through a thousand pictures since. De Mille, Von Stroheim, Brennon, and the many unnamed have all used it in one form or other. But none has reached irony empty of brutality—an unobstructed god-like view of the miscalculations of existence, yet touched by human compassion. There are no Hardys nor Chekhovs in the movies. *The Last Laugh* dribbled out into German sentimentality, although in substance it seemed familiarly like one of Constance Garnett's translations. The comedians—Keaton and Langdon as well as Chaplin—have touched near the edge of true irony, but only as children might. Chaplin rose to the intention in *A Woman of Paris*, but his forms were conventional and worn, cast in the clichés of irony of cheap fiction.

In the end, what remains wonderful about the movie is its instrument. Its ideas are still sentimental or bizarre, reflecting the easy hungers of life, and of today's shifting surface of life; it fails as yet to draw from the deep clear wells of human existence. Aside from its need of another kind of audience—even another world, a deep ironic point of view in the motion picture would require a great individual spirit equipped with a true knowledge of the medium. And none of this kind has arisen. He is rare in any art and any time.

Dial, Jan., 1927.

SUNRISE: A MURNAU
MASTERPIECE

Dorothy B. Jones

Among the works of the German-born director F. W. Murnau, *Sunrise* (1927) remains today a film which is still enjoyed and appreciated by discriminating cinema audiences, as well as by many average movie-goers when they are given the opportunity to see it. Despite the fact that *Sunrise* is a silent film, the average person enjoys it as a fascinating story told with honesty and sincerity. Others with more finely developed capacities for discrimination find additional pleasure in the profound understanding of human nature—implicit in all of Murnau's best work—and also admire and appreciate the subtle artistry with which he fashioned this picture.

Yet, strangely enough, *Sunrise* is a film which has rarely been given serious consideration by film critics. Although all have not expressed the scorn which Paul Rotha recorded in *The Film Till Now*,[1] most critics have either ignored it completely in their dis-

---

[1] (New York: Funk & Wagnalls Company, 1949), 182. This assessment of *Sunrise* originally appeared in 1930, but Rotha in no way amended it in his 1949 edition as he did by adding footnotes with respect to *Intolerance* and a number of other films.

cussion of Murnau's work or passed over it lightly as an unfortunate, Hollywood-influenced production unworthy of its talented
director. A quarter of a century, although possibly not an appreciable length of time for a film to live, may perhaps give us
the perspective necessary to reëvaluate *Sunrise* and to understand
why it has thus far stood the test of time.

Based on the short story "A Trip to Tilsit" by Hermann Sudermann, *Sunrise* tells of a young peasant whom a city woman se-
duces to drown his wife. He takes his wife across the lake to the
city but cannot carry through the plan. The young couple re-
discover their love for one another and spend a happy day in
the city. On the trip home however, a storm blows up, the boat
is capsized, and the wife is lost. The city woman, assuming that
her plan has succeeded, goes to the house of the man who is
nearly insane with grief and anger. He is choking her to death
when word comes that his wife is safe. The city woman leaves
and the man and wife continue their life together.

A motion picture telling such a story is bound to be a psychological melodrama. But in the hands of Fred W. Murnau, this
story is told with such striking simplicity that it has the universal
appeal of a fable. The film has a lyric quality which has rarely
been achieved in moving images. And the camera which focuses
almost exclusively on the young peasant and his wife is less concerned with the objective events of the story than with the meaning of the events to these two human beings.

A high tribute to the artistry of this film is the pervading naturalness and simplicity. For, although Murnau deliberately created a simple folk tale, he simultaneously has shown us the tremendously complicated human motivations and the subtle moods
which lie behind the actions of even the most simple people.
The postures and movements of the actors, the varying pace as
the story unfolds, the lighting, the camera movement, and, above
all else, the relationship of the central characters to the ever-
moving backgrounds in which they are pictured have all been
employed as means for helping us to share and understand the
human emotions which are dramatized in this film.

Thus, Murnau was not content to characterize the peasant (as
Sudermann did) as a boorish, overbearing and somewhat cunning
man whom one can readily imagine capable of murdering his

wife. Instead, the peasant in the film is pictured as an essentially simple, hard-working young man who loves his wife and child. By so doing, Murnau has given his central character greater universality; but, at the same time, he has raised the interesting psychological question of how it is possible for such a man to agree to murder his wife. In the opening sequences, Murnau sets out to provide the answer by detailing with remarkable cinematic skill and artistry the nature of the man's relationship to the city woman.

Under a low full moon, the man is seen moving slowly through the mists of the dark meadows to a rendezvous with the city woman. The camera slowly follows him, then moves on past him to a clump of willows, and finally on through the willow branches to reveal a clearing where waits the city woman, dressed in a tight-fitting black gown, sohphisticated, bored, twirling a flower in her hand. As she hears the man approaching, she hurriedly powders her nose; then she looks expectantly toward the camera as he comes toward her, and they embrace and kiss fiercely.

In the scene which follows, the city woman suggests that the man murder his wife. He is horrified, grabs her by the throat, and almost strangles her. As he gets up to leave, she comes after him. He tries to fight her off, but she holds him by the neck and then by the hair as she finally succeeds in kissing him passionately on the face, and then on the mouth. They drop to the ground; and bending over him with more kisses, she tells him, "Leave all this behind—come to the city." In large type, the words are repeated: "COME TO THE CITY."

Crucial to an understanding of the entire story is the rising emotional climax of the man's seduction by the city woman; and this is reproduced by the succession of carefully selected and combined background images, as well as by the actions of the players themselves. The sequence begins with what Lewis Jacobs has well described as a mood of "quiet sensuality . . . . [in which] The overhanging mists, the dew, the full moon, the sinuous and constant movement of the camera—all combined to create a dark, somnolent mood." [2] But this mood prevails only in the first part of the sequence. When the siren whispers in his

[2] *The Rise of the American Film* (New York: Harcourt, Brace and Company, 1939), 363.

ear that he should murder his wife, the scene becomes one of violent anger; and this mood, in turn, is transformed by the city woman into one of violent sexuality.

This last mood is accomplished, in part, when she forces him to submit to her kisses and is carried further up a rising scale of sexual excitement by the images (presumably of her creation) on the screen which suggest the excitement of city life. As the meadow behind them dissolves into a travel shot of a large city square at night filled with moving traffic, the couple appear to move into the center of the square, and eventually fade from sight as the whole screen pictures a succession of rapid travel shots. Whereas in the opening of the sequence the camera moves slowly and sensuously, now it moves rapidly and with abandonment in long breath-taking and dizzying strokes, peering down glittering streets and finally climbing recklessly up the side of tall buildings to take in the sky line of the metropolis alive with moving searchlights. The sexual significance of the dance-band and dance-hall images which follow is implicit: the dance-band leader with his back to the camera dominates the screen (the man who calls the tune and sets the pace for the dancers) while to his right, the screen features the dance floor with its scattered dancers; and this entire image moves in a circular fashion toward him as if gyrating to the wild music of his band.

But the movements of the dance-band images which next fill the entire screen are at an even higher pitch of excitement and are still more clearly sexual in their kinesthetic meaning. All of the musicians rise up and down in unison on the stressed beat; and, in the interim, they sway in unison from side to side. The sexual significance of this rhythmic pattern is once more related to the man and city woman when they reappear on the lower half of the screen where the woman is revealed on her knees doing a wild orgiastic dance to the music of the band. As the band fades from view, the city woman has obviously aroused the man into taking an active role as her sex partner. There immediately follows a blurry long shot of the village as seen from over the lake, with the full moon just beginning to pass behind a cloud. By means of its total imagery, this shot suggests the exquisite sensation of intense sexual pleasure (which, as suggested by this diffuse long shot, blurs awareness of objective reality);

and, at the same time, it symbolically suggests the imminent climax of passion (as the moon starts to pass behind a cloud). But even more telling is the contrast between the hazy beauty of this long shot of the village and the dark ugliness of the following close-up which shows the matted bulrushes to reveal where the pair have lain together. Further, as the camera pans slowly a little to the left, the deep mud close by is revealed; and the camera follows their footprints through the mire until her high-heeled patent-leather shoes come into view. Then, the camera tilts up to take in her black figure gathering together the rushes with which he is to save himself after drowning his wife. In these two successive shots, Murnau has contrasted the pure beauty of intense sexual feeling with the dark cold ugliness of the return to realities which follow when, passion spent, the man is left to face the meaning of his act.

This seduction sequence makes possible our understanding how such an essentially simple and boyish person could agree to murder his wife. The nature of the man's relationship to the city woman is clearly suggested by visual analogy in the early part of the sequence—before the murder of the wife has been proposed. From a view of the lovers, the film cuts to show the young wife seeking solace at the bedside of her child whom she holds on her arm and kisses. In the succeeding image, the city woman is holding the man on her arm as she kisses his face and neck, while he (in a comparable position to the child in the previous picture) lies back smiling. By this association of images, the relationship between the city woman and the man is defined: she, the worldly-wise woman, is as the mother; and he, as the child.

Also from the seduction sequence, we learn that this woman is sexually the active aggressor rather than a mere temptress. She has just suggested that he murder his wife, yet he allows himself to be seduced and thus commits himself to her and to her plan for murder. They have lain together on the rushes in the mud, the picture tells us; and he has become as cruel as she, for he has accepted her and is wedded to her and what she stands for. He feels guilt toward his wife, but he is bound by an even greater guilt to the city woman—the shared guilt of a sex act which has committed him to murder—which is made clear when we see him for the first time following his seduction. Gathering the rushes, the city woman turns to him and says, "After the boat has capsized, save yourself with these bulrushes. The rushes will hold you up—scatter them before you reach the shore and tell everyone she drowned by accident." (Throughout this scene, the man stands passive, his hands thrust into his pockets, his back to the camera, his shoulders hunched over in the depressed and somehow bestial posture, which remains characteristic of him until later when his resolution breaks, and he finds himself unable to carry through the city woman's plans.) The rushes are now symbolic both of the death plan for the wife and of the act of infidelity, two secrets which the man shares with the city woman.

Bearing the bundle of rushes, the man returns home and stealthily enters the barn. About to hide the rushes, the man is nosed by the horse and is so greatly startled that we become aware of how acute is his feeling of guilt. As he covers the bundle carefully with canvas, pressing it down out of sight with both hands, something in his manner and gesture suggests that in his own mind he is already hiding the dead body of his wife.

That the man's guilt centers upon this bundle of rushes is brilliantly suggested in his manner of awakening the next morning. In sleep, he moves slightly and turns his face toward the camera. Then his eyes abruptly open, and in sudden panic he sits bolt upright on the edge of the bed, his eyes wide with terror. There is a quick cut to a shot in which the camera moves in very quickly toward the bundle of rushes, now half-revealed as they lie under the canvas, and brings them into sharp focus in a close-up. Again we see his startled face, as he throws back the comforter and peers more closely. Realizing he has been dreaming, the man relaxes, puts his head down on his hands, and covers his eyes.

The camera's rapid truck in on the bulrushes, bringing them from a blurry to a clear focus, reproduces the startled sensation of awakening and carrying the fearful vision of a dream over into reality; and the man's reactions indicate the weakening sensation of relief which follows. More than this, we realize fully the man's great guilt as he awakens in horror to the thought that the rushes have been uncovered.

But Murnau uses still other means to show the man's acceptance of the city woman's plan to murder his wife. The very image of the murder which the man carries in his mind is the one originally supplied by the city woman. During their rendezvous in the field, the woman had first asked, "Couldn't she get drowned?"; and the caption dissolved into a picture of the husband standing in the boat and pushing his wife into the water. This image makes specific the woman's plan as her words urge him, "Then overturn the boat, it will look like an accident." Later when the man thinks of the plan to which he has become partner, this same image reappears and makes plain that *her* thought is dominating him.

Even more explicitly, the following morning the man weeps with remorse as he looks out through the doorway at his young wife feeding the chickens; and the ghost image of the city woman appears behind him, her hands going around him as she presses him close and kisses him. He averts his face, and her image dissolves, but now again, she appears below him, smiling, her lips lifted to his, inviting a kiss. At the same time, a large close-up of her, kissing his hair, appears behind him. The size of this close-up, a ghost image which takes up almost a third of the screen, suggests the overpowering influence of her presence. He presses his clenched fists against his temples, and the images slowly fade.

Throughout the entire first portion of the film, we see a man in deep conflict. This is perhaps most vividly summarized in a single close-up shortly after he has asked his wife to go across the lake with him to the city. She gaily makes preparations for the journey, obviously convinced that this is a gesture of reconciliation. Then there is a close-up of the man's hands as they move down slowly and deliberately around the bundle of rushes, like hands around the neck of a victim who is about to be strangled. His hands lift the bundle up slowly, and the camera tilts up to reveal his face, taut and glassy-eyed. The grim gesture in relation to the symbolic bundle of rushes makes clear that although he feels impelled to go through with the murder of his wife, he feels deep rage toward the city woman; and it is she, rather than his wife, whom he would really like to murder (for when the city woman first suggested the murder, he attempted to choke her; and later, at the close of the film, when he believes his wife to be lost, he does in fact almost murder her in this fashion). Yet there appears to be no way out, no way to resolve the conflict. The depth of his resultant depression is suggested by his stooped posture, his sluggish walk, his unshaven and generally unkempt appearance, his dark brooding countenance, and his complete self-absorption which sets him apart from all that goes on around him.

In all of this, Murnau demonstrates an intuitive understanding of the dynamics of personality. But *Sunrise* raises and convincingly answers the even more amazing psychological question of how a woman can accept and forgive her husband after he has planned to murder her. To begin with, the man and wife are shown to be simple peasant people, and their life together has been a good one. We catch a glimpse of this early in the film when the servant tells of what their life was like before the coming of the city woman: "They used to be like children . . . carefree . . . happy. . . ." And in a brief flashback, we see the man plowing the field while the wife and child sit under a tree close by; then he stops his work to play with the child. Clearly, this young couple loved one another and enjoyed life together prior to the arrival of the city woman.

But the real answer to the question is to be found in the characterization of the wife as a gentle, loving, and genuinely happy woman. Above all else, her womanly qualities of tenderness and compassion are repeatedly emphasized—as she weeps and fondles the baby after her husband has left her to meet the city woman, as she lovingly covers her sleeping husband and gently strokes his brow the following morning, and as she tenderly stoops to feed the baby chicks and shows kindness toward the dog.

Actually in the wife, Murnau has created an image of pure goodness, just as in the city woman his creation is one of evil. Never for one moment is there a shadow of jealousy, anger, or even resentment in this woman whose husband has not only been unfaithful, but has planned her murder. Yet so great is Murnau's skill and understanding as a master of character that we do not resent this perfection in the wife; in fact, we are scarcely aware of it. For he has succeeded in making this image of human perfection completely real and understandable by combining mature serenity and compassionate understanding with childlike innocence and simplicity. There is no trace of righteousness in this woman; indeed, her goodness appears like the innate goodness of an essentially happy child.[3] Although she is pictured as a mother, the wife appears to rely upon the servant who cares for the child. Indeed, the wife herself often seems to be like a child; for example, her appearance on the night of her husband's seduction: she is sleeping in the moonlight, and the long shot of the bedroom makes her seem small and childlike.

The wife's complete trust and reliance upon her husband is the key which makes her behavior appear believable. To her husband's infidelity and his attempt to kill her, she responds like a child whose trust in an adult has been broken; when he leaves her for another woman, she is heartbroken; when he attempts to murder her, her first reaction is one of fear and withdrawal, then of grief. These are the reactions of a child who feels his security completely bound up in an adult and who feels hopelessly incapable of doing anything to free himself from the relationship. Yet in the process of reconciliation, the wife shows a maturity and understanding which do not appear in the least inconsistent with what has gone before.

As the man and wife set out on their journey across the lake, an incident occurs which foreshadows the events to come. The dog, barking loudly, wants to follow them. (Perhaps the animal has sensed something wrong in the man's dark mood.) He breaks his chain, jumps the fence, and swims toward the boat. The wife wants to turn back at once; but the husband, with his hard and distant mood, turns a deaf ear to her pleas. (What is the suffering of a dog to a man who is about to drown his wife?) Only after the wife helps the animal into the boat does the husband turn back, unwillingly. As he walks the dog up the little hill back toward the kennel, the wife looks after him with troubled eyes. Now fully aware of his dark mood, she starts to rise as if to get out but soon relaxes, smiling a little at her own doubts; then sitting there with the rippling water filling the screen behind her, she begins to look genuinely frightened and again starts to rise. But the man comes down the path; and the wife, looking small and alone, sits back again in the stern of the boat. A moment later, they are pulling

[3] The concept of the innate goodness of children is one that predates our knowledge of personality development based on psychoanalysis. However, it remains a myth which our culture finds difficult to relinquish and which Murnau utilized in his creation of this character.

away from the shore—his body crouched over the oars, his dark face lowered, his thoughts centered within himself.

When they reach the center of the lake, the man rows more and more slowly and finally stops altogether. The wife leans forward toward him, her eyes wide with fear. He puts first one then the other oar into the boat and moves toward her, his hands hanging apelike by his sides, his face cruel, hard, and determined. The wife draws back in terror, then, as his figure looms over her, pleads for mercy. A close-up of his two hands outstretched as if about to throw her overboard is followed by a pan shot of his arms thrown in a sudden gesture across his face; the awful moment has come and gone, and his resolution is broken. Quickly he steps back and frantically rows toward the shore, as she sits in the stern, her face covered with her hands. A rapid series of brief shots spell out the empty moments as, head down, he rows desperately with increasing speed, and as numbly she sits with her hands covering her face. Neither looks at the other, but as the boat hits the shore, he moves toward her and makes a gesture to help her out of the boat. Suddenly activated by fear of her husband, she rushes past him, jumps onto the shore, and runs away while he, calling and pleading, follows her.

The sequence of the trolley ride into the city with its series of long unbroken shots is one of the most volubly expressive passages of the entire picture. The interminable agony of these two human beings huddled on the platform of the trolley—she numb and remote, drawn as far away from him as possible, he mute and miserable beside her—is more acutely felt because of the landscape which flows endlessly past the windows. Following its winding track, the trolley carries them along the edge of the lake (where, as if in mute reference to what has gone before, a lone boat is seen out on the water), through the woods, into the outskirts, and finally into the very center of the city itself. Despite the gradually increasing activity around them, they remain unseeing until the trolley comes to a stop at the end of the line in the middle of a wide city square.

In the city, the camera follows the couple as each moment brings them a little closer to that moment of understanding which is the rebirth of their love for one another. The simplicity, the subtle beauty with which this is achieved on the screen is difficult to describe in words. The dangers of moving traffic, the impersonality of the crowds, the strangeness of the city places—all help to draw them together as he protects and guides her through the streets. Filled with remorse, he tries to reassure her of his love; but though she accepts the food and flowers which he offers her, his kindness only makes her weep the more. Finally they go into a church where a wedding is taking place. Seated in one of the rear pews, they listen together as the wedding vows are taken. "Keep her and protect her from all harm," the minister tells the groom, and the husband too is finally able to weep. "Wilt thou love her?" the minister asks; the groom nods solemnly. And the husband, tears falling, gropes blindly for his wife's hand and puts his head down on her lap, as she caresses and strokes his head. Now she guides him (as he guided her when she wept) out of the pew to the side aisle. In the corridor of the church, they are shown standing together, her arms about him, his face hidden on her shoulder. He drops to his knees, hiding his face against her. A close-up shows her stroking his hair, and he raises his face to ask, "Forgive me." In answer, she kisses his brow. There follows a close-up of two bells in the church tower, swinging in alternate directions, yet tolling together. The man is weeping now in relief, and she kisses his cheek. He smiles, and she, smiling also, gently turns his face toward her (out of shadow into light) and kisses him tenderly on the mouth. There follows now a huge close-up of the two bells tolling in unison, ringing out the joy of new love and the harmony of human understanding.

The reconciliation of this husband and wife is one of the most moving stories ever told on the screen, and it is told almost entirely visually. (There are only half a dozen titles in this entire portion of the film—from the time when the man sees he cannot go through with the murder until the scene just described.) So well are these two human beings portrayed that at no moment is there any doubt as to what they are feeling. Their emotions are expressed not only in their carriage, movements, and facial expressions, but by the telling way in which they are pictured in relation to the scene around them. In addition to the examples already given, we have them leaving the church and walking out into the square, unaware of the traffic around them. The background itself dissolves to express their subjective attitude toward reality, for they are seen to be walking dreamily through a meadow full of flowers which indicates that they have returned once more to the country scenes in which they first fell in love. But it is of supreme importance that each successive stage of the reconciliation is pictured at considerable length. We do not sense briefly, but instead observe over a period of time and in some detail the full expression of each feeling and attitude; and thus, we ourselves become fully steeped in the subtly changing moods of these two people. Furthermore, this slowness of pace allows time for us to absorb the deeper meanings implicit in the physical posture and movements of the actors. For example, early in the reconciliation sequence, the wife looks into her husband's face as she accepts the flowers which he offers her and then weeps into them. We cannot help but be aware (though perhaps unconsciously) that the wife is holding these flowers exactly as a mother cradles a baby in her arms. By his direction, Murnau time and again subtly suggests the thought behind even the simplest act and gesture.

Naturally for a contemporary movie audience, *Sunrise* moves at a much slower pace than today's sound films. But if the observer adjusts himself to this pace at the beginning of the picture, he will be rewarded except possibly for a few individual scenes in which the actors' motions have been slowed down to the point of tedium, to detract from rather than add to the sense of reality. However, the artistry of this film is so great that even in such scenes, Murnau's intention may well have been to create deliberately a partial sense of unreality. For example, in the tense moments when the husband walks toward the wife in the stern of the boat, his actions are so slow that they appear almost as slow-motion photography; and his posture and movements are therefore exaggerated so that they become strange and unnatural. A sense of the unbelievable actually happening before our eyes was undoubtedly exactly what Murnau was aiming for to make this moment appear like some strange nightmare. Today, however, the sense of the unbelievable goes beyond what Murnau intended; therefore, the effect he desired is not wholly achieved, possibly because the contrast in pace intended in this scene has been heightened further by the conditioning our eyes have been given during the intervening years through a much faster tempo of movement on the screen.

Perhaps the most remarkable thing about this motion picture is the fluidity of its images, which flow freely from objective to subjective realities and back without any break in continuity. For example, after the man leaves the city woman and returns home, he is shown lying on his bed and looking toward his wife (and toward the camera) who is sleeping nearby. He continues staring in horror toward her, and slowly water begins to appear on the lower rim of the screen, gradually flooding it completely and obliterating all else but his outstretched figure. He appears to be completely surrounded by the rippling water, while his eyes remain open in the same fixed expression of horror. Then gradually his figure is obliterated by the water; and, as the morning sun catches the ripples, the camera pans up to reveal the shore line of the town shrouded in the morning mist; and this is followed by a picture of his wife, standing in the morning light, looking down on him as he sleeps.

In addition to the complete fluidity of images, this segment also illustrates another characteristic of the entire motion picture—the richness of meaning inherent in the images. The image of the man staring in horror toward his wife is seen sufficiently long for us to grasp what he is thinking. Then, as the water begins to appear at the bottom of the frame, we feel from the image itself how this thought (of the drowning) slowly hems him in and finally surrounds him until he loses consciousness in sleep (as suggested by the obliteration of his figure beneath the water itself). The image has symbolic meaning also, for we see it is he (rather than his wife) who is drowning—he is being lost because of his acceptance of the city woman's plan for murder, just as he was lost once he submitted to her sexual advances. Indeed in this image, Murnau again links the murder plan and the seduction, for the image of the man's outstretched figure being gradually surrounded and finally submerged by the rippling water is also symbolic of the sex act which sealed his acceptance of the murder plan. And this same image may be interpreted as having future reference as well, for the waters which, in this scene, shut off his sight of his wife, are, we are told, the waters of the lake near the village—the same waters into which he will peer hoplessly, after hours of search, believing that she is forever lost to him.

Murnau's method of cinematic expression in much of the film

is unique. As in the seduction sequence and others, the walk of the married couple into the center of the square outside the church conveys its meaning not by relating one completely fresh image to the next, but by retaining an image of the person (or people) and by slowly dissolving the background so as to make it expressive of the thought or mood of the person being shown. In some instances, the image of the person also dissolves into a mood picture which occupies the entire screen. Here, the step back to objective reality is taken by a brief intermediate one of the reappearance of the individual whose thought is being portrayed. This figure appears before the mood background disappears and before the original scene is reaffimed. Thus both the objective situation and the emotions or thoughts of the person being shown are visually interpreted, and continuity between them is unbroken. So, Murnau's film moves with ease from the act itself to the unconscious idea behind it, from the reality in which a character finds himself to his concurrent fantasy, and back once more to reality with complete freedom—all of which suggests again and again the depths which lie beneath the surface of human behavior.

Murnau uses other cinematic means for communicating the thoughts of his characters. For example, when a character speaks of a past or anticipated event, Murnau pictures it, and always in such a way that he distinguishes it from the immediate events of the story itself. For example, to represent a remembered scene (as when the servant recalls the happy days of the young couple), he slightly blurs the focus in order to contrast the vague quality of recollection with the more precise vision of reality. Or to picture a plan of action which is told by one person to another (as when the city woman outlines her plan of murder to the man), Murnau records the action in slow-motion which helps show that the act is one of passion rather than careful design. One of the remarkable things about all of these devices is that they are natural to the style of *Sunrise* and are consequently accepted without conscious realization that they are in any way unusual.

In this connection, and purely from a pictorial standpoint *Sunrise* is one of the most beautiful motion pictures ever made. Close study reveals that the composition of each shot in relation to the motion to be photographed within it must have been planned in advance and executed with great care. Unforgettable for their sheer beauty in composition and expressive motion are such pictures as that of the wife, framed in the doorway. As she makes the simple gesture of stooping down to feed the baby chicks gathered around her, a feeling of womanly tenderness is captured in an image of lasting beauty. Another memorable moving image is the city woman's view of the village street from her bedroom window, as the peasants with their lanterns begin to gather for the night search on the lake.

Fred W. Murnau was a true motion-picture artist. Perspective, composition, action, balance of motion within the frame, and lighting were all fully conceived in advance and were carefully worked out on the set before anything was recorded on film. All of the sets for *Sunrise* were built with the perspective of the camera in mind. For example, the ceilings of the interiors slanted downward, walls converged slightly toward the back of the set, and floors slanted slightly. Yet, as seen through the eyes of the camera, the interiors appear only to have unusual depth.[4] Those who worked with Murnau state that he was an artist who knew always exactly what he wanted and tirelessly aimed to achieve it.

Murnau expresses meaning frequently by means of subtle symbolism. The reeds which symbolize the man's act of infidelity as well as his acceptance of the city woman's plan for murder play a particularly ironic role in the closing portion of the film. After their reconciliation, the young couple spend a happy day in the city, sharing many small adventures. They sail home by moonlight, deeply content in their new love. But as they near home a sudden severe storm blows up. The man remembers the bulrushes which he had surreptitiously hidden in the prow of the boat and with which he had intended to save himself. Now he manages to tie the rushes with a rope to his wife's back as she clings to him in helpless terror.[5] A moment later the mountainous waves sweep

[4] This effect, known as "forced perspective," obviously requires that the camera on such a set be placed only in one position and remain stationary in photographing the action.
[5] By associative image, the film underscores his protective role by picturing next the terrified child at home clinging to the servant who holds the babe in her arms as she looks out of the window at the pouring rain and lightning.

over them both, and the boat is capsized. The man is washed ashore, but the wife is lost.

During the search which follows, the bundle of rushes plays an important and pictorially dramatic part. Summoned from their beds by the husband, the men of the village leave in their small boats to search the lake. We see a long shot of the dark water as from the top right corner of the frame the body of the wife, supported by the bundle of bulrushes, floats on the tide downward to the lower left of the frame. The search continues, and the husband leans far out over the prow of one of the boats, his lantern almost dipping into the dark water, as he calls her name repeatedly into the night. Again, we see the wife's body move silently through the water across the frame. But this time a trail of rushes marks her path for one bundle has scattered, and her head is slowly being submerged. This trail of rushes comes into the light of the husband's lantern, and we see his horror-struck face. There is a beautiful and dramatic close-up of his lantern held over the dark water as a bunch of the rushes which support her wet shawl move into its light, followed by another bunch containing the rope. Again, we see a close-up of his horror-struck face, then, a shot of the old man at the oars who, after looking toward the husband at the prow, silently removes his hat and bows his head. Now the husband collapses, and one of the men comes to help and comfort him.

Thus, to the end, the rushes remain symbolic of the man's betrayal of his wife. The outcome—or what appears to be the outcome when the search is abandoned—is exactly as the man and the city woman had planned: he has been saved, the wife has been drowned, and the villagers accept it as an accident. But the meaning of these events to the man himself has now been completely altered by intervening happenings: whereas before he wished his wife dead so that he could go away with the city woman, now he wants his wife alive; whereas before he desired the city woman, now he is certain that he loves only his wife. He must suffer not only the anguish of her death, but the horrible guilt of knowing that only a few hours ago he had wished for it.

There are innumerable other instances of the use of symbolism throughout this film. For example, the flowers offered by the man to the wife after they leave the restaurant have a double meaning: flowers are an expression of love not only for the living, but for the dead. Symbolically they are an appropriate offering: they remind us (and her) that he had wished her to be dead; and, at the same time, they express his present feelings of love toward her. Also the two bells in the church tower ringing out together are expressive of the harmony and joy that the man and wife are feeling together; they are the wedding bells which mark their reconsecration to one another.

Meaning in *Sunrise* is also frequently communicated by establishing significant contrasts, either within a given image or by contrasting a mood or circumstance to an earlier one which occurred in the same setting. For an example of contrasting a character and his background in a given image in order to heighten our awareness about the mood of the character we see the husband, his head lowered over the oars in dark brooding, against the lake which glitters brightly in the sunlight. Similarly, the city woman, with her sophisticated clothes, her affected manner of walking, etc., appears in striking contrast among the simple peasant folk. This latter contrast is seen in reverse in the barbershop and ballroom scenes when the man and wife with their quaint country dress and manners mingle with city people. For contrast of mood in the same setting, we have the gay mood of the young couple as they board the trolley to return home, for this cannot be seen without recalling the agony which marked their trolley ride into the city. Nor can the husband's grief as he enters the bedroom and passes his wife's empty bed be seen without recalling his earlier entrance after his seduction by the city woman. These contrasts in mood are strongly felt not only because they occur with the same people in the same setting, but also because the camera records the scene from exactly the same angle to intensify our unconscious awareness.

In any discussion of contrasting moods in *Sunrise*, the striking difference in feeling between the first and second portions of the film must be noted. Lewis Jacobs has written,

    . . . the first half was characteristically Murnau. . . . This half had a lyrical quality and was removed from the real world. . . . The

second half, obviously suffering from Hollywood interference, was
completely different. Its mood was realistic; the lyricism was dissipated by comic relief; the universality was destroyed by melodrama.[6]

The same contrast in the handling of the first and second portions
of the film has been noted by many other critics, and most of
them have similarly assumed that the shift was due to interference
with Murnau's original purposes.

Actually, however, when we grasp the underlying theme of
this film, no such interference is apparent. The mood which Murnau created in the first part of the film does indeed remove it from
the real world, and this is exactly as Murnau had intended. He
was picturing a situation of conflict which drew the man into a
world where his real values and his normal perspective on his life
had, through his infatuation with the city woman, been completely altered. A man obsessed, he moved in a strange and unreal world. This mood continues unbroken until the man finds
himself unable to go through with the city woman's plan for murder, and at this moment the spell is broken. The period of reconciliation forms the transition to the second portion of the film,
which Lewis Jacobs has correctly described as realistic. Now the
man is no longer being driven by emotions which run counter to
the main current of his life and remove him from reality into a
strange and unreal world. From a man living in torment, he becomes once more himself, a simple peasant who is in love with his
pretty wife. Consequently the entire mood and treatment become
realistic. Notably, humor begins the moment the reconciliation
has been completed: outside the church, people line the walks
awaiting the appearance of the bride and groom; but the peasant
and his wife come out of the church, their arms entwined, ob-
livious of all around them, and make their way through the aisle
of curious and amused onlookers. And as the pair, imagining
themselves in a flowering meadow, walk out into the square, our
smiles turn to laughter, especially when they find themselves embracing amid the confusion and hubbub of stalled traffic. Finally,
reaching the curb in safety, they, themselves, laugh heartily—not
only at the incident but in relief at being at long last in the fresh
air of normalcy. Here, the realistic mood and treatment, with

[6] Op. cit., 362.

accompanying strains of humor and gaiety, begin and continue unbroken until the tragedy of the storm when the man is once more thrown back into the world of nightmare. And now reality itself appears to have taken on the shape of that nightmare. The return to the earlier mood is tremendously effective, since it reminds us that reality often does confront us with circumstances which seem to reflect and stir up our deepest conflicts, throwing us into a torment which mocks the normalcy of our more healthy emotions.

Thus, not only are the changes of mood from unrealistic to realistic and back again completely in keeping with Murnau's purpose, but they come about gradually and understandably in terms of what is happening to the characters. With truly remarkable insight, Murnau has used the peasant's familiar background of the village to heighten the sense of nightmare and the unfamiliar scenes of the city as a background for the naturalness and genuine feeling between the husband and wife. And, with the three central characters themselves, the contrast also in a sense becomes one between the simplicity and naturalness of country life on the one hand and the complexity and synthetic qualities of city living on the other. (This contrast is humorously underscored, for example, in the series of alternating shots which place the natural grace and simplicity of the man and wife in counterpoint to the pseudosophisticated manner of a city couple who are among the onlookers during the peasant dance in the ballroom.) Although the realistic scenes of the city may not have the same lyricism of the earlier and final sequences of the film, they have a charm and warmth and reflect Murnau's sensitivity and understanding of people. Instead of detracting from the universality of the film, the sequences in the city add to it; for the two dominant moods of the picture, though in complete contrast, complement each other. They are "the bitter and the sweet" which Murnau refers to in his line of preface; they are what the modern psychiatrist might more accurately describe as the sharp difference of feeling which exists when we are dominated on the one hand by unconscious (socially unacceptable) drives, or on the other by conscious (socially acceptable) ones. That this contrast was Murnau's intent, rather than the result of interference from Hollywood, is born out by the fact that Charles Rosher, Karl Struss,

Frank Powolny, and others who worked with him on this picture all assert that Murnau worked entirely without studio interference of any kind and that the picture was, in every sense, one of his own making.[7]

The happy ending of *Sunrise* has also been marked by some critics as a Hollywood imposition. Some, among them the noted British critic Paul Rotha, apparently feel that the picture should have ended in tragedy, that the wife should have been drowned in the storm, leaving the man to face the bleakness of life without her. Such a point of view is in a way understandable since, except for the happy ending, *Sunrise* almost perfectly fulfills the definitions of tragedy outlined by Aristotle in his *Poetics*. To begin with, the man fits Aristotle's definition of a tragic hero, for he is "neither eminently virtuous or just, nor yet involved in misfortune by deliberate vice or villainy, but by some error of human frailty." Such a man is by far the best hero of a tragedy, Aristotle tells us, "for our pity is excited by misfortunes undeservedly suffered, and our terror, by some resemblance between the sufferers and ourselves." In this respect the man in *Sunrise* is an ideal hero, for his weakness, as dramatized in the film, is a universal one, existing in every human being to a greater or lesser degree. Actually, the man's weakness is inherent in his passive tendencies, his unconscious desire—existent in all of us to some degree—to be led, controlled, possessed, and perhaps even violated by someone stronger than himself. These tendencies are activated in his relationship to the aggressive and dominating city woman, and because of them she is able to seduce him into the idea of murdering his wife.

Tragedy in its highest form must also involve "discovery," according to Aristotle, "a change from unknown to known, hap-

---

[7] Charles Rosher, who photographed *Sunrise*, was in Berlin with Murnau when the director worked out his plans for the picture. According to Rosher, the film was completely planned by Murnau before he came to this country. Even the sets for the picture were designed in Berlin. Murnau signed a contract with William Fox with the understanding that he would first make *Sunrise* and that he would be given a free hand in carrying out this picture. William Fox kept his word. He assigned a unit manager to handle the business details of the picture, but all final decisions on the production were made by Murnau himself. Charles Rosher reports that no one but himself, Murnau, Karl Struss (who was also responsible for some of the photography), and the film editor saw any part of the picture until it was completed.

pening between those characters whose happiness or unhappiness forms the catastrophe of the drama, and terminating in friendship or enmity." In the Greek tragedies, this meant the discovery of blood ties between two persons, either one or both of whom were unaware of the relationship. In a modern drama, it is appropriate that the revelation should be one of a psychological rather than purely physical sort. Thus does the man in *Sunrise* discover that his wife, whom he has agreed to do away with, is actually the woman he loves. This "discovery" by the man of an already existing fact (which one feels is understood and fully accepted by the wife from the beginning of the story) is beautifully and subtly dramatized in the early city sequences, and culminates in their reconsecration to one another in the church.

Another primary element of tragedy as defined by Aristotle is "revolution" which he describes as "a change . . . into the reverse of what is expected from the circumstances of the action." This, indeed, is what occurs in *Sunrise* in the latter portion of the film. After a happy day in the city, the young pair plan to sail home by moonlight—"a second honeymoon." All is well between them, and one expects that they will return happily to their home and that the city woman will be sent on her way. Just as on the trip across the lake to the city, we had a sense of impending danger, now by the very contrasting circumstances of the homeward journey, we are assured of a happy and safe return. But the reverse of what is expected happens. Thus the climax of the story involves "revolution" in the Aristotelian sense.

But inevitably in evaluating *Sunrise* in these terms, we come to the crucial matter of the happy ending itself. Now the modern idea of tragedy rests primarily on the question of whether the ending is happy or unhappy. This factor was not so important in the judgment of Aristotle who applied the term "tragedy" to many plays of high seriousness which ended happily (for example, Sophocles' *Philoctetes*). In defining what he regards as the "perfect" plot for tragedy, however, Aristotle does specify that "the change of fortune should not be from adverse to prosperous, but the reverse . . ." And it might be argued that had the wife been drowned *Sunrise* would have been in form almost a perfect Aristotelian tragedy. Such a fateful ending would even have met Aristotle's requirement of implied design, for the man in the end was forced to suffer by chance that which he had originally intended should happen. Since the artistry of this film is so great, and since it has been substantiated that Murnau completed his picture without interference of any kind, the question then arises as to why Murnau rejected an unhappy ending.

Before answering this question it may be well to point out that the short story on which the film is based did have a tragic ending. In the story, however, the man is drowned while his wife survives: he could have saved himself, but instead, in his efforts to save her life, he loses his own. This tragic ending appears to be completely correct for the story as it is developed by Hermann Sudermann, for in it the man is shown to be far more villainous than in the picture. Also in the short story, the man schemes over a long period of time with the woman (the servant in the household of the young peasant couple) and cold-bloodedly plans his wife's murder. Sudermann has the man redeem himself at the end by dying in the act of saving his gentle wife. Through such an ending, good triumphs over evil: the good wife survives, the evil woman fails in her murder plan and loses the man, and the man proves himself essentially good through his act of sacrifice. Thus, Murnau had two possible tragic endings from which to choose. On the one hand, had the wife been drowned, the film could have provided the emotional catharsis found in the highest form of Aristotelian tragedy. On the other hand, had Murnau followed the original story more closely, the picture could have been a tragedy in the modern sense of the word, carrying with it a sense of finality, of heroic grandeur, of exaltation.

Actually, neither of these endings would have provided a convincing or satisfying conclusion for the motion picture which Murnau made, for his entire development of the story makes the ending which he chose the only possible one for this picture. Murnau rejected both these tragic endings because either one of them would have negated the film's underlying mood and theme and destroyed the remarkable unity of his work. For Murnau did not want to make us feel either purged of emotion (in the Aristotelian sense) or exalted (in the manner of the more modern tragedy). From his film in its entirety, he wanted above all else simply to make us feel the wonder of human relationships—the complex motivations which govern the lives of human beings (even the lives of a simple peasant and his wife), the nuances as well as the quiet depths of understanding which exist between a man and a woman who love one another, the subtle moods which color the days of our lives. *For the theme of the picture is that not events themselves, but their meaning to human beings and the use to which we put them is what matters.* This theme is inherent in the development of the story which writer Carl Mayer and director Murnau worked out together, and it accounts for the unusual cinematic techniques which Murnau used throughout in telling this story—techniques which, as we have already shown, made it possible for him to place primary emphasis throughout on the *meaning* of events to his central characters. This theme is likewise borne out by the film's ending. Murnau shows how the man's affair with the city woman, even his attempt to carry through the city woman's plan for murder, brings the man and wife to a new awareness of their love for one another, thus enriching their lives. And, significantly, it is the bundle of reeds (symbolic of the man's infidelity and the murder plan) which the man uses to save his wife. By the end then, the reeds become the very means by which these two people are able to continue their life together.

Thus in *Sunrise*, Murnau tells us that good and evil are both part of living, that our mistakes and our suffering need not ruin us, but that what these events mean to us and what we do with them is what matters, for they may indeed become the very means by which our tomorrow may prove to be a better day. Life goes on, Murnau tells us, and bitter or sweet is essentially good, for there is always the promise of the sunrise and another day.

The Hollywood Quarterly of Film, Radio and Television, Spring, 1955.

A DYING ART OFFERS
A MASTERPIECE

Richard Watts, Jr.

It must certainly come under the head of cosmic irony that, just as the silent cinema is giving a most realistic pictorial equivalent of the death rattle, a really great photoplay reaches town from overseas. That it is one of the few indisputable masterpieces of the dying inaudible photoplay, I am willing to assure you in all arrogance. A bit more modestly, though, I would beg to add my private belief that it is not only a magnificent film, but it belongs among the really significant achievements of modern art. The work is *The Passion of Joan of Arc*, and it comes to us from, of all places, France.

Among the more curious aspects of its arrival, one of the most striking is that it is a French picture. In the past, while such assorted nations as America, Germany, Norway and Russia have been making important advances in the cinema, France somehow has lagged lamentably and surprisingly behind. Most of its films have been almost unbelievably incompetent and only one of them, Jacques Feyder's *Shadows of Fear*, has possessed a strenuous merit. Now, just as the rest of us are pathetically on the verge of giving up the silent medium in the interest of synchronized dialogue, the French come along and manufacture a superb, enormously important work of art in the old manner.

Though *The Passion of Joan of Arc* is completely Gallic in style, acting and the locale of production, and certainly justifies Paul Morand's declaration that with it the French cinema art is born, the film offers additional proof of the importance of the international element in picture making. For example, just as most of the significant American films of an earlier day had a trace or two of the Teutonic influence about them, so did the French masterpiece require the direction of a Dane named Carl Dreyer. Such an admission is, however, not meant as a denial that the drama is entirely French in spirit and execution.

Though the picture belongs on that high level with *Potemkin* and *The End of St. Petersburg*, it succeeds in being entirely distinctive from them in manner. Among the many definitions of the motion picture that were brought up by the philosophers of the new art in the days when it seemed likely to amount to something, the most eloquent were those of Mr. Seymour Stern. One of the divisions he found for the cinematic form was, as I recall it, "sculpture in motion." That is the best description I can think of for the style and intent of *The Passion of Joan of Arc*.

It is not that the picture fails to make use of the methods of painting, poetry and the drama, also. Essentially, though, the French film is medieval Gallic sculpture suddenly and anachronistically galvanized into action. Reduced to cinema phrases, it would have to be described as a series of close-ups. The method is to offer, in the form of subtitles, transcripts from the testimony in Joan's trial and then photograph the reactions of marvelously carved figures to it. A subtitle will show you a question the inquisitors put to their victim and the camera will, with a superb sense of lighting and design, capture the fleeting changes of facial expression by which the judges accompany it. Then, Joan's reply will be given and, marvelously acted, you will see the victim's reaction to the persecution of her foes.

Subtitles have frequently been damned, even by admirers of the silent cinema, as crude handicaps to the medium of pantomime and as almost a justification for spoken dialogue. In *The Passion of Joan of Arc*, though, they are an essential part of the work, acting as sort of chapter headings to the mighty pantomimic drama that is to follow them. Were the questions and answers of the trial put to you audibly, the entire mood and intent of the picture would be ruined viciously. The whole effect of the film demands that everything be visual and even the captions, which provide a necessary key to the moving sculpture of the drama, are not an intrusion but an integral part of a magnificent work of art. Here is the complete justification of the sub-title.

The whole production explains, with high conclusiveness, the attitude of many of us to the talking pictures. From close-up to caption, *The Passion of Joan of Arc* is completely visual in its purpose and achievements. It is certainly not our contention that the audible films cannot produce effective, if imitative, dramas. When, however, their success threatens a purely pictorial form, capable of such mighty works as *Potemkin*, *The Passion of Joan of Arc* and a Chaplin comedy, in which talk would not only be unnecessary, but actually a tremendous handicap, I, for one, cannot feel completely friendly toward them. When synchronized talk imperils a definite art form capable of such things, I cannot help suspecting that its triumph means the blotting out of a very important manifestation of one of the grander aspects of the modern spirit.

What is undoubtedly the most important single contribution to the success of the picture, not even overlooking the magnificent work of the director, is the performance of Mlle. Falconetti as Joan. I realize that acting is so frequently the result of expert direction that it is usually ridiculous to make such a statement, but there are things this actress does that must certainly transcend all outside management. Mlle. Falconetti's Maid is a scrubby, puzzled, sorely tried little peasant, apparently without grace or distinction of feature. Yet, under the persecution of her judges, she frequently becomes transfigured, until, without change of make-up, she assumes a certain unearthly spiritual beauty; the internal loveliness and grandeur of a great soul. Never does she seem an actress simulating sanctity, and at climactic moments she becomes little short of overpowering in the mystic power with which she somehow invests her characterization. In the most difficult imaginable of histrionic feats, she achieves a triumph that transcends histrionism.

The rest of the characters are minor ones, but they have been chosen with a tremendously shrewd eye for medieval art. If, as one of the marvels of the picture, there is the creation of the feeling that in it the fantastic sculptured figures of the fifteenth century are in motion before you, it is the choice of types, as well as the skillful lighting, grouping and photoplay that is responsible.

As a philosophical contribution to the lore of Joan of Arc, the picture is probably not terribly important. It treats only of the trial and death of its heroine and it represents Joan quite simply, as a helpless, puzzled peasant girl and her judges as cruel, but equally puzzled, ogres, who grow more and more confused at finding themselves faced by such an unaccountable person. Shaw's *Saint Joan*, which, so far as I know, is still the most beautiful thing ever written about Joan of Arc, showed the inquisitors as upright men driven to the persecution by the inexorable logic of their intolerance. The picture attempts no such explanation, but, while showing the judges as saturnine gargoyles, it does offer them that excuse of a terrible bewilderment in the face of sainthood.

So far as I could discern there was no suggestion of the psychoanalyzing of Joan. If the film seemed modern in spirit, it was entirely because of the medium and through our own knowledge of the new psychology. The picture, though it employs such a recent art form as the cinema, always remains, so far as I could discern, an amazing transcription of medieval art and the medieval devotional spirit. The result is a thing of rare beauty.

New York Herald Tribune, March 31, 1929.

RUSSIA'S FILM WIZARD

(*a study of the career and achievement of Eisenstein*)

Evelyn Gerstein

With *The General Line*, or *The Old and the New*, as the title
has now been dissipated for a less technically minded American
movie public, Eisenstein makes his bow as a film ethnographer
and agriculturalist. For the first time since 1924 and since his
first film *The Strike*, which has never ventured outside of Russia, he has turned aside from the steaming heroics of revolution
and hitched his camera to a plough. As pure movie, as a swift,
kinetic design, his latest film is inferior to either his *Potemkin*
or *Ten Days That Shook the World*. It marks the passing of the
first revolutionary process with its breathless fury and strange,
insistent rhythms.

The revolution here is in the working of the land. In *The Old
and the New*, there is only the wildness and desolation of the
steppes, those long barren plains over which the clouds move
slowly at first and a solitary thatched roof breaks the awful monotony. Then, suddenly, in the midst of this primitive land, there
are the machines, moving in fantastic formation across the endless plains, blocking out everything else. It is all a somewhat satirical georgic in praise of cream separators, of model dairies, of

tremulous Nietzschean bulls and cows wreathed in daisies and ribbons of catapulting herds of sleek, prolific hogs, of bearded sheep luminous in soft focus, of shrewd immobile kulaks, imprisoned behind their rolls of fat, of suave Rasputins ogling Heaven for rain in the face of a sceptical folk, of the march of the plunging tractors weaving macabre shadows across the fields.

The Old and the New is exactly what its title so blandly implies: the old way of farm life in contradistinction to the new. It is Saint Tryphon supplanted by the spraying machine, prayers for rain forsaken in favor of modern irrigation, the three field system yielding to the six field system, and the taut, desiccated old peasants with their primitive ploughs yoked to their backs, giving way before an army of Fordson tractors. It is Eisenstein's song of the machines.

In *Potemkin* and *Ten Days That Shook the World*, Eisenstein based his cinematics on a firm sub-structure of drama, even if it was only a variation of the newsreel. In *The Old and the New*, there is no drama, except such as he has evolved in the filming of separate scenes. There is no progression, except from the wooden plough to the tractor. It is simply a paean of super bulls and super dairies, of the machine that ploughs up the land, and the machine that mows it down again, and of the staunch bearded peasants, weathered by the suns and storms of the steppes, who are now standing aghast before this irresistible god, the Machine.

Sheer propaganda for an improved peasantry and a more efficient working of the land. Yet as Eisenstein has filmed it, with his camera, in one instance, literally hitched to a plough, it is so vigorous in its composition and photography, so direct and satirical in its reality, that the spectator rises to cheer when the separator gets into its stride and rivers and oceans of buttermilk flow from it to the hilarious delight of the peasantry, and the tractor finally mills its slow insistent way across the hills of that bare country, with a whole, enraptured populace galloping behind.

It must be understood that just as in witnessing American films one unconsciously reverts to the philosophical conclusions of Hollywood, with its intimations of personal glory and boundless wealth and success as the supreme ends of life, so in all these

Russian movies one must for the nonce accept the "Communist Manifesto." In Hollywood, the Russian thing is dubbed propaganda; in Russia, the Hollywood convention is similarly described. In Hollywood, there are heroes and heroines and villains, and the end is the triumph of virtue over vice and the relegating of the villain to a movie hell. In Russia, the conclusion is the same, but the terminology is different; there, the masses are heroes and heroines, and the bourgeois and private capital are the villains, and virtue triumphs over vice in the person of the mass. As propaganda, they are equally insidious. But, in Russia, provided the director has accepted the tenet of communism, he is let alone; in Hollywood, the consideration of the box office is only the first step in censorship. But when, as in the case of Sergei Michailovich Eisenstein, the propaganda is touched with a leaping cinematic vision and a subtle sense of pictorial values, it is no longer propaganda; it has become art.

It is a strange paradox that this extraordinary young Russian, who at twenty-six had already made *Potemkin* and precipitated a world controversy, that the same Eisenstein who indulges in manifestos about the sheer beauty of mass production, who derides individualism both as a doctrine and as a practice, should himself be such an arrant individualist. There is no mistaking a film of his. No other director is so ruthless a satirist, so coolly realistic in the larger sense, so scientific in his approach to what is fundamentally an aesthetic problem, the creation of a film.

All those young Russians are materialists, Marxists, now. Their ecstasy over facts is a religion. Eisenstein's gods are Marx, Pavlov, the reflexologist, and Freud. He is a psychologist, rather than a philosopher, a propagandist, rather than a poet. He renounces art in favor of mechanics, and denies the existence of anything but facts and physics. He talks about composing his scenes with mathematic exactitude, of calculating the dramatic and psychological effect of eggs and steppes and rifles and Cossacks. He writes: "I approach the making of a motion picture in much the same way that I would approach the equipment of a poultry farm or the installation of a water system." He denies his sensibilities, although invariably they shape the design of his compositions, the placing of his scenes, and the rare loveliness of his out-of-door photography.

By profession, Eisenstein is a civil engineer. In the brief intervals in his study of mathematics and architecture, he managed a circus and a small experimental theater in Moscow. Before he was nineteen—he is thirty now—he had succumbed to two major passions, the drawings of Leonardo da Vinci and the Japanese theater, and he applied them, practically, to his theater designs. After his service in the engineering corps during the war, where he acted in the double capacity of engineer and staff artist, he became *regisseur*, assistant director and dramatist extraordinary for the Proletcult theater in Moscow. One of his first assignments there was the dramatizing of Jack London's story, *Mexicalia*. He joined Meyerhold and the revolutionary theater, but even that was not radical enough for him. So back to the Proletcult theater as director! Then, he went in for stressing movement, for circus acrobats, and satire. He produced Ostrovsky's classical comedy as a circus buffoonade, and began to evolve his theories of *montage*.

After he had produced *Anti-Jesus* in a setting that was really a gas factory in miniature, he renounced the illusions of the theater, and looked for something that would allow him to work more realistically, to get closer to actual life, to the factories, the streets and the masses. The camera was the logical instrument for him. It could reproduce reality with utter fidelity, it could range through space and time; it could be newsreel and abstract film all in one. Eisenstein made his first film, a mass film, *The Strike*, in 1924. Then he wrote: "The intellectual cinema should be an entirely new form, and create at the same time a synthesis of all the different kinds of cinema-emotional, pathetic pictures, actual newsreel and the 'absolute' film." Then he made *Potemkin*.

It was originally intended merely as a prelude to a longer, more vitriolic film on revolution. But *Potemkin* was vitriol enough for the rest of the world. There was something in the precipitousness of that film of the revolt of 1905 that upset the powers that be. Berlin forbade its showing; London refused it admittance; New York expurgated it. Hollywood, or rather the Hollywoodites who saw it here or abroad, grew rapturous, and talked nothing but "technique" and "rhythms" for days. Metronomes popped up all over the studios of the west coast, and for months the echoes resounded with *Potemkin*.

But few of them realized that it was Eisenstein, the director, rather than extraneous superimposed rhythms, that had to do with the flow of the film; that it was the swift impingement of scene on scene, the consistent contrasts of rushing mass movement and of slow, dull waiting, the climactic force of the slow, unerring march of the Cossacks down the long steps at Odessa, the terrific speed of that baby carriage plunging down into a film eternity, that created this emotional onslaught; that it was not alone the composition of each particular scene and the mass movement of all the scenes that evolved these fearful rhythms, but the passion of fear and terror and agony and joy that one read on the faces of each of its actors. It was the reality of the thing, its relentless catharsis, that shivered one.

In *Ten Days That Shook the World*, based on John Reed's book of those crucial, tortured days of revolution, Eisenstein had meal for his historian's reach. There is power and virility and imagination in each of its impending scenes, a lurking satire that is most pungent in his caricatures of Kerensky and the Woman's Battalion of Death. It is Eisenstein triumphant, a dispassionate god of inspired cinematic lightnings, a cool and ruthless scientist, with a strange elusive feeling for pictorial beauty. It suggests movement through space and time more than any other film that preceded it.

In *The Old and the New*, there are no lightnings, it is an Eisenstein gone pastoral, with his cows and bulls and sheep and sky soft focused, but his peasants in full tones. Unlike *The Village of Sin*, his peasants are outlined boldly, without pity, his satire on the Kulaks, who still infuse a little of the old regime into present day rural Russia, and of the bourgeois office class, is relentless. But one notices the sensuous delight that he has taken in his filming of wheat and sky. There, there is a new softness in his photography, that has always been cool and unyielding in its insistence on primary tones, even in the scenes of the Odessa harbor in *Potemkin*. In *The Old and the New*, the scenes are narrative and episodic in structure; yet there is no narrative. Like *Moana* and *Nanook of the North* and *Chang*, it belongs to the georgics of the films; and like them it is essentially pictorial, rather than cinematic, in form.

But, unlike his earlier films, Eisenstein reflects the intellectual passion of the man in every scene. The others were idylls; Eisenstein's film is rigorously scientific in its approach and suggested conclusions, and psychological in its treatment of race and civilization. But the scenes do not hold together, as in his earlier films. They happen, successively, and except for a few sequences, they do not dissolve, cinemawise, into each other. The taut symphonic structure that marked his other films, the underlying rhythm and movement is absent here. And although in individual scenes there is movement and play of light and shadow and rhythm, the thing, as a whole, is scientific rather than cinematic.

The Old and the New is Eisenstein's fourth film. His influence in Russia alone is amazing. He has already given rise to a school of neophytes who have in turn evolved into antagonists. The Germans brought the cinema its nuances, the half tones of a studied photography, the trick stuff that was disseminated all over the movie world in thin virtuosic streams. But Eisenstein has been the movie's Daumier, their caricaturist extraordinary, their first intimation of an intellectual approach. Without the intellectual approach, there can never be art, only photography that reflects life instead of illumining it.

Eisenstein is the materialist who made all the Glynish palaver that has sweetened the movies ever since their inception, seem the treacle that it really is. He has given the movies a criterion, an intellectual cinema that is neither esoteric nor decadent, an abstract film that is not too cerebral, a symbolism that is intellectual rather than emotional. Today, as the teacher of the theory and practice of direction at the State Technical Institute of the Cinema in Moscow, he is also in charge of the cinema division of the psycho-physical laboratories organized for the study of the spectator's reactions. He is also experimenting with sound, which he thinks is the ultimate for the movies. But it will be sound that is comparable to music and accentuates the abstractness and rhythmic quality of the cinema, as opposed to dialogue, which immediately tosses the movies back into the theater, and the speech that limits their absoluteness.

THE WORK OF PUDOVKIN

Jay Leyda

Vsevolod Ilarionovich Pudovkin was born in 1893 in Penza. His father, of peasant stock, was a commercial traveler. When Pudovkin was four his family moved to Moscow, where all his schooling took place. At the Moscow University he majored in physics and chemistry, but the outbreak of war found the student enrolled in the artillery and, by February 1915, a prisoner. After three years in a German prison (while G. W. Pabst was in a French prison) profitably spent learning foreign languages, he escaped and late in 1918 returned to Moscow. He worked as a chemist till 1920, and pursued old interests in painting and music by night. He has said that he took no interest in the silly cinema until Kuleshov, whom he met in 1920, took him to see *Intolerance*. Only two other films ever made as deep an impression on him—Eisenstein's *Potemkin* and Chaplin's *A Woman of Paris*.

In 1920 the First State School of Cinematography was opened by the Commissariat of Education under the direction of Vladimir Gardin. Pudovkin joined the school and became wholeheartedly absorbed in his new studies. Kuleshov had gone back to the front, and Pudovkin spent the two years until Kuleshov's return to Moscow under the tutelage and practical assignments of Gardin. His first film experience was a role (as a red army commander) in Perestiani's *Days of Struggle* (1920). In *Hammer and Sickle* (1921) Pudovkin not only played the leading role but collaborated on the scenario—besides assisting the administrator, the director and the property man. After one experience in the theater assisting Gardin in a staging of Jack London's "Iron Heel" at the Theater of Revolutionary Satire, he collaborated on the scenario and direction of *Hunger . . . Hunger . . . Hunger* (1921) which Edward Tisse photographed. Gardin gave him his first directing responsibility when he allowed Pudovkin and Tisse to work on one scene without him. After another scenario with Gardin (*Locksmith and Chancellor*, from a play by Lunacharsky) he was invited to co-direct the film with him, but Kuleshov had renewed his Workshop and Pudovkin preferred to join him.

The Kuleshov Workshop was Pudovkin's home for three years, when he left to work in the studio of Mezhrabpom-Russ. During these three years he became Kuleshov's closest assistant. Pudovkin assisted on the scenario and direction of *The Extraordinary Adventures of Mr. West in the Land of the Bolsheviks*, as well as playing the role of the chief villain. *The Death Ray*, which temporarily wrecked the Workshop, was written and designed by Pudovkin; he assisted in the direction of the film and again played the part of chief villain.

It is usually assumed that pupil and master parted because of basic differences but Kuleshov himself helped Pudovkin to find and hold his new job, and later even helped with some difficult scenes in *Mother*. Mezhrabpom-Russ was an amalgamation of the pre-revolutionary company Russ with the film department of Mezhrabpom, the Russian office of the Workers International Relief. They produced all types of films including purely educational ones. After a few unhappy days as assistant to Eggert on *The Wedding of the Bear*, Pudovkin was assigned to make a film popularization of Pavlov's studies in conditioned reflexes. Pudovkin's scientific background made him an admirable choice for the job and he approached the new work eagerly, less as an artist than as a scientist. Clearly as his "psychological resemblance to Griffith" has been indicated by Harry Alan Potamkin, a parallel with Pabst's development is often inevitable—particularly in comparing *Mechanics of the Brain* (1925-26) with *Secrets of a Soul* (1925-26), both begun as simple instructional films and both furnishing the director with a foundation for a realistic aesthetic, Pudovkin on Pavlov, Pabst on Freud.

CHESS FEVER—1925   During a pause in the filming of *Mechanics of the Brain,* Pudovkin was asked to make a topical comedy on the International Chess Tournament being held in Moscow's Hotel Metropol. The catch was that one could not ask the contestants, least of all Jose Capablanca, to act in a comedy. Shots of Capablanca, taken by a supposed cameraman, were brought to the cutting-table with shots of other actor's hands and of objects, and a minor role was thus created by the Kuleshov method that must have surprised Capablanca exceedingly if he ever saw it—which is unlikely as the film has never before been shown outside the Soviet Union. "Bits" were played by friends and members of the Mezhrabpom staff who happened to be around. The three druggists, for example, are played by the director Protazanov, Darevsky, then manager of the studio, and Raizman who was later to direct *In Old Siberia* (1928) and *The Last Night* (1937).

The film has a fund of simple satire and movie wit. The hero's extreme preoccupation with chess and the growing exasperation of the heroine (played by Pudovkin's wife) cannot be imagined apart from Kuleshov's ingenious cutting method. Widely separated figures and objects are brought into a related film concentration which Kuleshov termed "creative geography." Although it was the first film by Pudovkin to be released, *Chess Fever* was not a first step toward something higher but rather the last step in Pudovkin's study period.

MOTHER—1926   Gorky's novel was the base, but not the only source of Natan Zarkhi's scenario. He drew upon memoirs of the 1905-06 period, particularly events in the city of Tver, changing thereby the structure, but not the spirit or color of Gorky's treatment of the epoch. The history of the finished scenario is curious. It was first assigned to Yuri Zheliabuzhsky to direct, who—unable to find the right actress for the title role—asked Zarkhi to rewrite the scenario, transferring the character of the *mother* to a *father,* to be played by Moskvin. For some reason the plan was dropped, until revived by Pudovkin who brought back the original scenario with its simple theme of a down-trodden working-class mother rising to political consciousness through participation in revolutionary activity.

In the scenario, Zarkhi and Pudovkin consciously established a sonata outline through the various stages of production: first and second reels—*allegro* (saloon, home, factory, strike, chase); third reel—a funereal *adagio* (dead father, scene between mother and son); fourth and fifth reels—*allegro* (police, search, betrayal, arrest, trial, prison); sixth and seventh—a furious *presto* (spring thaw, demonstration, prison revolt, ice-break, massacre, death of son and mother). This early consideration for tempo is a contributing factor to the notable rhythm of *Mother.*

Most of the casting problems were solved by Doller, Pudovkin's assistant, who brought Baranovskaya and Batalov from the Moscow Art Theatre, and found Chistyakov, working as accountant in the studio, for the father. The bit-roles were discovered everywhere. For the colonel in the scene of Pavel's arrest, Doller found a former officer in the tzarist army—who played himself. The lesser officer in this scene was taken by Pudovkin, who always plays a small part in his pictures (also a habit of Alfred Hitchcock) and used to enjoy acting in the films of other directors.

In Anatoli Golovnya, a pupil of Levitzky, Pudovkin found a cameraman who, with him, made a working partnership as harmonious as that of Tisse with Eisenstein. The first scenes shot (the exteriors at the courthouse) established the character of the photography of the whole. One of the shots in this scene, the powerful composition of the standing policeman, called "an example of foreshortening which has become 'classic' in cinematic practice" (Vladimir Nilsen), gives us a key to another art drawn upon to contribute to the art of Pudovkin. The character and viewpoint of this composition comes from the well-known "camera angle" of Velasquez' "Bollo." We know that Pudovkin was not only acquainted with the best-known classical painting through reproductions, but had direct knowledge of the contents of Moscow's Museum of Modern Western Art, where the inspiration for the entire episode of the prison exercise hour is hung—Van Gogh's "Prison Courtyard." The carefully composed realism of

Degas, the haggard blue-period work of Picasso and the prints of Kathe Kollwitz are all contributors to the graphic representation of the mother. Another painting in this collection—Rouault's "Judges"—furnished the exact characterization for the three judges in the trial scene. The revelation of Pudovkin of the camera possibilities latent in the other medium came however from a film—*Potemkin,* without which the paintings may well have gone unused, in spite of Pudovkin's previous concern with that medium.

More important than any individual compositions in *Mother* is its continuation of the Griffith-Eisenstein tradition of camera as active *observer* rather than mere *spectator.* Lunacharsky remarked that the film carried a conviction as though an extraordinary cameraman had been present at the actual events. The photography of the actors is especially emotional in effect. Pudovkin has told how he establishes personal relationships with each actor in his films, a method that, particularly in *Mother,* renders them intimate to the spectator, helping to make this the most lyrical and intimate of the great cycle of Soviet films in the silent era. The mother's character is so firmly developed that her first smile (in her visit to the prison) usually breaks down any resistance that the spectator may have had.

During *Mother,* Pudovkin was also writing the first book of film theory by a practitioner—theory hitherto being the province of the critic. In two small booklets (condensed in English as "Film Technique") he makes a "simple and comprehensive introduction" to the new approach to film materials developed by Kuleshov and himself. The most startling (at the time) statement to foreign readers occurs in one of the introductions: "The foundation of film art is *editing.*" The fresh attitude toward this process tended abroad to blind followers to the other basic material in the book, even to ignore Pudovkin's cautious use of the word "foundation." The editing process is not the only one that made *Mother* great, but one can learn more of the value that Pudovkin placed on the process from this film than from the masses of *The End of St. Petersburg* (1927) or the technical tour-de-force of *Storm Over Asia* (1928). The expert cutting on human movement of *Mother* has been more widely absorbed into general film technique than its more intense cutting propositions. The clearest example in all of Pudovkin's work of the "associative" editing of unrelated scenes to form a "plastic synthesis," is still the episode of Pavel's joy in prison. Senses of smell (saloon, early morning), feeling (mud, blow of a fist), and sound (water drip, swollen stream) could not have been so strongly communicated with any other method. *Mother's* editing is the logical outcome of the disjunctive cutting introduced by Edwin S. Porter, enlarged by D. W. Griffith and others, and analyzed by Kuleshov. Although in direct opposition to Eisenstein's *shock* montage, Pudovkin used a linkage method far beyond Kuleshov's "brick by brick" theory, but (again) pushed there by *Potemkin*.

The individualized characterizations of *Mother* within the bold pattern of *Potemkin* is the first but not the only distinguishing quality that separates Pudovkin's work from that of Eisenstein. Leon Moussinac has further clarified this difference in an epigram, "An Eisenstein film resembles a shout while a film by Pudovkin is comparable to a song"—a song not lyrical alone, however, but in turn sad, bitter, angry, heroic.

Museum of Modern Art Film Library
Notes: The Russian Film Series, VII, 1939.

THE NATURE OF
THE CINEMA

André Levinson

Among the opinions of the sophisticated about the cinema are two which are equally foreign to disinterested discussion. On one hand is the special pleading of those friends of the seventh art who urge the films as a sort of cosmic agent that will change the face of the globe and transfigure the moral life of humanity. These enthusiasts already rejoice to see the major arts reabsorbed and abolished by the triumphant movies. On the other hand are those who hold the screen in utter contempt. It is, according to them, food for the vulgar, and a nursemaid to crowds wallowing in intellectual sloth. They reject it beyond hope of appeal and deny it any of the dignity of art. But panegyrics and invectives, the adulation of one faction and the heckling of the other, over-reach the goal at the same point. Their momentary struggles obscure the main problem.

As a matter of principle, the cinema—considered within itself—deserves neither this excessive respect nor scorn. If it has created a new point of view, like that which Louis Delluc discussed under the title of *Photogenie,* then film production and audience reaction obey immutable laws which preceded living photography, laws which govern all human understanding and sensibility, expression and perception. For the theorist, the cinema is a study in space, a specific aspect of the creative imagination; but it touches at more than one tangent on earlier art forms. It has its own technique; but it is grounded on several established principles of aesthetics.

To decide whether the cinema is an art, one must ask if this particular form of intelligence answers in substance and matter to the idea of art. It is not a question of whether the cinema is good or bad, but of whether it fulfills the conditions which distinguish a work of art from any other natural or manufactured product.

What makes a picture, symphony or novel a work of art? Above all, it is a fabrication, a new reality imagined and created by the artist. This fiction is accomplished by the selection of elements that nature offers—colors, masses, emotions and tones, and their regrouping according to an arbitrary arrangement. The choice of these empirical factors, and their ordering—balance of masses, harmony of proportions, musical or visual rhythm—everything, in short, which establishes mutual relationships between the parts of an object—are the property of a work of art which, by this name, becomes a cosmic thing. A third phase, equally important, concludes this effort at abstraction. A work of art is isolated from its surroundings, circumscribed by the limits of its form. Accordingly, every painting is, first of all, put upon a symmetrical surface. The frame attests that the isolation of this microcosm within it is a painting. Art encloses the infinity of phenomena in the finite quality of form. It is, then, the degree of abstraction, of stylization, which determines the hierarchy of the arts. The more complete the transposition—the principles of immediate reality finding themselves eliminated and replaced by equivalents—the more sovereign is the work.

In this sense, for example, painting is superior to sculpture. The sculptor places real masses within a positive space. The painter, at close quarters with a two-dimensional surface, pretends the volume of the figurative objects that he plans in a space that is illusory and suggested by artifice. The sculptor makes color an abstraction and works solely with mass and light. The theater has flesh-and-blood people acting on a stage, even if it is a real place. Yet living actors substitute themselves for imaginary beings, saying the things that the arbitrary playwright puts into their mouths. Scenic space, exactly limited, typifies an interior or a place. Fitted into the wall, this space opens only toward the footlights. Players and settings are thus seen only on the visual plane, facing the spectator. The theater, the quality of whose art is hardly questioned, is thus an anomalous melange of the conventional and the natural, of the represented and the direct, of fiction and reality.

In view of these proportions, where does the cinema come in? The major argument against it is its basis of photography and photo-chemical processes which, in automatic and objective fashion, establishes aspects of a reality that is not transposed. Must the film for that reason be fundamentally tainted? Has the play of lights on a plate or sensitive film anything in common with art? Photography figures in many laments as the death of painting. In calling the realism of a painting shabby, impersonal, without real life, traced from the object and inartistic, people are in the habit of saying that it is photographic—an unpardonable blemish! But the cinema is merely derived from photography.

Let us state the question this way: does the photographic plate offer at least some of the briefly enumerated characteristics of art? It certainly does, however much the hand of the painter which guides the brush is replaced by an objective lens. We have said that art is the selection and combination—in a voluntary order—of the elements of reality, volume, emotion and sound. This arbitrary and conventional grouping, which transforms raw matter into a work of art, we call form.

Has photography some elements of this convention which re-creates an object? Does it stamp a form with an image? Again, yes. Without being of purely artistic essence, and even while pre-serving some untransposed elements of reality, photography re-tains several elements of art.

For example, photography has this in common with painting: it projects masses on a surface plane. That is the first thing in its stylization. The solidity of bodies and the space in which they are situated are fictitious and illusory. The second convention is the delimitation of the visual field and the insertion of the image in a symmetrical frame. The third is the exaggeration of perspective, which in turn has impressed some painters as having Picasso values (gigantic hands or feet, out of proportion to the first plane of the canvas). The image is thus stylized and isolated; so much for the rules of artistic vision! In short, it is not the objective machine which dominates; that records mechanically; but it is guided by the eye of the photographer who adjusts its focus. Consequently, although photography is a technique, it can also be a means of artistic expression. The particle of the film, the image isolated in the little four centimeter quadrilateral, can have its own intrinsic beauty and a high quality of art. Its projection in a series gives it further values to be discussed below. Moreover, let us not forget that the image is intensified a hundredfold by the process of pro-jection; or that the other transposition, the "fade out," belongs solely to the magic screen. Whatever it is, the technique of living photography, whose astonishing results we recognize, is superior in its faculty of abstraction to the theater, whose raw material is often too much for a slender frame.

The true nature of the cinema is not yet clear to many people. They remain contemptuous and stubborn because they approach it with mental habits acquired by frequenting the other arts and particularly by their experience in the theater. That is their first mistake. The screen is clearly opposed to the stage. They differ completely in their methods, as in their object, even when both treat the same situations. It is neither the subject nor the theme which is the essential quality either of theater or cinema; it is the mode of expression, and in this they part at the same point as do music and sculpture. No confusion between these two types of art is possible. Yet they borrow from the same source: the creative emotion and the response aroused in us are perfectly analogous: a sense of harmony, of happy proportion or of a regular and pleasing recurrence of certain elements. The same is true for the cinema. It is not in what it has in common with the other arts that one must seek out its "open Sesame"; it is in its own nature, in its specific procedure.

The cinema differs from every other intellectual activity in the magic which operates at each turn of the crank. The operator's machine transforms space into time and vice versa. It is the greatest philosophical surprise since Kant—a prodigious and paradoxical mechanism which interlaces and substitutes, one for the other, the two categories in terms of which we consider the universe. Sculpture is material, spatial and immutable. Music, invisible and immaterial, lives during its duration. A film's projection is visible and transitory. Goethe, to quote a familiar analogy, called architecture frozen music. So the cinema is an animated painting—a motion picture—the very language of visual imagination. The speaking theater, on the contrary, proceeds by dialectic methods. It reduces the richness of human feelings and the complexity of the inner life to a verbal debate, a contradictory argument. The *dramatis personae* talk back and forth with more or less volubility. This is the basic convention that rules the theater. It gives expression to what happens within us.

The screen is, at the same time, freer and more conventional than the stage—conventional in so far as it gives us the reflection of the player and the place, not the real presence; free, since it is apart from the logic of verbal tilts and arbitrary unity. It does not need to localize action artificially, since it can follow its characters in ever multiplying settings and planes.

The silent art shows us things with the very richness of our inner vision, in the order in which they appear to our imagination. They emerge from our memory, are linked with our dreams. There is an end to the rigorous and abstract continuity of the syllogism. A theatrical setting of a passion or an idea is adjusted to the reason. But the association of images in our brain is irrational. They flock to the threshold of our consciousness, whirl among the shadows behind the door, strike upon that door and finally enter into the zone of light. The cinema treats images with that same ductility.

It is with a film's montage—whose general characteristics are forecast by the preliminary shearing away in the scenario—that the travail of style begins for the director. What is montage? It is the assembling and arranging of the units of a film, each in its own little frame. The isolated image, normally occupying the screen for a sixteenth of a second, is only an abstract unity; it is not perceived as a whole and does not function by itself. Like literature, the cinema is a living language not composed of isolated words drawn from the dictionary. It is their context, their fixed or free relation to other words which makes them live.

So in the cinema the unit of composition is the frame of the montage, whether it is a series of images photographed on the same plane at a uniform focus, in one setting and with its flow of action uninterrupted, or whether its significance is one of time. Therefore, too, the projection of a film, its form and carriage, depends essentially not on the individual unit, but on the relation of time and space between the juxtaposed frames and their relative value.

The montage of a good film has neither the rigorous alternation of poetic discourse nor the sweep of tunes infinitely repeated. Visual themes are unrolled in an endless melody, to paraphrase Richard Wagner; the structure of the most harmonious film is forcefully non-symmetrical, a rebel against stable balances. Its quality depends on the intensity of emotion expressed by the actors and impressed on the audience. The number of images which exhaust a sensation is indeterminate; an estimation of time duration in the cinema is subjective and variable. We may be struck by stupor, or frozen with fear during the projection of fifty centimeters of film. By concentrating one may reduce to a still less significant "shot" a prodigious gesture, a symbolic attitude concerning a great fundamental theme. One may, on the contrary, insinuate a state of soul over some dozens of meters by slow progression, envelopment and poetic torpor. Briefly, our sense of objective duration is abolished by the psychological factor, the emotional quality of direction.

Rhythm, the result of significant continuity, is the most persistent structural agent of the silent art; it is its form. Of course composition itself, the decor or the choice of the visual angle, the studied play of acting in the ensemble, is a first step of enormous importance. The functioning of scenery and point of view gives direction its matter. But in the final analysis, it is the latter which decides. It is the same path which, in writing and syntax, leads from a simple statement to the detailed elaboration of a novel.

I maintain this analogy, however suspiciously literary it may be, because it carries my argument forward. The two thousand meters of a film and the two hundred pages of a novel obey the same necessities and use the same means to affect their audiences.

When this relationship is clear, it is evident at once that it is not so much the theater which threatened the vogue of the cinema as it is the novel. The film is not the concurrent of the stage, but of writing. The cinema is a visual language. It makes us see things. The graphic quality of a book is, let us say, equally visual; we read with our eyes. But the writer uses letters and words, conventional ideographic signs and not direct images. Words are concepts which evoke moral or material realities, suggest them by associating them with others. In a book, it is an image which arises from a significant formula; in the cinema, it is the sense of an image that we must decipher. In the cinema, one extracts the thought from the image; in literature, the image from the thought. Here the differences stop, and the analogy starts.

The film and the novel are alike in that both are forms of cinematic art. Certainly the long strip of film and the book, each considered in its entirety, is an entity of fixed proportions and immutable context. They retrace a complete movement, an action arrested *ne varieture*.

But in the case of both the film and the novel, we perceive them not in their totality, but in a continuous succession of image-emotions or word-meanings. Their tempo is vividly the same; we take perhaps twice as much time—three or four hours

—to read a printed story as to watch a filmed one, a sufficient length of time in each case to relive events supposed to have filled long years. There are, then, the same continuity and the same compression of time.

Like the film, the novel is addressed to our imagination; more so in the sense that it only suggests by verbal artifices the visual images that the cinema projects directly on the screen. But if the reader is obliged to visualize the thing read, the spectator is required to read the image and discern the latent meaning of it.

The film has, in common with the novel, a mixed literary form: the abolition of all the unities—place, action, time; and, quite like the novel, it rescues from this complexity and apparent incoherence its inner unity, that of design, and a harmony of parts which should concur in forming a whole endowed with an organic life. The composition of a novel is equivalent to the continuity of a picture, each chapter, paragraph or other division forming a "shot".

If we consider a novel which is modern, but which proceeds remotely from convention, and then the much exaggerated influence of the cinema on literature, we discover there all the rhythmic processes of the film, the counterpoint of themes, their parallel and interlaced unreeling. It is the novelist's problem, as it is the director's, to play with the same psychological reactions, to seek the reader's attention in words or images; to prevent distractions and interruptions which would take the reader out of the magic circle; to appeal to his memory by flashbacks to that which has already been seen or done in the preceding chapters or reels.

While the first two thousand meters of film are unreeling and the two hundred and first page turns, one's memory keeps the living imprint of the two thousand meters already unreeled and the two hundred pages already turned. The novelist or the director appeals to these memories that have been stored away, at the same time associating the present moment to the persistent memory of what, half an hour ago, became the past. . . .

All these psychological methods, mnemonic and rhythmic, which are familiar to us in the novel, are brought to a head in the films by the supreme act of direction. By themselves they are the outstanding methods of two languages which differ at that point where suggestion is replaced by vision.

This much having been said, it would take us much farther along the way to enumerate the principal methods of direction by which the film maker arrives at his ends. For, as we have said, the image or the scene, the unity of vision or expression, attains its true goal only by its relationships with the other unities of a cinematic subject. But that is another story, and a long one.

Theatre Arts Monthly, Sept., 1929

GRIFFITH: PIONEER
OF THE FILM ART

Seymour Stern

AUTHOR'S NOTE: *This survey of the career and contribution of David Wark Griffith appeared, handsomely illustrated and under the title: "Pioneer of the Film Art," in the* New York Times *Magazine, Sunday, November 10, 1940. It caused considerable comment. Thus, while it was used unexpectedly as a study in English composition in schools of Binghamton, New York, it was also studied, for other purposes, in Hollywood, where Griffith, after almost nine years of enforced retirement, was attempting a directorial comeback. The leaders of the American film industry, far from having forgotten him, were reappraising his potential commercial value. The comeback failed to materialize, but, as an unintended by-product of this publicity, the references here to Griffith's religious films and exploitation of religious motifs were 'picked*

*up' by the trade as a cue to exploring the possibilities of renewing
the earlier production of such films. The time-dishonored fusion
of religion, profit and war, allied from antiquity, was considered
both more practical and more practicable by the commercial dic-
tatorship than a fresh gamble on rehiring the maker of* Intolerance.
*The author herewith makes it emphatically clear that these refer-
ences were included purely as a matter of record, and that their appearance as such does not necessarily indicate either approval or en-
dorsement, by the author, of Griffith's recourse to this type of
subject-matter and propaganda.—S.S.* (1959).

The films of David Wark Griffith, which for more than a quarter
of a century thrilled vast audiences with shimmering beauty and
towering spectacle,[1] have at last been added to the treasury of
native American arts. Thirty-two years after his entry into motion
pictures [1908], the legend, the achievements, the complex and
far-reaching influence of the king of directors, like the remembered
glory of an ancient world, have crystallized into what is now known
in film circles as the Griffith Tradition. A panoramic survey of the
high spots of this tradition will be made available to the public
for the first time,[2] when the Museum of Modern Art this week
launches an extensive show and exhibit devoted to Griffith's life
and work.[3] Among the pictures shown will be many of the cele-

---

[1] In the *Times*, the order of these five words was transposed from the original
text to read: "towering spectacle and shimmering beauty." The *Times* argued
that since beauty is of a higher category than spectacle, it should follow in as-
cending order of importance, a point which I readily conceded on philosophical
grounds. I have here restored the original sequence, however, in the interest of
the continuing debate over Griffith as the king of spectacle. I am frankly more
concerned today, as indeed I was twenty years ago, with tactical points and
strategy than with the logic of esthetics or the esthetics of grammar.—S.S.

[2] Actually, it was not the first time. Beginning in 1926, the Film Arts Guild,
headed by Symon Gould, launched the first "festival" in film history. Taking a
cue from the Wagnerian music-festivals of Germany, I publicized it in magazines and newspapers as the "Griffith Film Festival," and the word stuck. It
consisted, except in one instance, of extended consecutive runs of *The Avenging Conscience* (one night only), *The Birth of a Nation, Intolerance, Broken
Blossoms, Orphans of the Storm,* and *America.* All were shown either at the
former George M. Cohan Theatre or at the former Cameo Theatre, both in
Times Square, New York City.

[3] The accompanying art-exhibit at the Museum featured the work of the late
architect, Frank Lloyd Wright. Both exhibits were publicized under the title:
"Two American Masters."—S.S.

brated classics which have exercised, both singly and collectively, a dominant technical and creative influence through the years on the development of the screen.

Why is the name of D. W. Griffith still a synonym for the "father of film art"? What were the salient contributions which earned him world-wide and enduring fame?

Broadly speaking, his contributions fall into two major categories. First, the technical discoveries and inventions and creative adaptations. Griffith did not invent all of the devices which misinformed commentators of later years ascribed to him. The close-up, for example, appeared as far back as the quaint old primitive film, *The Kiss*, in 1895, and in some of the early German primitives, before Griffith entered the field. But he was the first to use the device for [both] dramatic and psychological effect—a contribution that shaped the entire technique of picture-making down to the present day. In addition, he himself added a multitude of more advanced methods, all of which have long since become an established part of film technique. Chief among these were the long shot, the vista, the vignette, the eye-opener effect, the cameo-profile, the fade-in and fade-out, the iris, soft-focus, back lighting, tinting, rapid cutting, parallel action, mist photography and the moving camera.

But far more important than any single one of these devices, or, indeed, than all of them taken together, is the second major category of Griffith's contributions, the content of the films themselves—i.e., the emotional, dramatic, intellectual and esthetic content, separate and apart from the mechanics of picture-making. For in the sustained acclaim of mechanics and technique, little attention has been paid to this aspect of the director's achievement. Yet it is precisely here that Griffith as an indigenous American artist made himself felt as the mightiest single shaping-force in the annals of the screen. Even before *The Birth of a Nation* [appeared] in 1915, his bold conception of the exalted purpose which the medium might serve lighted the horizons of the future for other directors and enabled them to chart their courses.

Griffith's versatile and elastic genius found itself at home in a variety of realms of thought and feeling—the social, the psychological, the philosophical, the poetic, and the religious. He stands alone among directors in having demonstrated, not once but many times, the capacities of the motion picture to project something more important and more lasting than mere entertainment. Long before the names of Eisenstein in Russia, Fritz Lang in Germany, Alfred Hitchcock in England, or Frank Capra in Hollywood were heard of, Griffith had brought to the screen important historical and philosophical themes, challenging social questions, visionary prophecies of the future. His epics abound in teeming canvases from the wide range of world-history. In *The Birth of a Nation* [1915] and *America* [1924], two mammoth films on the American Civil War [and the Reconstruction Period], and the [American] Revolution, respectively, he set permanent standards in the technique of staging battle-scenes and proved himself a master of the art of capturing the spirit of vanished historical epochs.

Orphans of the Storm, in 1922, combined magnificent spectacle with a great social theme. Griffith used the French Revolution as a platform from which he attacked communism and Soviet Russia, and at the same time, cited the historic fruits of the revolution as a vindication of liberal democracy and the democratic way of life. This was the first film to bring post-war [World War I] social and political problems to the screen. Its example was taken up by other producers and has come down to our time.

On an even grander scale, *Intolerance* [1916], with its four parallel stories, its stupendous re-creation of the Ancient World,[4] and its apocalyptic image-prophecy of the second coming of Christ, still stands as the supreme example of what can be done with masses and architecture on the screen. But here again, it was more than mere spectacle: *Intolerance* was the first philosophical film, the first attempt to base a scenario on an abstract idea, to which all the personal and dramatic elements were subordinated. In the excellent phrase of Terry Ramsaye, it was a "giant metaphor," the boldest [technical and creative] experiment in the history of the screen. Its influence, though unhappily filtered and vulgarized, has come down to the present day in two main lines: as a social and historical document, in the cinema of Soviet Russia; as a spectacle, in the [moronic] work of Cecil B. De Mille.

[4] Faulty proofreading caused the *Times*' text to keep the capital letters in lower case, in this reference to specific historic (Mesopotamian) rather than generic antiquity.—S. S.

But neither Griffith's directorial genius for colossal pageantry and the handling of crowds, nor his high seriousness of purpose and [his] passion for social themes [was] confined to the epic film. The development of the lyric, or poetical, film is one of the major movements in the history of the cinema, and for more than ten years it received its chief impetus from Griffith. In 1919, *Broken Blossoms* brought lyric poetry and high tragedy to the screen. Against a theme of [what Gilbert Seldes described as] "tragic love in the midst of terror," [5] Griffith made a passionate plea for a renewal of faith in Christianity and the Christian ideal. The poetic Yellow Man of the story became, in effect, a touchstone of the tragic failure of the Western World. He also served as a mouthpiece for Griffith's criticism of those "across the sea," whom a subtitle referred to as "the barbarous Anglo-Saxons, sons of turmoil and strife." And *Dream Street*, two years later,[6] carried these creative precedents a long step ahead by introducing allegoric symbolism as a part of dramatic method. In *Way Down East*, a folk-melodrama of New England life in the late Nineties, produced in 1920 [in New England and Mamaroneck, N.Y.], he had introduced the use of landscape and natural backgrounds as a vital dramatic and psychological element of the story. The continued application of the same method was beautifully demonstrated last year in John Ford's *Stagecoach* [1939].

The year 1924 saw Griffith's last important film, *Isn't Life Wonderful*[7]—a grim story of a family of Polish refugees in post-war [World War I] Germany. Famine, revolution, terror and death were its main ingredients. And with them, Griffith's final contribu-

---

[5] Seldes (in his book, "The Movies and the Talkies") applied the description to *The Avenging Conscience*. I quoted it in connection with *Broken Blossoms*, because it is equally applicable.

[6] Erroneously given in the original manuscript, hence in the *Times*, as "four years later." *Dream Street* appeared in 1921, after *Hearts of the World* (1918) and *Way Down East* (1920). It was preceded by two earlier efforts in the lyric vein, *The Idol Dancer* and *The Love Flower*, both directed with great personal feeling by Griffith in 1920. The final one of the lyric films of Griffith, *The White Rose*, appeared in 1923, four years after *Broken Blossoms*.—S. S.

[7] The title was erroneously given in the original manuscript, hence in the *Times*, with an exclamation-point following. On the screen, however, the main (official) title is followed by no punctuation whatever. The year was also erroneously given as 1925. *Isn't Life Wonderful* was released on November 30, 1924. The neighborhood-theatre run followed in 1925.—S.S.

tions to the development of cinematic technique. The influence of this film on foreign production, especially in Russia, was enormous. It was a direct anticipation of the present-day documentary, with this difference, that Griffith transcended the flat statement of the documentary method. He made "stark realism" more stark by heightening it with the philosophical query and the tragic overtone.

It would be futile to attempt to convey all of D. W. Griffith's complex and ramified influence over the destinies of the motion picture. His total output was nothing short of fabulous, since between 1908 and 1915, up to the eve of *The Birth of a Nation,* he had already directed about 440 films.[8] And always, at every point and turn, he conceived of the medium as a fore-ordained instrument for the expression of thought and feeling, an instrument which would have this advantage over the older arts—that it would reach the broad masses of the world and break down the babel not only of tongues but of whole cultures. All this, transmitted through his masterworks, had the most potent and fertile effect on film production as a whole. It inspired others—not only directors but producers, actors, actresses, cameramen, to view the medium in a new light. It gave dignity and stature to an art which, from its inception, had inherited nothing but social and intellectual contempt, or downright ill will.

Griffith was born on January 22, 1875,[9] in La Grange, Kentucky. By ancestry, spiritual heritage, education, and in the life of his childhood and youth, he was a true son of the Old South, a product of the last great romantic civilization of the English-speaking world. The Griffith family was typical of thousands of Southerners who had been ruined in the fall of the Confederacy; the future director of *The Birth of a Nation,* almost from the first moments of consciousness, was nourished on tales and legends of the Lost Cause. Indeed, it has perhaps never been sufficiently noted that

---

8 In the *Times,* the figure appeared as 2,000! This was a double error: for unaccountable reasons, I had written 200 instead of 400. The *Times,* as the manuscript was rushed to press, compounded the error, typographically, by inadvertently adding an extra "o."

9 The year appeared in the *Times* as 1880. This was not an oversight. It was the official, oft-publicized date Griffith himself had long given out as his birth-year, following an ancient asinine practice by theatrical folk, to underplay their ages in the hope of extending their years of employment.—S. S.

The Birth of a Nation is essentially, and in this very real sense, a regional film.

Griffith was in his mid-twenties when he drifted into the then embryonic movie world after several years of desultory wandering with a theatrical stock company. He tried his luck at writing scenarios and sold several to the Biograph Company, at 11 East Fourteenth Street [New York City]. Soon he was put on the payroll at $5 a day, and a short while afterward had learned all there was to know of the rudiments of film production as they existed at the time. In June, 1908, he made his directorial debut with an historic "short," *The Adventures of Dollie*.[10] It revolutionized the extremely primitive methods of story-telling, and its production marked the begininng of the golden age of film history, the age known as the Biograph Period.

Griffith made films at a time when studios were loosely organized, when there were no supervisors, no producers, no intermediaries between the director and the financial heads of the company. A certain sum of money was allotted to a production, and once the deal was set, the director had to work out his own salvation. From that moment, he alone was "boss." Thus, for seventeen years, from 1908 until the beginning of his [directorial] decline in 1925, Griffith enjoyed a degree of sovereignty and freedom such as has been the lot of only one other figure in screen history—Chaplin.

His working methods were intuitive, spontaneous, unplanned, except in grand outline. He never used a shooting script, and the entire production of *Intolerance* was shot from "mental notes." Inevitably, under such ideal [creative] conditions, he developed the "one-man show" philosophy. This is a theory of picture-making in which the director is a combination author, producer and cinematographer.

Needless to say, picture-making has changed radically, almost beyond recognition, since that bygone age, and the great thing, of course, that has gone out is the conception of the function of the director. In this respect, much, if not all, that Griffith stood for

[10] Erroneously given in the original manuscript, hence in the *Times*, as a "two-reeler." It was less than one reel (filmed in Old Greenwich, Conn.) and was released on July 14, 1908, the actual date of Griffith's directorial debut.—S. S.

seems to have been lost. Yet there are many signs of a healthy
stirring in Hollywood which, if they crystallize, would make the
director's role once more of supreme importance.[11]

11 About six months after this essay appeared, or in May, 1941, the function
of the director as the supreme creative command over all phases of a given
film-production, and with it the "one-man-show" articulation of filmmaking as
the artistic expression of a single mind, a single personality, were triumphantly
reaffirmed with the initial appearance of *Citizen Kane*. As a masterpiece of
conception, camerawork, cutting, acting, dialogue, sound-and-music, and,
above all, of directing, this film is unequalled to date in the era of the talking-
picture. Although many persons contributed to its making, it emerged as
essentially the product, and it bears the stamp, of one guiding mind and one
personality, a creative film-director in the Griffithean sense of the term, Orson
Welles.—S. S.

The New York Times, Nov. 10, 1940.

1930-1940

"Whatever experiments are made, in whatever direction they are made, they will only reach perfection as films where the artist-director grips at his medium as though it were his life, where the film is the first and final article of his faith, and he can find utterance in this and in no other way."

ERNEST BETTS

EISENSTEIN ON SOUND

S. Eisenstein

The old dreams of the talking films are becoming realities. Americans have opened the road to the technique of the talking film and have arrived at the first stages of the realization. Germany is working hard along the same lines. The world is saying that the great mute has found his voice!

We who are working in Russia know that, considering our technical possibilities, a really satisfactory realization will not be reached very soon. At the same time we find it timely to point out a number of doubts in principle and of a theoretical kind, especially as, so far as we know, the new improvement is to be used in the wrong way.

And a false conception of the possibilities of the new technical invention may not only hamper the development of artistic films but may threaten much that has been accomplished thus far in the matter of form.

The contemporary film, that works through visual forms, has a powerful effect upon human beings and rightly occupies a front seat among the arts. It is well known that the basic—and only—means of action that has raised the film to such a power is montage (editing). That montage is the most effective tool has become an indisputable principle, upon which the film is being developed on a world-wide scale. The success of the Soviet film on the screens of the world is mainly due to a number of accomplishments in the way of montage which it was the first to develop.

Therefore it seems that the only important things for the future development of the film are those that strengthen and broaden the effect of the montage upon the spectator. If we look at every new invention from this viewpoint it is easy to see the trivial significance of the color, as well as of the stereoscopic film, in comparison with the enormous significance of sound.

Sound is a two-edged invention. Probably its exploitation will follow the line of least resistance, i.e., that of satisfying mere curiosity. Here comes, first of all, the commercial exploitation of staple goods, and so we have the talking film. There are such films in which the sounds are produced in a natural way, the sound exactly coincides with the movements in the film and creates a certain "illusion" of talking persons, falling objects, etc. In the first method of sensational surprise this will not hurt the development of the film art. But it will be awful when the second stage of development will have been attained, when the first surprises of the new possibilities will have become faded and in their place will have arrived an epoch of automatic exploitation of highly cultural dramas and photographic performances of a theatrical nature.

The new technical invention is no mere incidental impulse in the history of the film, but an organic means of escape for the cultural cinematographic advance guard from a number of blind alleys which at first seemed absolutely barred.

The first blind alley is the film title, with all the helpless attempts to make it a real, constituent part of the composition of the montage. These include the breaking up of the title into separate parts and the changing of the size of the letters.

The second blind alley is formed by the "explanatory" parts; for example, general plans which only hamper the composition of the montage and slow down the tempo.

And every day the defining of the theme of the subject becomes more difficult. Attempts to solve the problem by means of tricks with the visual montage alone either lead to nothing at all or they mislead the director into the realm of artificial stunts calculated to make us fear reactionary decadence.

Sound, as a new element of the montage, as an element naturally coupled with the visual form, certainly will bring new means of enormous power for the solution of the complicated problems which today still seem insoluble to us, because of our incomplete methods based upon visual forms alone.

New York Sun, June 5, 1930.

THE FUTURE CINEMA:
NOTES FOR A STUDY

Harry Alan Potamkin

Thomas Hardy, in his early novel, *A Laodicean*, describes a woman thus: ". . . her stillness suggested the stillness of motion imperceptible from its intensity." In this description the future cinema finds its characterization. We are passing from motion whose transmission is impact to motion intensive. Someone has called it "static motion." The development, and it is a development in the full sense of improvement, is inherent in the very nature of cinema motion, which is motion organized in the image and with the image. The French, always alert to the necessity of an apt terminology, have called this twofold organization, "exterior movement," and "interior movement." The former comprises, to quote the excellent young French director, M. René Clair, "the movement of the objects enregistered: the play of the actor, the mobility of the decor, etc.;" the latter "the alternation of the scenes or motifs of the action." These two, with "the duration of each image," constitute rhythm, which is organized motion, as against the literal acceptation, typical of the American movie, of motion as recorded. Duration becomes more and more, in every cinema but the American, the paramount consideration of the cinematographer. In duration is an important means of accomplishing the cinema of the future, which will be philosophical or psychical as against physical or muscular, reflective as against the "emotional discharge," inferential as against literal. The quoted phrase, "emotional discharge," is from S. M. Eisenstein, the director of *Potemkin*. His commentary upon the necessities of the future is of great importance, in that the Russian cinema, which has been received with enthusiasm, recognizes that it has come to the end of the first epoch of the motion picture: the epoch of the muscular, physical, direct impact film. *Potemkin* is the conclusion of that epoch. The films of Pudowkin are a mingling of the first epoch with naive attempts toward the second. In the Ukrainian film, *Arsenal*, the first articulation of the principle of the future Russian film is discoverable: symbolism and not the symbol is the determinant. The symbol is a representation detail which runs into the inflation of sentimentalism. Symbolism is inclusive, unified, structural. The symbolism however must be achieved with the plastic materials of the first epoch: concrete objects, human values—the human actor, the common experiences, social conditions. Another inferential cinema will be evolved: the abstract . . . which will be formed of the effects of light, fluid color and created materials—of paper, of draughtsmanship, of pigment, of puppets.

I seem to have gone afield, away from the theme of "motion" expressed at the beginning of this consideration. But, in truth, motion does not determine the form or forms of cinema as much as the development of the interest of the cinema as an experience or an art determines the character of motion in the cinema. Every sententious young aspirant to the role of film-critic reiterates the platitude of motion as the key to the motion picture. Motion, however, is no such simple device as a key, it is a structure, a construction. To Matthew Josephson the literal record is motion: therefore the rudimentary American movie is ultimate cinema. Slater Brown, colleague of Mr. Josephson, apprehended the subtlety of film motion in his brief essay on "Sculptural Kinetics." In the epithet "sculptural" is contained the apprehension of movie kinetics as structure. Rhythm, Mr. Brown said, is "the progressive deformation of a theme." But the cinema is intensive as well as progressive. It is the intensive character that will be developed in the future. The most realized instance of intensive cinema is Dreyer's *The Passion and the Death of Joan of Arc.*

This film has indicated the importance of the composition and duration of the single image or picture. It has been, up until now, accepted that the fact of movement demands action, which, because of the domination of the American film, has been defined as antic and speed. The Russians have stressed the inclusiveness of the mounting of the individual image in the construction of the film and, although their realization of this montage is but an elaboration of the American impact film, this emphasis has turned the cinema to an examination of its basic vocabulary. With *Joan,* so consistent and complete in its intensiveness, as a statement of this vocabulary used for a nonphysical intention, the cinema enters into its profounder era. *Arsenal* is the beginning of the profounder era for the Russian cinema returning to its nativity in the traditional intensive, introspective Russian, of whom Dostoievski was the transcendent flower. *Joan* would be the beginning of the introspective American cinema, if that national folk-utterance had realized itself; for *Joan* in its stark unmodified lighting should be near to American practice, which stupidly, at this late day, turns to German studio-light, French multiple exposure and all non-literal details that it arbitrarily rejected yesterday. It is impossible to find a logic in the American cinema, as one was able to find it in the Swedish cinema of the golden age of Seastrom and Stiller, as one is able to find it in the German kino and Russian kino, and, yes, in the fragmentary French cinema. The American film worries about nothing but expedience. Expedience does not cherish experience.

There was one national film of this first epoch that was even then already in the epoch of intensiveness of treatment for intensity of experience. That was the Swedish film, so soon at an end. At an end in Sweden, but the Russian film, in its frequent poignancy, certainly not in its occasional arrogance, is the perpetuation of the Swedish film. This is not surprising: Sweden and Russia have always been close culturally. Emotionally there is a close relationship between Selma Lagerlof and Dostoievski. Between the Seastrom film, *The Phantom Chariot* (*The Soul Shall Bear Witness*) and the first of the post-Revolution Russian films, *Polikoushka,* for instance, there is an identity. And the Russian film of the Wufku, which I take as suggestive of the truer Russia and future Russian film, grown mature out of vociferousness and braggadacio, is very much like the Swedish film of Stiller, *The Treasure of Arne.* The present Russian film, where its formula is rendered stolidly, I think of *The Village of Sin,* still contains a veracity of experience that was not absent from the Swedish film of its golden era, when that film was at its end, in Molander's *The Accursed.*

We may say the cinema is now fulfilling itself as an experience. Out of Griffith comes Russian montage, out of the Swedish film the reflective Russian, which returns to its source—what folk is nearer its source than the Russian or the Swedish? I expect the imminent new era to bring with it a re-examination of the art of the cinema's first great artist, Seastrom, just as the termination of the first epoch led to a re-examination of the first great composer (not artist) of films, D. W. Griffith. Its interrelationship vindicates the cinema as an art with a tradition, the present instances of *Joan* and *Arsenal* assure it a future, in which it will attain to the heights of philosophic import and the depths of human experience. Intelligence will be contained in the intensive film structure, for concentration and organization are intelligence. Duration is sensitivity of the aesthetic intelligence. And duration is perhaps the most important single element in the rhythm of the future film. It is duration, contemplation and penetration of the image through the uses of time, which permits Jean Epstein, employing light and diagonal treatment of subject-matter, to rise above his puerilities and impurities to become the sole metaphysician of the cinema. Jean Epstein is an instance of the French cinematographer who has not yet realized his idiom, because he dwells in a confusion of an epoch whose mind is counter to his, which is the mind that will find a meaning for itself in the next epoch already developing. The French mind is pictorial, speculative, fond of stylization, sophisticated, intellectualized to the point of effeteness, reveling in irrelevances . . . *Arsenal* negates conventional continuity. This is a negation which achieved fluidity in the documentary montage-film, Vertov's *The Man with the Camera*. The French mind exploits dissociations: the cinema has fallaciously taken over the literary and graphic formulae of dadaism. But lately this dissociationism has—in Germaine Dulac's *The Sea-Shell and the Clergyman*—achieved unity (a first essential in the present cinema) through a central intention and a sustained flux of image-into-image upon a rhythmic scheme. Previously—*Entr'acte* by René Clair—the isolations were not re-established as a unity . . .

The question arises: Will the audible film, the optophonic film, survive into the speculative era? Certainly! There are two cinemas, as determined by the number of mediums employed: the simple and the compound. The simple cinema is the mute cinema, and it is subdivided into the linear and the composite. The compound cinema includes all compoundings of audibility, tactility, etc. with the visual (really the visual-motor). The compound cinema will exist in the second epoch and its form, sound-sight at the moment, will seek reflective utterance. It will find reflective utterance by dwelling upon two things: the integrated structure and speech-as-utterance. Speech in the visual-motor graph and speech as abstract sound . . . The duration of speech is of first importance in such organization, malleability and elasticity of utterance will be sought, and that search is a search for rhythm, "repetition in variation." Rhythm is always the answer, for, as William Carlos Williams once said, "rhythm is the poem."

What of dynamics in the future speculative, inferential cinema? Alexander Bakshy, who, more than all other critics, stresses the cinema as a dynamic art rejects films like *Chang* and *Joan* as being un-dynamic. To him dynamics is the physical "resultant of forces." *Chang* being a sequence upon a single line in a single direction would not be dynamic, lacking, as it does, plural play. But *Chang* is, nevertheless, cinema, rudimentary and forceful, of the linear simple form. *Joan* is certainly dynamic, it is plural: but Bakshy evidently recognizes only the progressive in dynamics, not the intensive. What of the resultant of two forces: a progressive and intensive? In physics, perhaps, one may deny such pos-

sibility, but can one, in aesthetics, as an experience of the be-
holder?

Pagany, Spring, 1930.

DISNEY AND OTHERS

Gilbert Seldes

The success of Mickey Mouse is so great that it overshadows not
only the competitors of Walt Disney in the field of animated
comics, but Disney's own more interesting work, the "Silly Symphonies." Mickey Mouse is a movie comic of the first order, but
I do not think its popularity depends entirely on its artistic merit;
it has some of the element of a fad, where it joins the kewpie and
the Teddy Bear, and I think because Mickey Mouse is a character, Disney finds himself forced occasionally to endow him with
a verbal wit and to give him too much to say, which is against
the spirit of the animated cartoon. The great satisfaction in the
first animated cartoons was that they used sound properly—the
sound was as unreal as the action; the eye and the ear were not
at war with each other, one observing a fantasy, the other an actuality. The words of Mickey Mouse are still disguised as animal
sounds, but the moment they are recognizable the perfection of
the animated drawing is corrupted.

This perfection can be observed in perhaps half a dozen of the
"Silly Symphonies." There was one called "Winter" (in a group
of the four seasons) in which all sorts and sizes of furry animals

watch the movements of the ground hog with anxiety and drive
him back into his hole, while his disembodied shadow dances
on the ground. In a dance of jubilation the rhythm of the movement and design made by the black and white figures on the
screen are in perfect harmony. The music to which they dance
is merely a guide to the rhythm. In "Busy Beavers" the ingenuity
and the inventiveness of Disney are at their highest point. Here
he reverses the favorite device of the animated cartoons. Instead
of transforming steam rollers and telegraph poles into fantastic
animal shapes, he transforms the beavers virtually into machines;
annihilating time and material, they strip and fell trees and build
dams at terrific speed, but always suggesting the sawmill, the axe
and the lathe. In a symphony called "Egyptian Melodies," he
takes you inside the Sphinx and after a beautiful comic dance
performed by mummies, the slaves, the soldiers, the high priests,
the chariots on the walls suddenly come to life and in the grand
climax all the hieroglyphics on two vast columns are animated
in a dance of extraordinary excitement and beauty.

These pictures are the perfection of the movie; they are the
movie developing in its own field, borrowing not at all from
inappropriate sources and transforming draftsmanship and musical composition to its own ends. They have reached the point
toward which the photographed and dramatic moving picture
should be tending, in which, as in the silent pictures, everything
possible is expressed in movement and the sound is used for support and clarification and for contrast. Disney's nearest rival with
whose work I am acquainted is Max Fleischer, and the best of his
cartoons is one called "Sky Scraping," in which a variety of animals carry the skeleton of a building beyond the crescent of the
moon and desert it at the five o'clock whistle. The "plots" of
drawn comics are seldom more complicated than this and that is
another point in which the regular movie might take a lesson
from them. I remember seeing this picture first on the same program with one of Harold Lloyd's early talking pictures and was
struck by the immense superiority of the simpler form. You see
two animal hodcarriers walk rhythmically along a steel beam; they
are stepping off into space when a derrick swings another beam
at right angles under their feet, and this continues until, having
established your confidence, the artist omits the saving beam the

last time and the two little beasts walk off unconcernedly into thin air. Red-hot rivets are used for golf balls and flatten themselves (the Anvil Chorus assisting) into their appointed places. And when the detail has been sufficiently shown, the skyscraper is thrown into a long shot and projects itself with enchanting rapidity, floor by floor, into the heavens.

Out of hundreds of animated cartoons, I can recall only two or three which were wholly bad; even the imitative ones and those lacking in ingenuity gave some sort of pleasure. This suggests that something in the form itself is a satisfaction to us. And that satisfaction, I think, is the childish one which the movie as a whole had in its beginning and which long custom and the injection of dialogue has taken away from the photographed drama. It is our pleasure in magic, in seeing the impossible happen. (The movies have also given us the pleasure of recognition in the newsreel, where we see what has actually happened, happen again.) In the early days we looked at a movie and marveled that a picture could be set into motion. Now we do not think of the picture—only of the actors. The animated cartoon shows us in movement something naturally inert, and it is essentially the satisfaction of magic that we get out of it.

Magic—not illusion. I cannot follow the admirers of Disney who attach a profound significance to his contemptuous handling of the Great God Machine. If the animated cartoon created illusion, you might take it as criticism, psychological rebellion and release from the tyranny of things. It remains a plaything, and in a very rudimentary form existed before the terror of the Machine Age set in. Mr. Terry Ramsaye notes, in his history of the moving pictures, that in China and Java silhouettes are cast in shadowy dramas against a screen and these are part of ancient folk plays. The contemporary animated cartoon uses machinery for the same simple process.

On the other hand, the perfection of this form is an American achievement and is bound to have some American qualities. It has no emotion in its comedy; it is repetitious (the reiteration of the musical, dance and chase motifs almost standardize the pattern); it is impertinent; it is genuinely gay.

And it strikes me that nothing is so much to the credit of the American movie public as the tribute it instinctively pays to the very best things the movie has done. I do not think I have ever seen an animated cartoon which at least half of the audience has not applauded at the end. This may not be true in the cathedrals and palaces of the talkies, but these real-estate operations are rapidly becoming the last place in which one can judge either the movies or their audiences.

The New Republic, June 8, 1932.

LÉGER AND CINESTHETIC

James Johnson Sweeney

Sergei Eisenstein has said that of the French no one has a truer understanding of the cinema than Fernand Léger. Recently the Levy Gallery in New York and the Arts Club of Chicago in presenting Léger's *Ballet Mécanique* made it possible for a wider American public to appreciate the quality of his pioneer work in this field. A film without scenario, relying solely on contrast and rhythm for its effects. "Pure" cinema in 1924—a date at which "montage" was little understood, much less the exploitation of rhythms as a temporal means of expression. This latter is even today little developed beyond the point to which Léger brought it.

However, for all this, his film might have represented an attitude of 1924. Eisenstein in making his statement six years later probably had something more actual in mind. As a matter of fact, theory as well as practice with Léger does follow a curiously consistent line of development; but what Eisenstein undoubtedly referred to was something in Léger's contemporary major interest—his painting—that appeared to him to be in close relationship with his own ideals for the cinema. For every formulation of Eisenstein's film-theory is an epitome of his total aesthetic attitude. Such an association would certainly not be offensive to Léger. Even aside from his respect for Eisenstein—if for no other reason than his abhorrence of "antiquarianism": an art should be "vitally of its epoch"; and in his opinion, "Cinema belongs to the age of the airplane. The theater belongs to the age of the horse."

In reporting the "Second International Congress of the Independent Cinema" which took place a few months ago in Belgium one critic writes *"C'est ce qui gouverne le plus clairement les cinéastes actuels: le gout des contrastes (dissonantes—ou analogies) . . ."* Eisenstein himself says in a recent number of *Close-Ups* that "conflict" is "the fundamental basic principle of every Art-work and every Art-form," and as a result "in the film, and characterizing it, occurs what we may describe as: Visual Counterpoint."

Toward the elucidation of this thesis Eisenstein predicates "the shot" and "montage" as the basic elements of the cinema and says that "to determine the nature of montage is to solve the specific problem of the film."

According to Eisenstein, older film makers were accustomed to consider "montage" as a means of bringing something before the spectator descriptively, "by sticking separate shots one on to the other like building-blocks." In his opinion true "montage" is not the recounting of an idea by "shots" or pieces of film following one another, but should produce an idea from the collision of two pieces independent each of the other. He calls this the "dynamic" principle, the other the "epic"—the terms being used in the sense of methodology of form rather than with reference to content or action. And he offers his well-known analogy from Japanese hieroglyphics where two independent ideographical signs (equivalating "shots"), placed in juxtaposition, explode to a new concept. Thus:

Eye plus Water—To weep
Mouth plus Birds—To sing.

The degree of incongruence between one "shot" and the next "conditions the 'impression—intensity,'—conditions the tension, —which in conjunction with that following becomes the real basic element of the peculiar rhythm." And this rhythm he claims is the only genuinely cinematic rhythm.

Shortly after the close of the war, Léger, in a letter to Leonce Rosenberg, published in *L'Effort Moderne*, wrote: "My ambition is now to arrive at the maximum of pictorial rendering through a contrasting of all the plastic means . . . My origins: influence of the impressionists from the point of view of color (Renoir, Seurat): from the point of view of form (Ingres, David). Before the war: no power of decision, a struggle with influences, with 'good taste'—timidity, uncertainty . . . Three years of War without touching a brush but in touch with the starkest most violent reality . . . Immediately on discharge I felt the benefit of my probation, grim as it was. I have found a power of decision. I model now in frank local tones and bold volumes without any concessions. I have gone beyond tasteful arrangements, grays, and backgrounds of dead picture-surface . . . So much the worse for 'good form' 'good taste' and 'style' as it is recognized—if there is any in my pictures someone will find it later on. For the present I am interested in producing 'live' organisms. For me a picture is the contrary to a wall, that is to say it should be a noise, movement."

Later, in an article on "Contemporary Plastic Experiment," he wrote that he was seeking primarily "a state of organized plastic intensity." To achieve that he said, "I make use of the law of contrasts which is the eternal means of producing the impression of activity, of 'life'." . . . "I strive to build up organized oppositions of contrary values, contrasting volumes, and contrasting lines."

And in his canvases from 1919 on we see a steadily growing definition, complexity of interrelationship, and emboldening of tension among these contrasts. At first his canvases were crowded with an infinity of minor "collision-plexus" in color, form and line. He could collect the whole turmoil of a modern metropolis into a single composition as in his huge "*La Ville.*" But there was a sense of crowding—restlessness as often as movement—a lack of some dominant, hence of the assertive unity essential to monumentality. And his colors still retained something of their impressionist fusibility.

But gradually we note an increasing simplification of content. A new interest in the fragment develops—now the enlarged fragment as we see it in a close-up; also a cruder apposition of contrasted fragments. From an article written by him in 1930 we read:

> "The cinema personalizes the fragment; it frames it and offers it in a new realism of which the consequence can be incalculable.
>
> A collar button under a lens and thrown on a screen may become a radiant planet."

The close-up unquestionably offered him a field of unspoiled plastic monumentalities. But his interest in contrasts persevered, in fact, became even more assertive. With the simplification of major forms, naturally his line- and volume-contrasts became fewer, more evident and sooner exhausted. It now lay with color to play the contrapuntal lead, always of course supporting the broader graphic, volume-representational effects. And color assuredly offered a subtler field through which to set the rhythm of the whole.

As Eisenstein says:

"A color tone imparts to our vision a given rhythm of vibration. (This is not to be taken figuratively, but actually physiologically, for colors are distinguished from one another by the number of their vibrations.)

The adjacent color tone is in another rate of vibration.

The counterpoint (conflict) of the two—the received and the now supplanting vibration rates—yield the dynamism of the apprehension of color play.

Hence we have only to make a step from visual vibrations to acoustic and we stand in the field of music."

It is unquestionably these "rhythms of contrast" we find in every element of Léger's work—or perhaps better his peculiar courage of sensibility to tension among such rhythms—that gives it its quality and individuality. His gift is the courage and ability to strain a composition almost to the breaking point, or to urge a contrast to the verge of a plastic incompatibility. The day Léger first admits a compromise, the result will be a banal effeminate prettiness.

Creative Arts, June, 1932.

NOTES ON HOLLYWOOD DIRECTORS

Dwight Macdonald

"A good Ph.D. thesis," commented Eisenstein after he had seen what many consider the finest American talkie: Milestone's *All Quiet on the Western Front*. The remark is significant. It sums up the American movie. What Eisenstein meant is that *All Quiet* shows that Milestone understands his medium, that his technical proficiency entitles him to a Ph. D. in cinematics. But, also that the film is not a creative effort. "Now that you've shown that you know how to make a movie, let's see you make one," is what Eisenstein in effect was saying. As we shall presently see, neither Milestone nor any of his contemporaries in Hollywood have been able to carry out Eisenstein's injunction. For all its technical proficiency, Hollywood gives birth to perhaps one movie a year that is not aesthetically stillborn.

The explanation is simply that the Hollywood director has nothing to say. For the artist to create, however lamely, he must believe in something—realism, romanticism, Communism, his own importance, it doesn't matter what. He must have standards of some sort, and feel a certain pride in maintaining them. He may let himself be bent by outside pressure to a greater or lesser extent, depending on his temperament, but his sense of integrity must draw the line somewhere. None of these things is true of even the most talented Hollywood directors. They are not artists. They are craftsmen, specialists, technicians who turn out, perhaps with stifled boredom or indignation, whatever the industry requires of them. Sometimes a talented director gets a good scenario to work with, and the result is a film that is at least superficially interesting. More often, able directors waste themselves on hopeless scenarios. Whether the material is congenial or not, the Hollywood director accepts it without protest and dutifully sets to work on it.

Chairs can be made this way but not works of art. There is something lacking in American movies, even the best of them, and that is a sense of personal conviction. In my opinion, Hollywood has produced only two directors whose work is comparable to that of the greatest foreign directors. There may be more competent technicians in Hollywood than Von Stroheim and Griffith (though, making allowances for time, I doubt it), but there is no one with Griffith's ardent belief in abstract ideas, no one with Stroheim's passion for realism. That belief and that passion supply the driving force behind *Greed* and *Intolerance* and *The Birth of a Nation*. In such films one feels the director actually had something to say and that he was going to say it if the heavens fell and Mr. Zukor frowned. Furthermore, both Stroheim and Griffith were extreme egoists, who insisted on making their movies just as they thought they should be made and who didn't hesitate to kick over the traces to get their own way.

But the Hollywood director of our day is neither an egoist nor an idealist. He is a good little boy who swallows, perhaps with a wry face, whatever the Zukors and the Laemmles ladle out to him. This prevailing attitude makes it difficult to evaluate the American cinema of today in terms of its directors. For the same individual's work varies widely according to the quality of the scenario. There are able directors who have made dozens of utterly insignificant films. And there are quite undistinguished directors who have, by some fluke or other, managed to produce a single excellent film in the course of a misspent life. There is, furthermore, the matter of actors. The Hollywood rule seems to be that the best directors never get the best actors. Thus James

Cagney's genius for portraying the Irish mick is usually hampered by mediocre direction. John Barrymore gives distinction to many a commonplace film, and Garbo has only once in her Hollywood career had a first-rate director—Feyder, who made *The Kiss*. And so, with good directors making poor pictures and poor directors making good ones, with the actors often taking over a film entirely, it becomes difficult to write about American movies in terms of their directors. Perhaps the twenty-first century critic will consider the Hollywood cinema as an impersonal, or rather multipersonal engineering product similar to the automobile. For the present, however, it is easier to think in the old terms and to regard the director as the decisive factor in the creation of even a Hollywood moving picture.

DAVID WARK GRIFFITH at fifty-three is the dean of the world's movie directors. He started out as an actor (he still affects the high striped collars, pearl gray derby, and British accent of old-school Broadway) and took up directing under protest. Almost from the beginning of the movies, when he was making two-reelers such as *The Lonely Villa* and *One Avenging Conscience*, he was recognized (and rightly) as The Great American Director. In 1914 he made his first important picture, *The Birth of a Nation*, one of the sensational hits of all time. Two years later he produced an equally sensational box-office failure: *Intolerance*, a lengthy and lavish super-spectacle which remains his peak achievement. (Both Eisenstein and Pudovkin testify to its influence on their work.) Important works followed: *Broken Blossoms* (1919), *Way Down East* (1921), *Isn't Life Wonderful?*, *One Exciting Night* (1923). Of late years his work has been consistently mediocre—*The Battle of the Sexes*, *The Sorrows of Satan*, *Abraham Lincoln* et al. Since the dismal failure of *The Struggle* last year, he has done no directing. He has been speaking on the radio this winter on a program advertising Pond's Face Cream.

Unhappily D. W. Griffith has no place in a survey of American directors who are doing current work of interest. The utter collapse of Griffith, indeed, is one of the most tragic spectacles The American Cinema has to offer. His historical importance can hardly be overstated. He was the first director to build a movie in

terms of cutting, or montage, which he used with magnificent
effect in *Intolerance* and which was later adopted by the Russians as the cornerstone of their cinema. To Griffith goes the
credit for the close-up, the fade-in, the fade-out, the 'masked
shot' and many other technical devices that have long been com-
monplaces. And, most remarkable of all, a few of his films, despite
their archaic photography and moth-eaten sentimentality, still
have cinematic vitality. But it seems hopeless to expect anything
more from him. At fifty-one he is 'through.' He has simply not
grown into the present and has nothing to say to it. For Griffith
is a profoundly unreflective artist. He shows no understanding of
his own work, and the fact that King George liked *Intolerance*
obviously pleases him more than the chorus of critical acclaim
that still salutes that masterpiece. Lacking the intelligence to understand either himself or the world he lives in, Griffith's equipment for aesthetic survival consists only of an instinctive mastery
of technique and a few intensely-felt moral ideas. Today his
technique is obsolete and his ideas outmoded. There is nothing
left for him except to reminisce twice a week, from 10:00 till
10:15 over WJZ.

KING VIDOR, once the brightest of Hollywood's bright young
directors, will celebrate his fortieth birthday next year. Perhaps
it is old age creeping on him, perhaps some subtler cause, but in
any case he has done nothing of interest since 1929. He began
directing in 1912, at the age of eighteen, and has been steadily
at it ever since. His most celebrated silent movie is *The Big
Parade* (1925), 'America's war epic,'—though an intelligent mi-
nority prefers his *Wild Oranges* (1924), from the Hergesheimer
novel. He also directed Marion Davies, whose talents as a come-
dienne have never been properly exploited, in two excellent
satirical comedies, *The Politic Flapper* and *Show People*. His
talkie career began impressively enough with *The Crowd* (1928)
and *Hallelujah* (1929) but has petered out into potboilers since
then.

It is a peculiar condition of Hollywood cinema that even the
most gifted directors make an appalling number of second-rate
films. The only American director who has never turned out a

mediocre production is Von Stroheim, who has made a scant dozen movies in his long career, who insists on getting his own way in all matters, and who scoffs: "Turning out pictures with the regularity of a sausage-machine is bound to make them as alike as sausages." The gibe goes directly home to King Vidor, who for two decades has been grinding out movies with sausage-machine regularity. By 1923 he had produced a long string of completely forgotten works—*The Sky Pilot, Love Never Dies, Peg O'My Heart*, and so on. His later silent productions include *His Hour, La Boheme, Proud Flesh*, and *Bardelys the Magnificent*. As for his talkie career, consider such recent efforts as *The Champ*, sentimental hocum of the worst sort, the routine *Cynara, Billy the Kid*, which wasn't good even for a Western, and the sloppy, antiquated *Bird of Paradise*. It is the privilege of the American director, working against time for unsympathetic masters, to descend into mediocrity. But Vidor abuses the privilege.

Even the best of Vidor's productions have been overrated by the critics. *The Big Parade* was exciting enough in its day—though credit for the "epic" scope which was its most impressive quality goes to Irving Thalberg, M-G-M's boy production genius. It was Mr. Thalberg, according to the story, who saw a chance to make the super-super movie of the Great War and who had Vidor shoot the whole thing over again on a bigger scale. But *The Big Parade* has been completely overshadowed by Milestone's *All Quiet on the Western Front*. Only a few sequences are alive today: the transformation of the rookie material in the training camp; the girl's figure against the background of trucks and guns moving up to the front, the line of soldiers advancing through the woods. In *The Crowd* Vidor had a fruitful theme: the submergence of the individual in the masses of a big city. But the film soon turned into a pathetic little story of a young married couple who haven't enough money and whose child is killed by a truck. The theme is lost in a mass of human interest, and the picture is destroyed as an organic whole. While Vidor shows some personal conviction in the early parts of the film, he was spineless enough to make three endings—happy, ambiguous, unhappy—which were tacked on according to the type of audience. Perhaps Vidor's essential weakness is that he has enough imagination to choose significant themes, but not enough to sustain them. Thus in both *The Crowd* and *The Big Parade* he bit deeply into American life, but chewing what he had bitten off was another matter. It was the same with *Hallelujah*, the most ambitious film of Negro life that has yet been made. Here, certainly, was the chance of a century, and Vidor made every effort to rise to it. But his conception of the Negro was banal. Just as one met in *The Big Parade* the stock war characters—the vivacious French girl, the hard-boiled sergeant, the lanky company humorist—so in *Hallelujah* one finds the routine slices of Negro life: revival meeting, cabaret, cabin in the cotton. And these elements are handled in the routine way—as, for example, the scene in the Church with its uplifted hands, Tuskegee-choir voices, and arty lighting. There is also a technical inadequacy in the directing. The movement is too slow. The chase through the swamp, effectively photographed as it is, lasts twice as long as it should. Structurally, the film tends to break up into episodes, for Vidor has neither the Griffith sense of construction nor Sternberg's rhythmic drive.

There is no point in discussing Vidor's more recent productions. Of late he has divorced his wife, left Metro-Goldwyn-Mayer, and turned independent. Perhaps all these shocks will shake something good out of him in the future.

ROUBEN MAMOULIAN was born in Armenia in 1898, the son of a banker and an actress. Educated in Moscow and Paris as a lawyer, he drifted into directing plays in London. There he was discovered by the late George (Kodak) Eastman, who brought him to Rochester, N.Y., as director of the American Opera Co. After three years of this Mamoulian began to direct plays in Manhattan: *Porgy, Marco Millions, A Farewell to Arms* and others. Paramount brought him to Hollywood in 1931 to make *Applause*, starring Helen Morgan. There he has remained ever since. He has made *City Streets*, whose scenario is said to be considered a model in Russia, *Dr. Jekyll and Mr. Hyde, Love Me Tonight*, and is currently directing Marlene Dietrich in *Song of Songs*.

Like Michael Arlen, Mamoulian is a bright young Armenian. Also similarly, his productions are glib, imitative, chic, with a fake elegance, a pseudo-wit and a suggestion of Oriental greasiness. They are marked with that vulgarity which is continually straining for effect, which cannot express a simple thing simply. A Mamoulian production can be depended on to overstress the note, whether pitched to lyricism, melodrama, fantasy. Thus his *City Streets*, a gangster melodrama, is directed as heavily and pretentiously as if it were *Greed* or *Sunrise*. There are brooding shadows, shots of pigeons flying beyond prison bars (freedom— get it?), weird angle shots of sculpture. Thus, too, in *Applause*, a sentimental little back-stage tragedy, he put Helen Morgan through her extremely limited paces with all the solemnity due a Sarah Bernhardt. The trashy emotionalism of the story, which a more honest director would have restrained, Mamoulian plays up for all it is worth. His *Dr. Jekyll and Mr. Hyde* is a cheaply sensational affair compared to the silent Barrymore version. The brutal exaggeration of Hyde's make-up, physically so much more revolting than Barrymore's, spiritually so much less so, is a typical Mamoulian touch.

To Mamoulian's other cinematic crimes must be added that of plagiarism. *City Streets* is almost pure von Sternberg. And his latest film, *Love Me Tonight*, is a René Clair film plus some Lubitschisms and minus Clair's freshness, wit, and charm. To make up for Clair's wit, Mamoulian has gone in for bigness. His country house is an enormous castle in the most opulent Hollywood tradition, with swarms of aristocratic inmates, long lines of servants, acres of sparkling polished floors. There is not one comic old spinster—there are three, which of course makes it three times as amusing. (Mamoulian, by the way, has more of Cecil B. de Mille in him than his admirers suspect.) For Clair's freshness, Mamoulian substitutes a hectic experimentation with trick effects. Sometimes this is pleasing enough, as the use of slow motion in the hunting scene. But Mamoulian uses his tricks unintelligently, without taste. The shot of the horn-blowing huntsman, for example, taken from an Eisenstein angle, strikes a heroic note that is absurdly out of key in a musical comedy featuring Jeannette Macdonald and Maurice Chevalier. For Clair's casual charm Mamoulian can make no substitution. To be light and casual is simply not in him. The opening sequence, in which Chevalier's impromptu morning song is caught up by one person after another, and the closing episode, when the princess gallops after her lover's train and stops it by planting herself, on horseback, across the tracks—such things cry out to be treated lightly. Alas, the Mamoulian touch, too heavy even for melodrama, quite crushes the life out of such frail little blooms of fantasy.

The only reason for considering Mamoulian's work at such length is that he is taken seriously by many otherwise intelligent persons.

ERNST LUBITSCH is the only director in Hollywood with his own complete staff which works with him on every picture he makes. They are mostly Germans, for although Lubitsch has been working in this country for nine years he is still more Teutonic than American. The son of a Berlin shopkeeper, he progressed from a job with Max Reinhardt to acting in movie comedies to directing comedies himself. But the films that made his reputation were two big-scale heavily wrought historical dramas: *Passion*, with Pola Negri as la Pompadour, and *Deception* with Jannings as Henry VIII. On the strength of these (together with his *The Flame* and *Sumurun*), he was brought to this country in 1924 and, with characteristic Hollywood intelligence, put to work directing Mary Pickford ("America's Sweetheart") in *Rosita*. Luckily, he came under the influence of Chaplin's *A Woman of Paris*. Stimulated by this pioneer film, he made a series of subtle, witty, smoothly made boudoir farces, all of them with a distinct "Lubitsch" quality. *The Marriage Circle* (1924), *Kiss Me Again*, and *So This is Paris* were the most notable. He also made what Paul Rotha (whose book, *The Film Till Now*, is an invaluable mine of facts about the movies) considers his most brilliant film: a satire on the Hollywood movie called *Forbidden Paradise* (1924). In his last silent film, *The Patriot* (1928), with Jannings as the mad Czar Paul, Lubitsch went back to heavy "costume" drama. His talkies have been disappointing—perhaps because he insists on tinkering with the spoken lines, despite his sketchy knowledge of English. Also, just as Sternberg has gotten into a rut with Marlene Dietrich, so Lubitsch repeated himself tiresomely in his Maurice Chevalier-Jeannette MacDonald Series: *The Love Parade*, *The Smiling Lieutenant*, and *One Hour With You*. It is significant that his two best talkies, *Monte Carlo* and the current *Trouble in Paradise*, are not Chevalier films.

There are, in a sense, two Lubitsches. There is the Lubitsch who began as one of Germany's most popular screen comedians and who has developed as a highly individual director of boudoir comedies, with precisely the witty, sophisticated, deft, ironic touch needed for those delicious little affairs. And there is the Lubitsch who began as Reinhardt's assistant and who had always had a hankering for pretentious dramas with plenty of emotional fireworks and historical background. This second Lubitsch seems to me inferior to the first. A film like *The Patriot*, for all the impressive trappings of technique in which it is swathed, has something static, cumbersome and *dead* about it. As a "serious" artist, Lubitsch has nothing to say. The moral earnestness of a Griffith, the emotional drive of a Stroheim, Murnau's psychological insight, Sternberg's shadowy, somewhat "arty" lyricism with the camera—Lubitsch has none of these. His vital qualities are called into play only in comedy. When he takes himself seriously, it is as if an excellent vaudeville star should insist on appearing in Shakespearian tragedy.

About once a year—sometimes not so often—Hollywood turns out a movie that can be accepted without innumerable reservations. In 1931 it was *Little Caesar*. Last year it was Lubitsch's *Trouble in Paradise*. That this should have been so excellent a production is more than a little strange. It is true that Lubitsch enjoys the greatest reputation of any director now active in Hollywood. But, this is based largely on his silent films. Of late he has made *The Man I Killed*, a dismally slow-paced Teutonic tearjerker, in which he indulged his weakness for being taken seriously and which he therefore considers his *chef d'oeuvre*; *One Hour With You*, a routine Chevalier film; and *The Smiling Lieutenant*, another Chevalier film, which was a vulgarized, heavyfooted version of that charming German production: *The Waltz Dream*. There was therefore no reason to suppose that *Trouble in Paradise* would be anything more than just another movie.

It is, with all qualifications, superb. Within the admittedly drastic limitations of its genre, it comes as close to perfection as anything I have ever seen in the movies. The opening shot of the Venetian garbage barge with its discordant gondolier strikes the note of sophisticated burlesque that is held throughout. The pace is fast, as it should be: each shot is held just long enough to make its point, and the point is never hammered in. "Lubit-schisms," those touches of wit that no other director quite captures, are scattered everywhere with a prodigal hand. There is enough "camera interest" for a dozen movies. When the lovers embrace, for instance, they are pictured rapidly (1) in the flesh (2) in a mirror (3) as shadows on a satin coverlet. As always, Lubitsch makes great play with the swinging camera, but he also gets some very nice effects with rapid cutting. Sound is used with especial brilliance. There are no "songs" arbitrarily set into the narrative like plums in a pudding. Instead, the action is accompanied by a running commentary of music. Like the old movie-organ pieces (still the best solution to the problem of movie music) this makes no attempt to be "good" in itself and is quite satisfied to serve as a background for what happens on the screen. Finally the decor, by Hans Dreier, is the best "moderne" job I have yet seen on stage or screen. Most cinematic excursions into modernism are either grotesque or tasteless, but Dreier's clocks, staircases, windows and chaise-longues are original, delicate and even refined.

Only Lubitsch, who works out every detail on paper before he shoots a single scene, could master all these sound and cinematic devices and put them smoothly to work in a single film. Varied and brilliant as is the technique, it never becomes obtrusive. It is always used to carry on and give point to the narrative. (Which, by the way, is banal—and quite unimportant.) Consider the climax of the movie, certainly one of the classic scenes in film comedy, when Filibo suddenly remembers where he has seen the mysterious Duval before. Here the crashing chorus of mock-dramatic music, the excited jumping up and sitting down of Filibo, and the mad gyrations of the camera to follow him—all these elements come together with shattering effect. There is also the fact that Filibo is played by a master of light comedy, Edward Everett Horton. This suggests another of the film's excellences—the acting of Herbert Marshall, Charles Ruggles, and Kay Francis. But the list of virtues is endless. Enough to say that *Trouble in Paradise* almost makes one believe in Hollywood again.

HARRY D'ABBADIE D'ARRAST, according to an acquaintance, is "nervous, somber, ugly, continually making faces and
slightly hysterical." He was born of a good French family in the
Argentine in 1897. He learned his cinema abroad and came to
Hollywood in 1922. For three years he was one of Chaplin's as-
sistants, notably on A *Woman of Paris* (1923) and *The Gold
Rush*. Later he made a series of sparkling Menjou comedies:
Serenade, Service for Ladies, A Gentleman of Paris. In 1930 he
collaborated with Donald Ogden Stewart on the story for *Laughter*, which he directed. After a lapse of over a year, RKO-Radio
set him to work on a film version of the French comedy, *Topaze*.
This is currently running and appears to have re-established his
reputation.

It was d'Arrast's work with Chaplin on A *Woman of Paris* that
bent his twig in the direction it has held ever since. When Chaplin undertook his only experiment in directing a serious movie,
he could never have foreseen the enormous influence his effort
was to have on the Hollywood cinema. Superficially, A *Woman
of Paris* was an unpretentious little story of a *boulevardier*
(Adolph Menjou) and his mistress (Edna Purviance, leading
lady in most of Chaplin's comedies). But in a quiet moving way
it brought to the screen for the first time a sophisticated analysis
of human relations. There was subtlety in it and psychological
penetration. Hollywood took over Chaplin's discovery, but with
a difference. The film's witty, gay, ironic, deftly sophisticated note
was at once appropriated, but the sensitive feeling for human
realities, the pathos and the irony, were never recaptured. The
comedies of Lubitsch and his followers, more numerous today
than ever, all stem from Chaplin's film. Menjou, whose flair for
sophisticated comedy Chaplin discovered, has been playing a
cheapened, externalized version of his *Woman of Paris* ever since.

But the most faithful disciple has been d'Arrast. Most of his
comedies have the glitter of A *Woman of Paris* with none of its
human warmth. The demand for sleek Parisian *roués* and satin-
walled boudoirs is apparently inexhaustible. Every now and then,
however, d'Arrast makes a movie that cuts beneath the surface.
In the silent days it was his significantly titled A *Gentleman of
Paris*, a sort of Maupassant novelette done with lots of cold style.
And he has made two talkies of exceptional interest. *Laughter*

is memorable because it attempts (not entirely successfully but with a bitterness unusual in the movies) to satirize this money-built civilization, because it has some brilliantly insane dialogue by Donald Ogden Stewart, and because of fine performances by Glenn Anders, Frank Morgan, Frederick March, and Nancy Carroll. The current d'Arrast production, *Topaze*, is smoothly and intelligently directed. In it John Barrymore gives the finest performance of his screen career. Why an actor with such a sense of high comedy should be consistently given heavy romantic parts is one of the trade secrets of Hollywood. Also to be noted is Myrna Loy, in my opinion the most attractive, intelligent, and charming of present-day movie actresses. It is also a mystery why for years she has had to get along on "vampire" parts in Fu Manchu thrillers.

HENRY KING, born and raised on a Virginia plantation, began his career as a blackface song and dance man. After ten years in "legitimate" (vaudeville, burlesque, circus, stock) he went into the movies as an actor. His main achievements in this line seem to have been appearances opposite Lillian Lorraine in *My Lady of Perfume* and Baby Mary Osborn, first of the infant stars, in a series of films directed by himself. He has made every sort of movie, from archaic Pathe serials to the once famous Ronald Colman-Vilma Banky affairs, but his reputation rests entirely on two silent films: *Tola'ble David* (1922) and *Stella Dallas* (1925). While I was disappointed in his current *State Fair*, it is better than anything he has done for some time and at least has revived interest in his work.

"I rehearse my pictures just like a play," King once remarked, "and during the rehearsals I build up my continuity." This approach, diametrically opposed to that of Griffith, Eisenstein, and all who understand the movies most deeply, does not make for great cinema. And King is important neither for his photography nor his filmic structure. But he has a quality that is rare in Hollywood: a delicate, sure human sympathy. At his best he can make his people real and can induce one to follow their doings with emotional intensity. His feeling for people shows in the casting of *Tola'ble David*. His selection of Richard Barthelmess to play David was sheer genius. It was the first time Barthelmess played this type of part, and he has been playing it ever since, most lately in *Cabin in the Cotton*. King also took a Scotch musical-show comedian, Ernest Torrence, and made him into a really terrifying villain. "Torrence was so vehement," he explains later, "so full of needful expression, so intelligent at grasping what was wanted of him, that I found myself building on his part and curtailing the business of another."

Most Hollywood movies are about the very poor or the very rich because social extremes are always dramatic. Such movies as do not fall into these categories—films about gangsters, for instance, or actresses—usually deal with some picturesque minor social group. The epic of the externally undramatic middle classes has yet to be screened. The nearest we have come to it is King's *Stella Dallas*. There is no question that *Tol'able David* is a more successful work, is indeed one of the most *perfect* movies ever made. But *Stella Dallas*, in my opinion, was a more remarkable film. The theme was Mother Love, a temptation for any director. But King presented it not as shrilly sensational melodrama but as a deeply felt drama of a middle class mother and her middle class daughter. The mother (Belle Bennett) is just a bit "common" according to bourgeois standards, and the daughter (Lois Moran) realizes that her mother is the chief bar to her marrying the "nice" young man of her choice (Ronald Colman). This the mother learns by chance (for her daughter is too fond of her to say anything) and to insure her daughter's happiness, steps out of her life. For Hollywood this plot is a triumph of originality, for the castastrophe is precipitated by nothing more sensational than the bourgeois idea of some people being "nice" and others being "common." That this conception has, in real life, given rise to more drama than all the gangsters in Chicago—this is beside the point as far as Hollywood is concerned. The scene is mostly a summer resort and here again King admirably recreates, entirely without satire, the tone of such fortresses of the American bourgeoisie—the tennis, the wicker chairs on the porch, the flashy roadsters, the white flannels and the 9-to-12 dances at the Lake House. Now there have been summer resorts and, God knows, mothers enough in the movies. The only difference is that King's direction, warmly and delicately sympathetic, makes them seem true—"realizes" them in Cèzanne's pregnant phrase. The greatest distinction of *Stella Dallas* is that it presents a mother-and-daughter relationship in which one believes and which is therefore intensely moving.

About King's latest work, *State Fair*, I find it hard to write with the proper critical restraint. I am not one who insists that a work of art shall be judged by its social implications, or lack of them. But there is a limit to the detachment of art from present-day realities. At a time when the American farmer is faced with ruin, when the whole Mid-West is seething with bitterness and economic discontent, a movie like *State Fair* is an insulting 'let them eat cake' gesture. The vaudeville rusticity of millionaire Will Rogers, the 'cute' little doll face of Janet Gaynor—thus Hollywood embodies the farmer! There was no excuse for the cheerfully trivial tone of the whole thing, the studied avoidance of anything more serious in the life of the farmer than whether his hog will win the state championship. And the slick, marshmallow-sweet Hollywood photography was in itself just cause for a national farmer's strike. What a chance for a realistic, documentary film of American farm life in these times! And Hollywood gives us a movie about as earthy as the gingham overalls in a musical comedy number. In spite of his scenario and a flagrantly inappropriate cast (what has become of King's flair for casting?) King manages to get in a few nice touches—the night ride to the fair and the rain at the end, for example. But the whole fabric was rotten with evasion of reality, and no amount of good directing (which King didn't give it anyway) would have been any use.

ERICH OSWALD HANS CARL MARIE STROHEIM VON NORDENWALD was born in Vienna forty-eight years ago, the son of a colonel on the Austrian general staff. He was graduated from the Imperial Military Academy in 1906, badly wounded in the head (only his protruding frontal ridge saved his eyesight) in the trouble with Bosnia-Herzogovina in 1908, cashiered for quarreling with his commanding officer. In 1909 he landed, penniless, in the United States. For five years he knocked around as a fashion correspondent, soldier, boatman, section hand, dishwasher, stable man, vaudeville actor and fly-paper salesman. In 1914 his knowledge of European military and court etiquette got him a job on a movie called *Old Heidelberg*. The war brought Stroheim suddenly into demand to play villainous Prussian officers in such pro-ally films as *For France* and *The Unbeliever*. He became known as "The Man You Love To Hate." Griffith gave him a mob part in the biblical episodes of *Intolerance* ("He's one of those guys yelling 'Crucify him!'" explains Griffith) and used him as art director in some later films. When the war ended, so did the demand for Stroheim. After months of starvation, he showed Carl Laemmle a scenario he had written and managed to get Laemmle to get him to make a movie from it. The maximum cost would be $25,000. The result was *Blind Husbands*, a melodrama of amorous intrigue done in the Continental manner. It cost $85,000, but it was a box-office success. It was followed by *The Devil's Passkey*, a $75,000 production that somehow cost Mr. Laemmle $185,000 before it was finished. Stroheim now embarked on his masterpiece in this genre: *Foolish Wives* (1922) which he wrote, directed, played the lead in, and which was positively not to cost over $250,000. After he had shot 200,000 feet of film and spent over $1,000,000 the frantic Laemmle induced him to bring the picture to an abrupt end with a subtitle. But *Foolish Wives* was a great success. He was working on *The Merry-Go-Round* when Irving Thalberg, the curly-haired, cold-eyed Boy Wonder of Hollywood movie executives, took charge of Universal's production end. Thalberg has the keenest nose for box-office values in all Hollywood. Shrewdly he sensed that Stroheim was a dead beat and forthwith fired him. Stroheim now went over to *Metro* which, in reckless disregard of Thalberg's judgment, gave him *carte blanche* to make a super-spacial movie from Frank Norris's novel *McTeague*. It is said that Stroheim had wanted to make the film ever since he had found the book, years before coming to Hollywood, in a cheap boarding house room. After he had run far over his allotted time and money, Stroheim presented Metro with a brutally realistic movie, completely lacking in sex and box-office appeal, that took ten hours to show. They cut its forty-two reels down to ten reels, called it *Greed*, and sent it out to the theaters. It was a complete failure. Those who have seen *Greed* in its entirety (no one seems to know just what has become of it now) pronounce it one of the greatest American films. In spite of everything, Stroheim was given *The Merry Widow* to direct. He turned out a frothy, sophisticated film that was a commercial success. In June, 1926, Stroheim began making a movie for Paramount to be called *The Wedding March*. He took a year to make it, another year to edit it, and finally suggested that it be run in two sections, with an intermission for dinner. Over Stroheim's protests, Paramount cut the first half to ten reels and released it in 1928. So resoundingly did it flop that the second half, *The Honeymoon*, was never released. Next he wrote, directed and acted in a white-men-in-the-tropics film starring Gloria Swanson and called *Queen Kelly*. But something happened—the talkies came in or Miss Swanson wasn't pleased—and *Queen Kelly* was never shown in public. Since the talkies, Stroheim has been forced to fall back on acting. He has played, and well, in *The Great Gabbo*, *Three Faces East*, *The Lost Squadron*, and *As You Desire Me*. Recently Fox set him to work directing an affair called *Walking Down Broadway*, called him off when he had taken twenty-six reels without any commercially tangible result.

The career of Stroheim presents in an intensified form the dilemma of every serious artist in Hollywood. His conflicts with the commercial end of the industry are those of his colleagues, and his frustration is theirs. But whereas they all compromise, more or less successfully, between Art and Mammon, such compromise is temperamentally impossible to Stroheim. He is a remarkable example, the only one Hollywood has to offer, of an artist who subordinates everything to what he considers his art. When he makes a movie, he loses all sense of time, of money, of human endurance. He keeps his actors at work until four in the morning, and he sees no reason why an audience should not be willing to sit through ten hours of a movie—if it takes ten hours to adequately express his idea. He is, in fact, as indifferent to the reactions of the public as he is to the interests of the producers. "I never go to see my pictures in the theaters," he once declared. The amazing thing is not that Stroheim has been thwarted at every turn of his career but that the producers have let such a lunatic spend as much of their money as they have. Stroheim obviously has no place in Hollywood. To me, he is the most interesting director out there.

Greed is generally considered Von Stroheim's masterpiece, but the only one of his films with which I am very familiar is *The Wedding March*. My estimate of his ability is therefore based chiefly on that remarkable film. Since, as we have seen, it has been released only in a mutilated version, there is no point in criticizing it as a whole. Looking at the parts, one is impressed most of all by their great variation in tone. With the flexibility and resource of a virtuoso, Von Stroheim adapts his style to the particular mood or emotion he wants to convey. His love scenes are lyrical with moonlight, appleblossoms and soft focus effects. His butcher shop and his brothel are presented with the most realistic insistence on the sordid and physical. The beginning of the film is in still another key: it is cool, deft analysis of social situations—a prodigal son asking his parents for money, a flirtation in a crowd. This flirtation is a lengthy episode in which, by a directorial *tour de force*, one's interest is held with only the slightest instruments of expression—a raising of the eyebrow, a glance, a discreet smile. To heighten the effect of this scene Von Stroheim places it against a background of an entirely different tone: the pomp and circumstance of the Corpus Christi procession. This same principle of dramatic counterpoint is followed in the treatment of the characters. The minor actors are not suppressed to form a neutral background to the "stars" as in most American movies, but on the contrary their personalities are strongly underlined. Thus when they come into contact with the principals or with each other, situations are created that are rich in the complexity of varying motives and emotions. The final wedding sequence, which assembles all the characters of the film, is built up wholly on this sort of counterpoint. *The Wedding March* is a most ambitious picture, as vast in emotional scope as *The Birth of a Nation* is vast in physical scope. Its greatness rests in the fact that it is ambitious without being heavy, serious without being dull, at once deeply felt and expressed in effective cinematic terms.

With Stroheim realism is a religion. His favorite author is Zola. There seems to be no limit to his appetite for reality. When he was a boy, he used to compete with his brother in picking out military insignia. "There were 106 infantry regiments in Austria with special markings and stripes. Yet I knew them all," he boasts. And again: "Somewhere in my subconscious mind I have a sort of photographic place. I see everything in the form of a scene for a picture." Innumerable legends have grown up around his attention to detail: how he spent two weeks teaching a squad of extras to salute in the Austrian manner; how he insists that cinematic grand dukes shall wear crests on their silk underwear and cinematic beggars shall wear tattered underclothes; how he blackened the hooves of a squadron of cavalry horses with shoe polish. The triumph of Stroheim's realism is *Greed*, which is pure Zola from the opening shots of the cheap dentist's office to the dead mule and salt-caked faces in the Death Valley sequence at the end. If *Greed* is Zolaesque, *Foolish Wives* and *The Wedding March* are Balzacian mixtures of melodrama, passion, and sophistication. Balzac would appreciate the worldly penetration of their analysis of personality, the richness of detail with which they define a social atmosphere, and the passion with which their characters pursue their ends. One recoils in amazement at the emotional intensity Stroheim can put into the melodramatic situations of such films.

"If I can dominate a player," Stroheim once remarked, "I can get anything I want from her." Actors to him are mere tools of his craft. They express *him*, not themselves. This was also the attitude of Griffith, who used to keep his actors in ignorance about the plot in order to keep the control more completely in his own hands. If they insisted on knowing something, he would purposely mislead them. No director gets more out of his actors than Stroheim. The doll-faced Mae Murray detested him when he directed her in *The Merry Widow*, but he forced her to really act for the first and last time in her career. He picked Zasu Pitts out of comedies and made her the tragic heroine of *Greed*. She has gone back to comedies, but Stroheim, and many of those who saw *Greed* call her the greatest tragic actress in Hollywood. (Milestone had her play the mother in *All Quiet*, but the executives couldn't take her seriously, and he had to re-take her scenes with Beryl Mercer in her place.) He found Fay Wray in Westerns and gave her the lead in *The Wedding March*. Stroheim himself is an actor of extraordinary power. His playing, like his directing, combines meticulousness with emotional intensity. With the utmost economy of means—a raised eyebrow, a slight motion of the lips—he gets terrific effects. His friend James Cruze, who directed him in *The Great Gabbo,* declares, "Von can steal any scene with the back of his fat neck."

In the twenty years Stroheim has been in Hollywood, he has made just seven pictures. Some directors—and able ones, too— turn out almost that many in a single year. Le Roy made six last year, Wellman made five. To such men a movie is merely a technical problem: how can this banal situation be dressed up to the best advantage, what directorial tricks will inject the greatest amount of synthetic vitality into it? But to Stroheim making a movie is an intensely personal experience. He takes it all much too seriously. He doesn't understand that Hollywood exists to make money and that it is the business of the director to turn out, as cheaply and speedily as possible, a picture that people will pay to see. But then Stroheim has never had any sense of money. He has worked a year without salary just to get a movie finished the way he wanted it. Stroheim is a foolish fellow indeed compared to a director like the high-powered Clarence ("Never Made A Flop") Brown, who gets $300,000 a year for putting Joan Crawford and Greta Garbo through their paces. He is stubborn, naive, conceited, wrong-headed, Quixotic. Inevitably he has made an utter mess out of his career: only one movie in the last five years, and that never completed; his wife reduced most of the time to one dress; he himself forced to play small parts under directors who don't know a tenth what he does. But Stroheim has one quality which the slick, facile technicians now dominant in Hollywood somehow don't seem to develop: a sense of personal integrity. No pressure can make him do what he doesn't believe in. He stands up for his own ideas in spite of everything. He has guts. His career is a warning to most young directors, an inspiration to a few.

JOSEF VON STERNBERG, according to Paramount's handout, was born in Vienna in 1894 and was graduated from the University of Vienna "with several degrees." Furthermore—"He has sandy brown hair, and blue eyes that give the impression of being dull. That is when he is brooding." Sternberg spurns as a *canard* the rumor that he was born Joe Stern of Brooklyn. Like every one else in Hollywood, he has a "gag" whereby he calls attention to himself. His particular gag is that he is an artist

—aloof, temperamental, not to be imposed on by mere $150,000 a year studio executives. Strangely enough, there is a certain amount of sincerity behind this gag of Sternberg's. In its interest he had unhesitatingly shattered to bits his Hollywood career, and not once but several times. After a decade of apprentice work as film cutter, cameraman, scenarist, and so on, Sternberg entered on his career in 1924 by getting some one to put up $5,000 for a picture he wanted to make. This was *The Salvation Hunters*, a grimly realistic drama acted mostly by amateurs and photographed mostly against a mud scow in San Pedro Harbor. Chaplin saw the film and was impressed enough to give Sternberg $20,000 for a half interest. But when a Hollywood audience snickered at the pre-view, Chaplin pretended it was all a big joke —on Sternberg. The film was never released for a public showing. Perhaps as another joke, Chaplin had United Artists hire Sternberg to direct Mary Pickford. The film was never made: America's Sweetheart just didn't get along with Sternberg. He next went over to Metro-Goldwyn-Mayer, made two pot-boilers, and then broke his contract ("by mutual consent"). Once more Chaplin took him up. He directed Edna Purviance, Chaplin's leading lady in the older comedies, in *The Sea Gull*. "Beautiful but not human," was Hollywood's reaction. The film was never released. It began to seem as if Sternberg was temperamentally incapable of making a commercial movie. When, in 1926, Paramount gave him a contract, no one was very much excited. Sternberg surprised every one, Paramount included, by turning out *Underworld*, a high-powered melodrama that is the ancestor of all gangster films. It was the biggest box-office success of 1927 and won Sternberg a bonus of $10,000 from Paramount. He has been with Paramount ever since then. Notable among his silent productions were *The Dragnet, The Last Command, The Docks of New York,* and *The Case of Lena Smith*. His first talkie he made in Germany for U F A: *The Blue Angel,* starring Emil Jannings. To play opposite Jannings he picked an obscure German musical comedy actress named Marlene Dietrich. The story is that he chose her after hearing her say her one and only line in the show: "Hurray for the gentleman who has won the Grand prize!" When he returned to this country, Dietrich came with him. His direction plus Paramount's astute publicity made Dietrich into a star of the first magnitude, the pretender to Garbo's crown. Except for *An American Tragedy*, every picture Sternberg has made since *The Blue Angel* has been built around Dietrich. There was *Morocco* in 1930, *Dishonored* in 1931. *Shanghai Express* and *The Blonde Venus* last year. His contract with Paramount expired several months ago and has not been renewed—largely because of a bitter quarrel over *The Blonde Venus*. He sailed for Germany in February—to work for U F A, was the report. But the Nazi revolution barred him (despite the "von") from a U F A job—as it is said to have also caused U F A to fire its most talented director, G. W. Pabst—and he sailed back to this country. There are rumors he is joining a new production company.

Perhaps the best approach to Sternberg is through Stroheim. The two are linked together in many ways. The "von" in Sternberg's name may well be a furtive tribute to the man who taught him the use of significant detail. From Stroheim he also acquired his taste for realism, his meticulous attention to lighting and composition. His first movie, *The Salvation Hunters*, which he still considers his best, was made soon after Stroheim's *Greed* appeared. Its brutal heavy-handed realism was precisely that of *Greed*, which Sternberg is said to have studied closely. Some interesting parallels can be drawn between Sternberg's *The Case of Lena Smith* and Stroheim's *The Wedding March*. Each was released in 1928; each was the last silent film by its creator; the setting of each was pre-war Vienna; each centered around a love affair between a young officer and a girl of the people; the full-scale reproduction of the facade of Corpus Christi church, one of the triumphs of Hollywood realism, was used in both films; and, finally, *Lena Smith* was dedicated to the mothers of the world, *The Wedding March* to the lovers of the world. Even Sternberg's well-known "signature," the black cat which appears in each of his films, may be traced to Stroheim. A black cat figured prominently and effectively in the climactic murder scene in *Greed*.

Sternberg presents that mixture of temperament and affectation which marks the man of talent—as contrasted with the man of genius. Stroheim is far more *outré*, and at the same time less affected. He has the passionate sincerity, the naive directness of genius. But there is always something small and self-conscious about Sternberg's gestures. Stroheim is believable when he shaves his head and wears a silver bracelet. Sternberg is suspect even in so innocent a matter as the cane he carries. There is more than a little of the "art" director about Sternberg, and his films often have a slick "artiness" about them. Both men have fought for their aesthetic integrity, both are known in Hollywood as "difficult," which means "honest." But one feels that Stroheim is irreconcilable because it is in his nature to be so, Sternberg because he wants to keep in character as an "artist." A case in point was the uproar with Paramount over *The Blonde Venus*. Sternberg had written the scenario himself (it is notable how many of the directors considered are also skilled scenario writers) and he resented certain proposed changes—including, of course, a happy ending. When Paramount insisted, Sternberg took the train for New York. Paramount threatened to sue for $100,000 damages for breach of contract. ("One hundred thousand dollars? Is that all? I think they are trying to humiliate me," observed Sternberg, unimpressed.) Things were finally patched up, however, and Sternberg completed the picture. After seeing it, I wonder what all the shooting was for. There is nothing in it that makes the slightest difference, one way or another. It puts Sternberg in the ridiculous position of defending bad art against the onslaughts of commercialism. The pity of it is that there is a good deal of sincerity mixed up with Sternberg's faking and posing. And, of course, a great deal of talent. The talkie career of von Sternberg is a study in degeneration. For him Marlene Dietrich has been far more of a *femme fatale* than for any of her cinematic victims. Each of her films has been just a little worse than its predecessor.

In his silent films Sternberg was as interesting a director as Hollywood had to offer. They were cut so smoothly, with such a delicate sense of rhythm, that they had that finished, complete quality which few American films possess. Their photography was the best in Hollywood: luminous gray tones, rich dramatic chiaroscuro, with each shot a well-thought-out composition in itself. A scenarist himself, Sternberg knew how to tell a story, how to keep it moving and give it suspense. His films moved along smoothly and swiftly, with the minimum of waste motion. Skillfully he kaleidoscoped the narrative so as to get pace and avoid wearisome exposition, as in *Underworld* when the murder is followed immediately by the judge pronouncing sentence of death.

All of these gifts Sternberg had—and still has. But they have degenerated into the hollowest, most patent kind of technical trickery. His latest movie, *The Blonde Venus*, is perhaps the worst ever made. In it all Sternberg's gifts have turned sour. The photography is definitely "arty"—a nauseating blend of hazy light, soft focus, over-blacks and over-whites, with each shot so obviously "composed" as to be painful. Sternberg's rhythm has declined to a senseless, see-saw pattern. And his kaleidoscopic cutting has reached such a point that the film is all pace and nothing else. The scene changes often, simply because Sternberg didn't have the vitality to get anything much out of any one scene. Therefore his camera flits restlessly, and fruitlessly, from New York to New Orleans to Berlin to Bueños Aires. The whole thing reminded me of the galvanic twitching of a corpse. As for the story, the characterizations, and the cast—never has there been anything more naive, more absurdly artificial and Holly-woodish. To survive in the hostile atmosphere of Hollywood, it would seem, the artist must have something more than talent.

MERVYN LEROY is the current Boy Wonder among Hollywood directors. He is short, slight, and looks much younger than he is. When he went to a Manhattan theater recently to see a play he was going to direct, he was unable to convince the man in the box office that he wasn't his own office boy. To lend himself dignity, he puffs solemnly on a large cigar. It is rumored that his real name is Lasky and that he is a nephew of Jesse Lasky, the producer. He was born in 1900 in San Francisco, and in 1920 he got a job as a cameraman at First National. He has stayed there ever since, which is something of a record in Hollywood. From playing bit parts and writing "gags" for Colleen Moore pictures, he progressed to directing Mlle. Moore (said to have had the largest fan mail any star ever received) in several of her innocent little *operas*. Thence he rose to directing less innocent but equally ephemeral productions: *Hot Stuff, Showgirl in Hollywood, Broadway Babies, Ritzy Rosie*, and so on. In 1931 he surprised every one by turning out *Little Caesar*, a gangster melodrama that was an enormous success at the box office and with the critics. Since then he has made a vast number of films, most of them mediocre, a few worth recording. Notable are: *Five Star Final*, which had a moral and emotional force rare in the American cinema: *Gentleman's Fate*, an excellent gangster picture in which LeRoy extracted from John Gilbert his first decent talkie performance; a fast-paced farce called *High Pressure*; *Local Boy Makes Good*, wherein LeRoy managed to restrain the appalling antics of Joe E. Brown enough to make him human and amusing for the first and last time; the somber *I am a Fugitive* and the trivial, smartly directed *Tonight or Never*. When his wife divorced him last summer, his salary was $91,000.

I should not hesitate to call *Little Caesar* the most successful talkie that has yet been made in this country. The credit goes chiefly, though not entirely, to LeRoy. He gave it a dynamic, driving pace which carried through to the very end. By skillful cutting he carried the rhythm of his episodes and related them so closely that, unlike most American talkies, *Little Caesar* seems to be an organic whole. He adroitly modulated the tone from tense melodrama (as in the gangsters' inner sanctum scenes) to satire (as in the superb banquet episode) to the bleakest realism (as in the last reel). And he precisely caught the atmosphere of his night club, of his cheap flophouse, of his lunch counters and hideaways. But there was also the performance of Edward G. Robinson (whom, to be sure, LeRoy picked, more or less out of the air, to play the part) which would have triumphed over any direction. And there was an excellent script and a plot which was both dramatically and psychologically effective. It was a remarkably fine touch in the grand tragic manner, to have Caesar's ruin brought about by his one human feeling, which is also his one weakness; his friendship for Joe Massara.

According to Hollywood legend, LeRoy had long been eager to make a movie out of W. R. Burnett's novel, *Little Caesar*. When he learned that First National had bought the rights, he determined to get the assignment. Afire with enthusiasm, he spent weeks wandering about the Los Angeles waterfront, closely observing the way real gangsters acted and talked. His bosses were so impressed by his underworld erudition that they let him make the picture, which would normally have been assigned to a more eminent director. (LeRoy at the time had nothing to his credit except *Broadway Babies* and the like.) To avoid any possible interference from company executives, LeRoy refused to show them a single foot of the film until it was all taken, cut and assembled. Then when it was beyond their power to tinker or tone down, he ran off the completed film—and knocked them out of their chairs. They released it just as he had made it, and predicted a big success at the box office. For once, they were right.

I have yet to see a dull movie by LeRoy. Whatever his movies fail to do, they always *move*. He knows how to give speed and pace to a film. His recent picture, *Hard to Handle*, for example, is a commonplace affair as to plot and dialogue, just another press-agent story. But LeRoy keeps the mechanism purring along at such a smooth, swift pace that one is not bored—until after it is all over and one has time to reflect. He makes his actors talk and move rapidly. He gets impetus every now and then by a quick succession of short shots dissolving into each other every five seconds or so. Above all, he doesn't dot his i's. Once his point is made, he moves on at once. Essentially, it is the vaudeville black-out technique.

LeRoy is perhaps the most efficient director in Hollywood. He is prolific, as the five full-length pictures he made last year testify. And he is versatile. Melodrama (as, *Little Caesar*), human document (*Two Seconds*), social propaganda (*Five Star Final*), farce (*High Pressure*), comedy of character (*Local Boy Makes Good*), sophisticated "drawing-room" comedy (*Tonight or Never*)—all are grist to his mill. LeRoy, in a word, is the answer to every producer's prayer: a director who has talent but who will do what he is told. It might be better if he had some of Stroheim's egotism and personal conviction, if he were a little more the individual artist and a little less the merely clever technician. But LeRoy makes no pretensions to being an artist. He is just a nice, modest, well-liked youngster, the boy friend of Ginger Rogers, the intimate of Jack Dempsey and "Junior" Laemmle. "Mervyn," gushes a Hearst writer, "Mervyn is known as 'a great little guy' on both coasts. He doesn't pose as a prodigy, a genius, a 'von' LeRoy. He's just a young feller trying to get along." Which is precisely the trouble.

LEWIS MILESTONE, whose actual name is said to be Milstein, is stoutly built, ruddy, blue-eyed. He has a nice sense of humor and it is rumored about in Hollywood that he reads books. He was born in Russia in 1895. Sent to school in Germany by his father, a well-to-do manufacturer, he ran away to the United States. He worked in a photographer's studio and, on the outbreak of the war, entered the photographic division of the Signal Corps. After the war he went to Hollywood as a film cutter at $20 a week, met a director named Milton Seiter, and collaborated with him on a series of piffling productions: *Daddies, The Little Church Around the Corner, The Foolish Age* and so on. In 1924 he got a job as director with Warner Brothers. He proved to be so useful that he was constantly being lent to other companies to help out with pictures that were not going well. This worked until the day he discovered that Warner Brothers were paying him $400 a week and charging other companies a minimum of $1,000 a week for his services. He revolted, broke his contract, and went through bankruptcy to satisfy the judgment Warner Brothers won against him. A free man once more, he signed a four-year contract with Howard Hughes, who was just beginning his high-powered career as an independent producer. He made two excellent pictures for Hughes: the picaresque *Two Arabian Knights*, a rowdy, vulgar and very funny comedy, and a gangster melodrama called *The Racket*. But Hughes, too, kept farming him out, which usually meant that he had to work on second-rate pictures. Milestone finally bought up the rest of his contract and once more regained his freedom. When Carl Laemmle in 1929 bought the screen rights to *All Quiet on the Western Front*, he sent for Milestone, already known as a director of ability and integrity, and had him make the movie. In 1931 he joined United Artists. He has made three films for them: *The Front Page*, which was widely considered the best movie of 1931, *Rain*, a very poor picture indeed, and *Hallelujah, I'm a Bum*, which is even more painful. He seems to be through with United Artists—perhaps wisely, considering his last two pictures—and to be pondering his next move. There was a rumor last fall that he was to go to Spain with Sidney Franklin and Ernest Hemingway to make a movie about bullfighting. And a few months ago the papers printed an even more fantastic report: Milestone is to join forces with Lubitsch, Vidor and Sternberg in an entirely new producing company: Eastern Service Studios, Inc. Behind the new company is mysterious Captain Baynes. Behind Captain Baynes is the Electrical Research Products Corp., which makes talkies equipment. And behind the Electrical Research Products Corp. is Western Electric. Captain Baynes is reported to have already leased the Paramount Long Island studio, idle for many months, and to have made practically sure of his four directors. The present moment is a propitious one for getting them together. Milestone is at loose ends. Vidor has been working on his own for several years. And Paramount's contracts with both Lubitsch and Sternberg are reported to have expired without being renewed. If Captain Baynes gets all four directors into his company, it will amount to a corner on Hollywood's best directorial talent.

To executives who grow worried when he is in the middle of a movie, Milestone quotes scripture: "O ye of little faith!" He will brook no interference once he has begun to work, and he insists on doing all his own cutting. His attitude is scrupulously, absurdly (from a Hollywood viewpoint) conscientious. Thus his break with Selznick two years ago, which killed the newborn Selznick-Milestone Pictures Corp., came about because Selznick wanted him to assume responsibility for seven pictures a year. Milestone didn't think he could satisfactorily oversee so many pictures, and so he gave up an excellent chance to become an independent producer. When he was making *All Quiet*, he was continually pestered by the producers' insistence on a "happy ending"—which he didn't give them, by the way. Finally he called them on the phone and said: "I've got your happy ending. We'll let the Germans win the war."

An enormous amount of praise has been heaped on *All Quiet on the Western Front*—more, I suspect, for its obvious sincerity and emotional integrity than for its cinematic qualities. It is a very fine movie, but I am inclined to think it has been overestimated. There is much talk of the picture's realism, but I found the sets extremely artificial and the lighting very much in the overdramatic, glossy slick Hollywood manner. The French cottage had a property cow and a property cart posed in just the right place before it, the whole forming a composition reminiscent of a Royal Academy landscape. The daylit battle scenes were reeking with California sunlight (compare the grim gray tone of Russian war films), and the night tableaux were full of calcium star shells, melodramatic shadows, and fake moonlight. There were too many dug-out scenes, and they were too full of confusion and squalor. Hollywood dugouts are always phony looking, anyway. Furthermore, the film is monotonous. Milestone is said to have cut it from 18,000 to 12,000 feet, but another 2,000 feet could easily have been taken out. The class-room scene was much too long: the effect of the teacher's patriotic monologue on his students could have been suggested in half the time. Another example is the scene where the boys look at the girl on the poster. This took several minutes, much too long in view of the minor point made by the episode. Milestone's use of the close-up seemed to me excessive. His trick of showing five or six faces in rhythmical succession, while effective as a means of presenting the boy soldiers as a group of individuals, became an annoying mannerism. He has a way of shoving his camera into the face of the speaker—a trick he repeats in *The Front Page*. This gives a powerful drive to the spoken lines, but it gets tiresome. Also, the lines aren't worth so much emphasis most of the time.

The limitations of *All Quiet* are most apparent when it is compared to a war film like Dovzhenko's *Arsenal*. Whereas the Russian has an inexhaustible variety of attack on his material, getting all sorts of contrasts and harmonies of scale, angle, distance, lighting, tempo and film texture, Milestone repeats himself tiresomely, his close-ups (even the infantry charges are done in close-up), his pearly gray lighting, his sluggish rhythm. Nor are there any such moments of intense imagination in *All Quiet* as occur in every reel of *Arsenal*. Even so absurd a war film as Griffith's *Hearts of the World* contains passages better than anything in *All Quiet*. I refer to certain panoramic shots, mostly at the beginning of reel five, epic in their sense of mass and distance and God's-eye scope. This is pure cinema—a matter of visual values entirely—and this is where Milestone is weakest. His flair is for human, not abstract, drama. One is moved by his characters, whom he presents with sensitive awareness, but their cinematic realization leaves one cold.

Of what might be called the "younger generation" of Holly-wood directors, Milestone and LeRoy are perhaps the most talented. Their work differs greatly. Milestone's movies tend to be slow-paced, brooding, emotional, Teutonic, while LeRoy's are speedy, hard-boiled, nervous, American. But they are significantly alike in one essential. I have already commented on LeRoy's extraordinary diversified output. And the writer who called Milestone "an efficient chameleon" was just about right. What is the common denominator of the rowdy slapstick of *Two Arabian Knights*, the dogged, bitter realism of *All Quiet*, the noisy melodrama of *The Front Page*, the gentle whimsicality of *Hallelujah, I'm a Bum*, and the cheap theatrics of *Rain*? To make for the last time a point I have already suggested several times before: the type of director now in the saddle in Hollywood is technically competent, clever, even intelligent but somehow lacking in individuality. It is not precisely a matter of "integrity," in Milestone's case at least. As we have seen, he compromises very little with his ideals and has suffered considerably through his insistence on making movies his own way. Rather it is a matter of personality. There is a certain individual quality to the work of the best of the older generation—Griffith, Lubitsch, Sternberg, Stroheim. Their movies may be very poor indeed, but they are unmistakably *theirs*. No such personal note exists in the work of the younger generation. They have, it seems, nothing to say.

Symposium, March-June, 1933.

Note by Dwight Macdonald, September 1, 1959: *The late Theodore Huff and I went to school together at Phillips Exeter Academy in the early twenties; I remember him as a tall, mild-mannered esthete, one of a group of schoolboy intellectuals which was remarkably large and self-confident (not self-assertive, but one could hardly expect that in a boarding-school). Recently I came across a letter he wrote me in 1934 pointing out some inaccuracies in my "Notes on Hollywood Directors." Partly to keep the record straight, partly because it is an interesting document in itself, full of the scholarly devotion and excitement of the early cinéastes, I reproduce it below, with cuts.*

97 *Engle Street,*
Englewood, N.J.

Dear Dwight:

While looking about for the October issue of "Spicy Parisian Nights" in one of those back number stores, I came upon a magazine called "Symposium" with your article on Hollywood directors. Imagine my surprise! I never knew that you were such a student of the cinema. In the old days, I never heard you discuss pictures seriously and my impression was that you looked down on them as all the intellegensia [*sic*] of the time did (including Lincoln Kerstein [*sic*]). To be very frank, I am very jealous of you and Kerstein being such authorities and critics today. It's my proudest boast that I didn't have to wait for Eisenstein, Pudovkin and Clair. I considered movies an art years before and I have seen everything from "Cabiria" on. If you never heard me discuss films, it was because of the general attitude of the aestheits [*sic*] of the day. Fort Lee, near Englewood, was the first Hollywood, as you know, so I was brought up in the atmosphere. . . . Some of my earliest memories are watching Mary Pickford and others "on location" in Englewood with their yellow faces and purple eyelids. Did I ever tell you how (before Exeter days) I used to bicycle to Mammaroneck (32 miles round trip) on Saturdays to visit Griffith's studio and to watch (from afar) "Way Down East" and "Orphans of the Storm" in the making?

But what I started out to say was that I was very much impressed by your Notes. . . . Why don't you go on, list the foreign directors in the same way? . . . I could be of help as I have hundreds and hundreds of stills. . . . also I have the scenarios of many of the pictures you mention ("Woman of Paris," "Intolerance," for instance). I used to take them down in shorthand.

Just between ourselves, it seemed to me that many of the early pictures you discuss you hadn't actually seen but had done research on them. [*True, true*—D.M.] This criticism below of minor mistakes is only to show off what a "book of knowledge" I am on the subject when it comes to *facts*—even tho I can't write like you.

GRIFFITH:

"*The* Avenging Conscience" was a five-reeler Mutual picture, 1913-14, and not one of the old Biograph two-reelers.

"Intolerance" was not produced two years later than "The Birth"; it was made the same year (though the Babylonian part wasn't made till 1915) and *released* in 1916.

Under "Important works followed," it was a mistake to list "One Exciting Night," a frank program picture, and to leave out "Hearts of the World" (1918), "Orphans of the Storm" (1921), and "America" (1924).

I don't like "archaic" photography either. Remember in an old picture you are apt to see a dupe or a dupe print. I consider parts of "Intolerance," for instance, far superior to the murky, artificial photography of today. And "Way Down East" is the high-water mark of photography for me. [*I now agree wholly about the "archaic" photography, especially after seeing "The Birth of a Nation" this summer for the fourth or fifth time; the photography, in its clarity and harmony of tones, seemed miraculous—far better than anything one has seen on the screen for decades.—D.M.*]

VIDOR:

He first attracted attention with "Jack-Knife Man" (1920), a story of great simplicity and *no love interest*. It made his reputation.

"The Crowd" was not a talkie—it was made in the late silent era.

MAMOULIAN:

I'm glad you don't like him. He certainly is a great imitator.

LUBITSCH:

You pulled a great boner in saying Negri was La Pompadour. It was DuBarry of course. . . . He came to this country not in 1924 as "Rosita" was made early in 1923 (during our Upper-Middle year at Exeter). . . . And here is the remark I don't like: "With characteristic Hollywood intelligence, put to work directing Mary Pickford (America's Sweetheart)." It sounds too much like Seymour Stern, Harry Alan Potamkin or some other "highbrow" critic. Mary *brought* him over to direct her. . . .

HENRY KING:

You left out "The White Sister" (1923) in his reputation-resting films. Surely this was one of the most beautiful pictorially ever made—taken in Italy before the days of "process" shots. Also his rehearsing like a play is not "diametrically opposed" to Griffith as D.W. used to rehearse for weeks in advance & work out things before going before the cameras.

VON STROHEIM:

"Foolish Wives" was released in 1921, not 1922. I saw it at Exeter on a Wednesday, disguised in old clothes as a townie. [*Friday night was student night at the local movie house, the Ioka; Huff risked expulsion to gratify his scholarly passion.—D.M.*] If I had known you were interested, what fun we would have had seeing it. It really was, tho, an absurd mess even tho it is often spoken of today. . . . but it did give the feeling that the director was an individual of "driving force". . . .

VON STERNBERG:

I don't agree that his films move swiftly and have pace. I think his films are very slow & languid. Who else ever uses such . . . slow dissolves (10 or 15 seconds) and general sluggishness? Also his annoying trick of always having something in the way! His characters are always obscured by palms, vines, gratings or shadows.

I hope you haven't minded these criticisms. . . . I really got a big kick out of the Notes. You took the words right out of my mouth when you said that the directors of today do not stand out as individuals; they are all on a competent dead level. . . . By the way, I had a job as cameraman and assistant last summer on a 16mm film made by a Yale man—John Flory '32. He got a seven-year contract with Paramount on the strength of it ("Mr. Motorboat's Last Stand"). He certainly was lucky. It's almost never happened before. . . . Well, I must stop.

Sincerely yours,
Ted Huff

FORMAL CINEMA

Kirk Bond

[1]

It is often remarked that cinema is an art unique. Commonly the reason is found in its technique, involving as it does collaboration to a greater or less extent, as well as a degree of reality which for many people effectually debars cinema from becoming an art at all; occasionally someone sees beneath this the essentially dual role which cinema, far more than literature must play.

It has always been characteristic—unfortunately, if you wish—of the genius of English-speaking peoples to mingle art with other affairs of life, with the consequence that their only artists of the first rank are poets. It is difficult for us to understand the Latin or the Teutonic ability to make something out of mere patterns in light or sound, and, what is stranger, apply them in the business of life. We incline to the heresy that art is the better for associating with man, improving his daily life, rather than providing on state occasions the opportunity for creating or absorbing particular attempts to reach an absolute Idea. Herein, of course, we are deficient, but we must know this if we are to criticize cinema, for, like the other formal arts, it is based upon a direct impression made on the senses.

On the other hand, cinema is, unlike all other arts, a medium of intelligent communication. To a minor degree in the ordinary newsreel or educational film, eminently in montage, it is a language, an undreamed-of successor to the ancient hieroglyphics. Never before, with perhaps the slight exception of Oriental calligraphy, has there been an art to combine such opposites. It is scarcely surprising that the two rarely receive their due together.

Generally formal cinema has been the one to suffer. With no little show of reason it has been demonstrated that dependence upon the sensory impressions of the film leads to nothing. It has been considered impossible, by artists and laymen alike, to express feelings of a high order in nothing more than a moving photograph. And the futile, if amusing, romps of so many experimenters do much to confirm this opinion. They are seldom prepared to defend their work against criticism, for they have not taken it seriously, and their best efforts exhibit a virtuosity and a lack of conviction that in themselves almost persuade one of the barrenness of this field.

Formal cinema, however, remains. It has had its serious-minded workers, its moments of intuition, and it demands aside from this the utmost attention as a theoretical case. Barring actual achievement, the medium requires a sensuous expression. If there were no such expression, we might say, it would be necessary to predict one. Whatever the common result, cinema is in its origin a medium of moving light and shade. The reality of most films is impressive, but it is purely an effect, and its dispensability is clearly evident in the slightest attempt at pictorial impressionism, or symbolism. It is perhaps analogous to the life-like realism of last century painters and sculptors, or to "tuneful" music, except that its proper basis is more difficult to discern. One can, without advocating the strict "functionalism" of an Eggeling, reasonably ask for some recognition of the two-dimensional, monochrome character of the screen.

In stricter terms, we may define cinema as the observed motion of light and shade on a limited plane surface. It combines primary elements in a wholly new order. It is dangerous, of course, to found aesthetic judgments upon physical data; nevertheless it is possible to say that cinema supplies the one missing order. Of the two higher senses—sight and hearing—the latter is served by music both statically, as in the East, and dynamically, as in our own age, while there has been developed a plethora of arts based on visual form or design. It only remained to discover an art appealing to the eye through motion—motion, that is, conventionalized in a definite medium.

There are serious objections to the newly-invented cinema as a satisfactory solution of the problem. Indeed there is some reason for supposing the problem insoluble, a purely theoretical union of elements impossible save in a devitalized age of sophistication and mechanical ingenuity. For all that, whatever the validity of a "fourth order", cinema does supply one, and as far as we can tell does so legitimately. It is rigidly restricted, yet it offers almost unbounded possibilities for motion in space and time. Again and again intelligent critics have stressed this point in deploring the customary reliance of commercial and amateur films alike upon well-worn dramatic actions or simple documents. It is for the future to decide, but it seems fair to assume that moving values on the screen can have a quality comparable to that of similar values in the finest musical compositions.

The single fact of their motion definitely removes cinema from competition with the various graphic arts. Few people realize the vast difference caused by the simple incident of motion. The photograph is still to be judged by the canons of painting, composition, light, tonality, and because so much is determined by external conditions, photography can scarcely hope to do better than a romantic impressionism. Let the same photograph be put in motion and it is subject to a wholly new set of values. For the line of the artist is substituted the moving light of the artist. It is the distinction between a landscape with clouds, and the actual clouds shifting against the sky. A more pointed illustration is an ordinary fire. Painters, with rare exceptions, have passed it by for the obvious reason that there is nothing to paint, it is all motion. Yet there must have been some who wished to catch the bright, fluid colors of the flames, whose fascination is the very opposite of that of the pictures we are told to see there. Somewhat as color has come to be used in painting as a functional equivalent for line, so on a larger scale the brush-made line gives way in cinema to the rhythmic ordering of less precise masses of light and shade.

One cannot urge too strongly that this obviates dependence

upon structural composition of line and mass. It is too often thought that the rhythmic, dynamic basis of cinema consists in the proper organization of pictorially composed images, each in some sense flowing into the next. Nothing could be more misleading. Such a conception logically forces one to trim the motion to suit the composition, which is nonsense. To maintain a particular composition through a sequence is only to bring the theater onto the screen, whether the actual content be realistic or highly abstract. Naturally, proper composition of the motion will normally guarantee reasonably sound static composition, but it must be clearly understood that this will be due not to the direct application of the principles of graphic art, but to the more general principles of aesthetics inherent in good cinema. Whenever the one is definitely violated, the effect of the other will justify the sacrifice.

[2]

In cinema there is not the slightest necessity for pictorial completeness. A Turner or a Cézanne as well as a Phidias must present a finished design, for his success depends upon the immediate aspect of his work. The totality of his meaning exists without reference to the element of time. The cinemist, on the contrary, has to project his meaning through a temporal continuity, in which the single image, so far from being important, is fundamentally nonexistent. Although still tied to the physical facts of frame and canvas, he is free from responsibility towards them as graphic materials. Their excuse is that a three-dimensional medium (such as Edison envisaged, for example) is artistically inconceivable. In this respect the stereotyped products of Hollywood are more essentially cinematic than some of the films of the painters of avant-garde, though to be sure the former's inartistic theatrical nature more than cancels this advantage. The image that exists only in the mind's eye as an arrested moment in a sequence, or as used as a dimly suggestive still, has not sufficient consequence to demand attention as a subject for spatial design.

Cinema possesses a greater affinity with music. Even here, however, the relation is more useful in philosophical than in technical discussion. Music—Western music, that is—employs likewise temporal continuity, and the two are thus what might be called fourth-dimensional homologues, but they are not so similar in actual detail as to merit the many comparisons made, and the conclusions that have been drawn. .

Music is composed of harmonic units, bearing both in quality and quantity exact mathematical relations to one another. Involuntarily it possesses a beat, which is taken for granted in any musical criticism. In cinema there is neither unit nor beat for it is only a continuous photograph of nature. Of itself, although it exists in time, it does not possess the aesthetic quality of time. It is thus futile to compare the basic elements of the two for rhythm or harmony. It may not be too fanciful to suggest that this difference is demonstrated in the formerly universal custom of employing music as an accompaniment to a film. Just because the film itself lacked a definite rhythm, was it possible, and commonly preferable, to add to it a tom-tom, as it were, to mark the tempo? The underlying reason, of course, is that one sense restricts itself to a particular, ordered phase of its field, whereas the other embraces the entire field. One can no more combine pictures of objects in an exact rhythm (excluding as before montage) than one can the objects themselves, although the purest abstractions have some claim to this closer sort of musical analogy.

Nevertheless cinema is not a cognate art for nothing. If it is dissonant by nature, it can be worked into melody by the artist. Upon the material of painting he will impose the temper of music, but with the purpose of painting—to impress upon the physical world an ideal order. Obviously the result will be in large part incommensurable with that of the musician. Their chief similarity is simply their dynamic approach. The aim of both arts is an aesthetic expression in time, and on this level the two can be profitably compared. Cinema, no less than music, may have a fine subtle rhythm, a powerful crescendo, a light-hearted scherzo, or solemn processional. For the harmony of notes and scales it merely substitutes a harmony of nature drawn up in ordered patterns of continuity. This, however, introduces the whole question of the real meaning of formal cinema.

If cinema is an aesthetic expression in time, it is still true that it is also a visual, and so a plastic art. Except in the purest abstract work, it is necessarily concerned, to some degree, with a represen-

tation of the physical world. It is, therefore, although closely related to neither the fine arts nor music, a sort of hybrid of the
two, and cuts across the established distinction between them.
Heretofore there has been either the art of form, expressing directly the beauty of nature, or the art of continuity, expressing in a
more abstract fashion the essential rhythm we find in the beauty
of nature. Quite naturally architecture, the first of the arts, is
called frozen music: music is the final, free form of those principles which begin with the master craftsman and the builder. They
gradually become clearer and more explicit through the several
stages of sculpture (the final form for the Greeks) and painting,
but in music their expression changes from the relatively concrete to the relatively pure and abstract. The latter is not necessarily the superior; it does form, however, a distinct and separate
order.

Into this tidy classification has come the film. A few hoped at
first, through the proper composition of lines and masses, to attain a visual art similar in character to music. That the abstract
film has not lived up to expectations is a story only too well
known. Despite early hopes it seems to have done little more
than the efforts of the Cubists and others in painting and sculpture. It may be illogical, but it is a stubborn fact of experience
that neither the painter nor the cinemist can seek his Idea beyond
the limits of natural material. Consequently the film is thrown
back upon this material at the same time that it is demanding a
musical freedom for its quality of motion. The result can only be
a compromise. Forced to be too realistic both for a purely plastic
art and for an abstract art, the film must hope to be able to fill
up successfully a measure of half and half.

This necessity would seem to point to a permanent equivalent
of the dance and of that harmonious extension of the dance the
Greeks called music. The same principle—temporal rhythm of
natural material—lies at the base of both, and in itself is an answer to those who do not admit the validity of formal cinema. For
always there has been an art of "visual music", perhaps before any
other art, only it has perforce been of transient interest; it is but
reasonable to assume that the film can represent this art in a
permanent and therefore more flexible form. The difference, however, is considerable. No plastic form created on a basis of real life

can involve such a conflict of means as does cinema. Its rhythm is a purification rather than a sublimation of the rhythm of nature. Nature necessarily combines the visual with the temporal, the concrete with the abstract, but to turn this into a strictly formal art is another matter altogether. While the conception is simple enough, the execution presents a formidable problem, and it is here that theory breaks down, leaving the critic to be guided by the actual achievement that has gone before.

[3]

Those films which, irrespective of purpose, may be regarded as wholly or in part formal fall naturally into three groups. At one extreme is the purely absolute film; at the other the sensuous film drama, most notably represented by the school of *Caligari*. The borderline between these two is the proving of the film-poem which, if we may be permitted to judge cinema by Aristotelian standards, will be the most satisfactory of the three. Whether this conclusion is allowable or not, the film-poem has much in its favor. I cannot think that the absolute film is superior to the abstract film. It is subject to the same criticism—that mere functional patterns, just as in painting, cannot of themselves suffice. The eye demands a familiar scene in visual art, and will not recognize the idea of beauty of the artist who does not supply such a scene. No amount of theory can dispel our instinctive conviction that a picture must be a picture of something, a statue of something, and similarly a picture of some action, and not a congeries of idle shapes and objects. Motion for motion's sake is a legitimate rule only if it is a motion familiar to us, and which we expect to see in a continuity of motion. Arbitrary motion may please us for a while, but in the picturing of movement we look for a representation of such movement as we know, the movement of life, and we do not readily respond to artificially propelled heads, coffins, violins, dice, and the like. In short we demand a causality of motion.

On the other hand, the sensuous film drama is too close to reality, and is already chiefly of historical importance. The distinction is not always made, but by this term I understand narrative which replaces the psychological semi-montage of Griffith and Pabst by a sensuous background and atmosphere. *Caligari,* of course, is the prototype (although less typical, and closer to Pabst than is generally imagined), while *Faust* is the culmination. Films of this sort still appear from time to time, but they are obvious throwbacks to the Old German school, poignant reminders of what we have lost. The great value of the school lies in the fact that it was really the final expression of the ancient German culture, of the spirit of the Nibelungenlied, Till, Duerer, and Faust. It was impossible for this spirit to see beyond the pictorial qualities of the screen. It did not and could not know the meaning of "cinematic value" as an end in itself. In utilizing the film it only sought to retell old stories and legends in an imaginative medieval setting composed for the purpose. When Murnau, therefore, in *The Last Laugh* handed over, as it were, the leadership of German cinema to Pabst, and revealed in the perfection of *Faust* that the old spirit was dead, there was no one to take up where the Germans had left off. Modern cinemists are at the beginning rather than the end of a tradition, and want either some form of montage, or formal cinema by way of genuine filmic means and not simply a filmic background. The old films can always be inspiring for their static qualities, but as a technical genre they belong to the past.

If I have not been too indefinite there should be a certain amount of room between the two groups I have just mentioned, room for action that is rather a pattern in itself than played within a pattern. Such cinema will avoid the exaggerated purity of the abstractionists and the absolutists, as well as the impressionistic counterpoint of the Germans. In it the elements will be controlled and unified to produce an aesthetic whole, which will yet be credible and reasonable. Normally it will depict human beings, for the same reasons that the best painting and sculpture does; normally it will, however, in contradistinction to painting and sculpture, be artificially or formally composed, although some future genius may succeed with sheer naturalism. It will, moreover, have space for abstract or absolute sequences, which may perhaps be compared to figures of speech in literature.

To build on practice; it is more important to give experimenters a free hand than to try to lay down for them laws which must inevitably be superseded. It is, however, the critic's privilege to cast ahead and indicate the general scope of a subject, as it seems to him, and I think it is not too much to claim that, of the several divisions of formal cinema, that roughly defined by the term film-poem is the most likely to be the cinema of the future.

Experimental Cinema #5, 1934.

WHAT IS A MOTION PICTURE?

James Shelley Hamilton

The motion picture (or cinema, or movie, whatever is the habit of calling it) is still young, as one has heard often for many years. More important, it is still growing. Growing, and therefore changing, as an art form. Ten years ago an imposing list of master-pieces had been made, and critics (not reviewers) were pretty sure they knew what "cinematic" meant, and exactly what a true movie was, aesthetically. Then sound and spoken dialogue came into use on the screen, and critics uttered pained cries: their definitions didn't fit any more: the "pure" art of cinema had been bastardized.

Such cries are still uttered from time to time, but no one who has kept his head believes any longer that good movies stopped being made when Al Jolson could be heard when he sang, as well as seen. As more years pass other things will inevitably happen to change the form and technique, and the effect, of the motion picture. Is it possible to discover if there are any fundamental principles that make a motion picture a motion picture, in the sense that poetry is poetry, or music is music, no matter what changes happen to the form?

A thing has to be before it can be defined. Many short stories had to be written before the aesthetic analyst could investigate them and decide whether merely being short made a story a short-story, or whether other elements weren't necessary. The definition of a novel, though the form is some two hundred years old, has to be kept elastic, for too much rigidity leaves no place for the occasional new departure from accepted forms which still has to be called a novel because there is nothing else to call it. Even such a mild difference in narrative procedure as Aldous Huxley uses in *Eyeless in Gaza* has made a good deal of disturbance among reviewers. Can it be a "good" novel, they ask, perceiving a difference of form without appreciating its effect. Bound by their previous conception they have to call it bad, or change their rules.

The movie is still very much in the process of becoming, and the maker of definitions has to keep open-minded. Something may come along next month—and oh would that it would!—to stretch today's notion of good movie-making into something broader and deeper.

Any such rigid definition of form as that, for instance, of a sonnet, would be rash and silly. The number of feet in the length of film used, or the dimensions of the frame in which the picture appears, obviously have little to do with the essentials. Other elements just as obviously have so much to do that merely to name them seems superfluous: that a movie is made with a camera, that it consists of a series of pictures so made, put together in such a way that when they are projected upon some surface where they can be looked at they give the illusion of continuous motion.

In other words—to go on with the obvious—those little frames of pictures are what the movie-maker uses to create with, as the musician uses tones, the writer words, the painter paint. If the pictures are colored, or have a third dimension, or a fringe of sound embroidered on the edge, there is no essential change: they still are pictures, to be put together into a movie. The important question is what does the movie-maker do with them? And most important of all, what does he do with them that couldn't be done as effectively with paint, or musical tones, or words, or on a stage with actors in the flesh?

There is a general habit of thinking of the pictured story as the most important kind of movie—it is surely the most popular, though the material movies can use is limited only by what can be visualized. News is material for motion pictures, and geography, and history, many of the sciences, even political campaigns. But not many movie houses flourish if they show only such material. People generally seem satisfied with as little actuality as possible in the movies: they want an improvement upon actuality, a selection and interpretation. For selection and interpretation you have to have understanding and imagination, and once you have those working creatively you are on the road that leads to art.

So there are two good reasons why the pictured story is worth looking into: because it is the most widely interesting, and because it is the type most likely to produce something on a level with the best in literature or the drama or music. Any intelligent person not averse to examining the emotions with the mind can work out a standard for these movies not necessarily too personal, without fear of being on the wrong track. For so far no absolutely right track has been laid out—the motion picture has no Aristotle who has set final rules for it. If one wants to go a bit further than merely saying "I like it" or "I don't like it," all that is necessary is first to understand the nature of the movie (just as one has to understand something of the nature of music before venturing to form and judgment that goes beyond mere personal preference) and then to examine the quality of the special example under consideration. Quality is of course what finally makes a movie good or bad.

Some widening or correction or reassurance of judgment almost always comes out of any intelligent discussion of movies among a group of alert and inquiring minds really interested in the essentials of what they are talking about. But if the discussion is to be more than haphazard there ought to be some aim and form to it—a kind of program, or at least something in the way of a definite subject. At the risk of sounding like an examination paper, here are some suggestions that might be considered in a preliminary inquiry into the nature of the motion picture, with some reference to the quality of special examples.

The important thing in the first place is not to be led astray by something that may turn out to be unessential, as so many aestheticians were by the silent films. Look back at a couple of "old masters," if you happen to have seen them:

The Cabinet of Doctor Caligari used to be called the perfect motion picture because it was all pictures, with no sub-titles. A few years later came *The Passion of Joan of Arc*, which seems in memory to have been pretty nearly half sub-titles, and yet it was called a great film. Did the matter of sub-titles have anything to do with the greatness of either? What is the memorable thing about them both—story, characters, or total effect? What was the effect, and how was it created? Could a play or a book have done as much and as well?

The old sub-titles are gone for the most part, though occasionally a screen-writer uses one to cover time lapses—a quicker, and, it usually seems, a lazier way of getting the story along than contriving that the story get itself along. Speech has taken their place, and the term "talkies," which isn't heard so much now, is really its own criticism of itself: it implies that there is more talkie than movie, that the screen uses words more than action. What is the limit where a motion picture contains too much talk to be a true motion picture? You hear a man making a speech in a newsreel— we see it on a screen, created by the machinery of motion pictures but no more what we mean by a movie than a man exercising on a rowing machine is what we mean by a boat-race. Often in "shorts" we fidget through a reel or two of chatter-chatter, usually intended to be comic—is it tiresome merely because it fails to be funny, or because after all what we are looking for is to see something happening?

The heart of the question seems to lie in the word itself: motion picture, movie. There is movement in it. It is getting along, in some direction, to some end, and getting along not only in the dimension of space but in the dimension of time. One foot of film adds itself to another, and it moves. And with movies that have the greatest effect we find that they move not only intransitively, visually before our eyes, but transitively: they move the spectator, doing something to his emotions. And with all this the question of words—speech or sub-titles—is not a question of words or no words, but a question of how words (or other sound, or color, or what-not) help or hinder.

There's another point about movement: is it mere motion, which like a machine operates automatically in space, or growth, where in the dimension of time we can see and know that something is building itself, adding with each passing moment something to what has gone before and creating the illusion of a living organism?

People who take their movies as something more than mere pastime, like picking up a magazine story or casually turning on the radio, cannot help becoming critical, and as they become more consciously so they find themselves giving attention not only to how a thing is done but to what is being done, often deciding that a given thing wasn't important enough to have been done at all, however well. But leaving out the question of importance for a while, the question of quality depends to a very interesting extent on what is being attempted.

The business principle that makes all the other producers hurry to follow suit with any type of film that one of them has made a success with, supplies plenty of field for comparison of quality in similar but different attempts.

Take the perennial Western. (And by the way, why is the Western perennial? Is it anything more than the constant arrival among audiences of a new generation of youngsters to whom the type is new?) What is a Western, essentially? How is an elaborate production like King Vidor's *The Texas Rangers* any better than some film of Buck Jones', or John Wayne's, or Bob Steele's, which aren't nearly so elaborate? Do Westerns really get any better? What is the matter with them if they don't?

Take detective stories, which for some reason that hasn't been explained never used to go well on the screen in the silent days, but which flourish mightily now that the actors can talk. What made *The Thin Man* a model which every maker of detective films seems to try to follow? Was its appeal in its plot, or in something else? How far can mere plot carry a detective story to success?

Take the kid pictures—the films which exist for Shirley Temple or Freddie Bartholomew or Jane Withers, or the occasional others in which the most important character is David Holt, perhaps, or Sybil Jason or some other child. Are they for children, or about children, and are the children real? Where would *The Devil Is a Sissy* stand among such films? Have any of them any standing as real motion pictures?

Take the musicals. Those with singers—Lawrence Tibbett, Lily Pons, Grace Moore, Nino Martini. Those with dancing—the Astaire-Rogers films, or the various Melodies and Broadcasts. Are they just shows, or are some of them really movies?

There are other groups, each one of a more or less definite class, and after the more immediate personal question of whether you care for the class or not, and find entertainment in it, you can examine them more searchingly and find out where they stand among the films that are remembered, and which there is an audience for year after year.

National Board of Review Magazine, Nov., 1936.

JEAN VIGO

Siegfried Kracauer

I saw Jean Vigo for the last time in the summer of 1934. He looked even younger than he was—an adolescent with a pointed face, about to die from tuberculosis. Very few people knew his name then, or his work. *A propos de Nice* has been shown in a few theaters only, *Zero de conduite* had been considered too "harsh" for general release, and, if I am not mistaken, *Atalante* had not yet been released. As a rule, rebels are not popular, and in the motion picture industry probably less so than anywhere else. And Vigo was a rebel, on two counts: against the screen formulas and, even more intensely, against the established order of things. He used the camera as a weapon, not as an anesthetic.

In today's France, Vigo's pictures are shown in the neighborhood theaters.

VLADIMIR POZNER

Jean Vigo—who died before he was thirty, in the autumn of 1934—left only a few films. His first film, *A propos de Nice*, can only be mentioned here, since for years it has been inaccessible.

In 1933, this satirical documentary was followed by *Zero de con-duite*, a film influenced by Rene Clair and the French avant-garde, depicting a students' revolt in a boarding school. The brief series ends with *Atalanta* (1934), a masterpiece that brought Vigo to the forefront of French motion picture directors. Among them, perhaps only Vigo and the Rene Clair of the great Parisian films have been able to discover and conquer territories reserved exclusively to the film. And although Vigo lacks Clair's wonderful lightness, he surpasses him in his profound concern with truth.

His very method of composition reveals an original relation to the screen. Vigo's plots are not the classic, hermetically sealed constructions designed to produce suspense by themselves alone; rather, they are light, very loosely knit, and not at all pur-poseful. The plot of *Atalante* could not be simpler: Jean, the young master of the river steamer *Atalante*, has married Juliette, who soon longs for Paris, away from the monotony of cabin, water, and landscape. She deserts her husband, who, jealous of Paris and the whole world, would be lost in the city if it were not for Pere Jules, his old factotum: Pere Jules brings Juliette back to poor Jean. The emphasis is on the numerous little single episodes, each more pregnant with suspense than the common-place story itself. These little episodes compose the plot without, however, depending on it for structure and meaning. The open-ing passage, in which Jean and Juliette in festive attire proceed like strangers, silently, side by side, through the forest across the field to the beach, far ahead of the wedding party, is a perfect piece of poetry. By stringing his episodes like pearls, Vigo en-dows a technical fact with esthetic significance—the fact that the celluloid strip is virtually endless and can be interrupted at any time.

More important are the conclusions Vigo draws from the fact that the camera does not discriminate between human beings and objects, animate and inanimate nature. As if led by the meandering camera, he exhibits the material components of mental processes. In *Atalante* we experience with all our senses how strongly the fogs of the river, the avenues of trees, and the isolated farms affect the mind, and how the sailor's relationship to the city is determined by the fact that he looks at the lodgings perched on the quay from sea level. Other film directors, too, have identified objects as silent accomplices of our thoughts and feelings. But Vigo goes still further. Instead of simply revealing the role objects may play in conditioning the mind, he dwells upon situations in which their influence predominates, thus exploring camera possibilities to the full. And since increasing intellectual awareness tends to reduce the power of objects over the mind, he logically chooses people who are deeply rooted in the material world as leading characters of his two full-length films.

Immature boys are the heroes of *Zero de conduite*. Early in this film two of them ride to school at night in a third-class railroad compartment; it is as if they were left to themselves in a wigwam that imperceptibly fuses with their dreams. We see a man's legs on one of the benches, and then, on the other bench, we see the upper half of a sleeping traveler. This halving of the sleeper, marking him as an inanimate being, increases the impression of isolation from the world, an impression already aroused by the smoke which shuts out the world behind the car window. The partition of the compartment lies somewhat obliquely in the picture, an angle which points to the fact that this entire sequence cannot be located within real space and time. Their adventurous ride stimulates the two boys to pranks. From unfathomable pockets they produce alternately a spiral with a little ball springing out of it, a flute, shriveled toy balloons blown up by the younger boy, a bunch of goose quills with which the older one adorns himself, and finally, cigars a yard long. Photographed from below, they squat exaltedly as the smoke of the locomotive mingles with the smoke of the cigars, and in the haze the round balloons float to and fro in front of their pale faces. It is exactly as if the two in their magic wigwam were riding through air. With a jerk, the sleeper falls. "*Il est mort!*" One of the boys cries, frightened. With the balloons hovering around them, they get off the train; outside we read the sign: *Non Fumeurs*, and immediately the wigwam is retransformed into an ordinary railroad compartment.

While the objects in *Zero de conduite* participate in childish play or occasionally frighten the boys, they become fetishes in *Atalante*. As such, they possess Pere Jules. Michel Simon's Pere Jules ranks among the greatest characters ever created on the screen by any actor or director. The old man, a former sailor, takes care of the *Atalante* in company with his accordion, innumerable cats, and a feeble-minded boy. Grumbling to himself inarticulately, he walks up and down between the steering wheel and the cabin in a sort of daze—so much one with the *Atalante* that he seems carved out of its planks. All that affects him is physical actions, which he, however, does not experience consciously, but immediately translates into similar actions. Jean lifts Juliette with whom he stands back to back: witnessing this amorous scene, Pere Jules begins to shadow box. Juliette tries on him the coat she is sewing: the coat induces him to imitate an African belly dancer, and since Africa to him is not far from San Sebastian, he avails himself of the same coat, as he would of a red cloth, to irritate an imaginary bull. He does not remember the events, but reproduces them following certain signals.

Instead of using the objects at his disposal, he has become their property. The magic spell they cast over him is revealed in a unique episode in which Pere Jules shows Juliette all the mementos he has brought home from his voyages. The piled-up treasures which crowd his cabin are depicted in such a manner that we feel they have literally grown together over him. To evoke this impression Vigo focuses on the objects from various sides and on many levels without ever clarifying their spatial interrelationship—using nothing but the medium shots and close-ups made necessary by the narrowness of the cabin. The alarm clock, the musical box, the photograph portraying Jules as a young man between two women in glittering dresses, the tusk, and all the bric-a-brac emerging little by little, form an impenetrable wickerwork constantly interspersed with fragments of the old man himself: his arm, his tattooed back, his face. How accurately this piecemeal presentation renders his complete submission to the rarities around him can also be inferred from the fact that he preserves in alcohol the hands of a deceased comrade. The idols, on their part, display triumphantly their inherent powers. At the head of their great defile Vigo marches a doll which, when set into motion by Pere Jules, conducts mechanical music from a puppet show like a bandmaster. The magical life of the doll is transmitted to the curiosities that follow in the parade.

" . . . *un documentaire bien romantique*," Brasillach writes in his *Histoire du cinema* about *A propos de Nice*, "*mais d'une belle cruauté, ou les ridicules des dames vieilles et amoureuses, des gigolos et de la bourgeoisie decadente étaient ferocement stigmatises.*" Responding to the overwhelming appeal of material phenomena, Vigo, however, more and more withdrew from social criticism. In *Atalante* it appears, indeed, as if he actually had wanted to affirm an attitude hostile to intellectual awareness. Could it be, then, that Vigo's career had taken a retrogressive course? But in *Zero de conduite* satire still manifested itself, and perhaps he indulged in the magic of mute objects and dark instincts only in order, some day, to pursue more thoroughly and knowingly the task of disenchantment.

The Hollywood Quarterly, April, 1947.

PRELIMINARY TOPICS
IN DEFINING CINEMA

Paul Goodman

To define cinema, as music may be defined as tone in movement, is extraordinarily difficult, yet fundamental; so I trust the reader will bear with me while I lead him through the mazes of a topical discussion and offer no principles but only thorny problems. Then, first, comparing cinema with other arts: the only arts that seem to be obviously unlike cinema are sculpture and architecture, apparently because they do not move. (One may take a cinema of a building, carrying the camera around it; but the quality of this will not be architectural.)

Yet paintings and photographs do not move and are like cinema. The first name of cinema is moving-picture; the first film, I think, showed a walking horse, and the remarkable thing about it, clearly, was that it was a photograph that moved. Critics of a more advanced state of the screen must not forget this primitive magic, yet few consider it any more. Elie Faure, in a little book called *The Art of Cineplastics*, thinks almost entirely in pictorial terms, in terms of the plastic composition of color or shade coming into movement, as if a Vermeer or a Van Eyck were to come to life. (This is the effect, e.g., of many parts of Murnau's *Sunrise*.) Faure, to be sure, has the pre-occupations of a critic of painting; but when Eisenstein, on the other hand, speaks contemptuously of those who judge a scene of cinema as they would a landscape, he betrays a preoccupation with the cutting-room and the script, rather than with the screen. The fact seems to be this: so long as we remain within one shot or scene and have no cut or dissolve, therefore no montage, the criteria of a moving picture are relevant, and painting and photography offer valuable suggestions; but once we cut, edit, and construct the film, the whole effort is to break down the quality of painting or photography, to effect something else. To effect what? One possible answer to this brings us back again to painting, namely: to effect, by the analytic device of montage, a compound image. Seymour Stern, for instance, speaks of the basic image-idea that creates and synthesizes the analytic montage. (*Experimental Cinema*, Feb., 1930.) Is this unlike a cubist decomposition? I think not. But obviously the cinematic analysis or decomposition can be either of a still image or of a moving image, such as breaking a dish. These are two kinds.

On the other side, let it be remembered that the effect of a still picture is altogether unlike that of a moving one. As Faure himself says: "Stop the film a moment, not even a memory of the filmic emotion survives." Yet there is also such a thing as motionless cinema, where the motionless shot is not still, but is the limit of slowing down. How is this paradox to be analyzed?

A second name of cinema is photoplay, *Lichtspiel*. Once past the stage of mechanical experimentation, cameras immediately began to turn comedies and melodramas, as if the theater were the nearest art. And except for the fact that novels, with their wider scenic scope and more diffuse plot, have largely taken the place of plays, this has since been "the common practice of mankind." The first duty of cinema, holds a critic of this persuasion (Buckle: *Mind and the Film*) is to tell a story; the first critical discussions should concern the fundamental instincts governing human action, namely: Love, Anger, Fear, Self-Preservation. And so he goes on. This, I repeat, is the general current practice of cinema, reflected in the newspaper reviews which mainly describe the plot. At the same time, there is a strong supposition that this practice, of using cinema to tell more or less complicated stories, is absurd malpractice and a perversion of the proper nature of the art. For it is not evident, but has only been taken for granted, that the end of cinema is to tell a story. Let us dwell on this awhile.

Eisenstein, in the manner of Hegelian dialectics, distinguishes two periods of the relation of literature and cinema: the first literary period, when the camera worked over the finished product of book or stage, to heighten it emotionally; and this led to the discovery of "trick photography"—and the present literary period, when only the literary conception is taken, and is worked up cinematically, the photography now being at the heart of the invention. (*Close-Up*, April, 1929; cf. *Film Art*, Spring, 1934.) This insistence that the conception be treated cinematically is, of course, shared by all the critics, by Braver-Mann, Arnheim, Klingler, Pudovkin. But the question is this: ought the conception itself to be literary? or cinematic? (and what does cinematic mean?). Eisenstein defines his present practice as "the direct screening of class-useful conceptions," and this is indeed the nature of *The General Line*, for instance. The conception is literary. And though, almost continually, the screen is occupied by scenes of cinema, these are ordered not to their own end but to the end of the story.

Let us take another tack. Rudolph Arnheim, in his book *Film*, points to certain incompatibilities between literature and cinema (putting aside for the moment the talkies): "A simple phrase like 'she lived absolutely alone in her cottage' is extraordinarily hard to express on the screen, because it does not indicate a passing event, but a permanent condition which cannot easily be made clear in any momentary scene." Again, he points to the fact that images used as symbols—e.g., a head of Lenin—are not so universally intelligible as words; but used as pictures in a pictorial movement they are clear to all who can see and sense movement (though community of experience is necessary for any art). From such considerations, Arnheim concludes as follows: "Almost any film might be turned into a novel, but hardly any novel will make a good film." The reason for the second clause is evident, but is it so sure that any film can be turned into a novel? How does Arnheim come to this idea? Obviously because he feels that a cinema is a story, and by describing the scenes, instead of filming them, always maintaining the same story-structure, we obtain such a novel as might be written by a visualist. (Apropos, it is a curious question to what extent cinema has influenced modern prose.) But supposing the scenes of a cinema were ordered, not to telling a story, but to some more natural end? Then one could no more describe them than describe a painting or a tune. This is very important; let me illustrate: In *Potemkin* it is necessary to bring out the rebellious mood of the sailors at the putrescent food served them: Eisenstein has one of the crew break a dish on which are glazed the words "Give us this day our daily bread." This scene is considered excellent cinema, for two reasons: (a) because the incident clearly illustrates the story, (b) because it illustrates it not by literary means but by a thrilling motion, brilliantly decomposed and rebuilt by Eisenstein. Now obviously it is (b) that is cinematic, but it is (a) to which the incident is ordered. Suppose, then, the incident ordered to (b) itself, to bring out, by certain proportions, the cinematic quality of this very motion: it might then be part, for instance, of the sequence, "A locomotive rushing head-on—breaking a dish—a slow motion swan-dive backwards—culminating in a still shot of the grinning bust of Socrates." Now the incident in *Potemkin* might be put into a novel: "The sailors were so angry they broke the dishes." But the incident ordered to cinema could not profitably be told in words, but must be seen or visualized.

At risk of fatiguing the reader, let me return to this just once more. The following three propositions of B. G. Braver-Mann (in *Experimental Cinema*, Feb., 1930) seem to me typical of the way critics most often miss the point. He says:

1. "The medium of cinematic art is motion."

Yes, but what is the object imitated in that medium? Is it a story or is it the cinematic aspect of actions, thoughts, character?

2. "Motion as an art-medium is self-sufficient and has no affinity to such media as words, music, painting."

On the contrary, cinematic motion has great affinity to words, music, painting, and can therefore procure great assistance from these.

3. "Motion applied to a succession of images can transmit thought, stimulate emotion, indicate time, place, character, sound, speech, atmosphere, physical sensation, and state of mind."

Yes, yes—to a degree all of these. But what of transmitting—the proportions of cinema?

But on the reverse side, let us again stress that what I have argued is against the almost universal practice, including Chaplin and Rene Clair, Pabst, Pudovkin, and Murnau, *The Birth of a Nation* and *Potemkin*. It is perfectly evident that we have here art of a high, almost of a very high, standard. And this would be incredible if the practice of the art were altogether unnatural. This side of the argument I shall set forth in the next installment.

In important respects, cinema approximates music: and perhaps it is to this art that it should be most compared by nature, just as to literature by practice, and to photography by history and appearance. The criteria of painting, it was said above, are relevant so long as we remain within a single shot; for the movement between the shots, the movement of cutting and dissolving, music, it seems to me, furnishes important critical apparatus. Montage may be correctly, though of course only partially, described in musical terminology. For instance, the strips may be cut to proportionate lengths in waltz-time, in march-time, in common-time; this is called metric montage. It is partially the correct manipulation of such musical cutting that gives a film swing and flow. Within the scene itself there is a musical accent, perhaps the rhythm of the camera work. And the climactic progress of the film as a whole, what Potamkin used to call the "steady forward march," is not foreign to the nature of the musical climax: the thickening of the counterpoint, the freer dynamics. . . . "With the play-book before me," says the Japanese director, Shige Sudzuki, "and looking at a chronometer, I make a continuity of the film and mark musical technics on it, just as does a music conductor." (*Close-Up*, March, 1929.)

Nor must we omit the cinematic relevance of another art: miming and dancing. For it is clear that on whatever theory of cinema, the kinds of action that will be of the highest interest to us, will be the motions and expressions of human-beings. But the topics of discussion under this heading are obvious—the importance of Chaplin, of the close-up, of the closing-in of the iris to attract attention to one feature or gesture—and they need not here be drawn out.

Trend, May-April, 1935.

THE FUTURE OF COLOR

André Sennwald

To base a judgment of the color film on the success of *Becky Sharp* as a dramatic entertainment is to become the spiritual kinsman of the fellow who predicted that the automobile would never supplant the horse. *Becky Sharp* happens to be a bad picture which will probably assume a position in the history of the cinema as lofty as that occupied by an even worse picture—the first all-talking film, *Lights of New York*. The fact is that the new Technicolor process has been employed here and there in the photoplay so brilliantly as to bludgeon the intelligent spectator into the belief that color will one day become an integral element in the cinema.

Its function on the screen will be equal in importance to the function of music. It may, properly used, become as basic an element in film technique as photography and sound. *Becky Sharp*, from the color standpoint, so far surpasses the ten or twelve films which Warner Brothers produced several years ago in the two-color process as to lift color out of the novelty class and insure *Becky Sharp* a place among the distinguished milestones in the advance of the cinema.

That is approximately how this column feels about the first full-length photoplay in the new Technicolor three-color process. The critical opinion of the town, as represented in the film columns of its daily newspapers, is about evenly divided on the future of color as reflected in *Becky Sharp*. Almost unanimously the reviewers agree that the picture is a dreary film edition of a tedious dramatization of *Vanity Fair*. Thereafter they divide into two camps, consisting of those who see a revolution on the basis of the film's employment of color in the new process, and those who still want to be shown. Here are significant excerpts:

"The most important cinematic experiment since moving shadows first became articulate. As a dramatic entertainment it has its faults, and some of these stem from the experiment itself, but as the first serious step in an uncharted field it is a considerable triumph." —*The Herald Tribune*.

"Not that the black and white film is to vanish overnight, but it is in the death throes, and the knell was sounded with the arrival in glorious raiment of *Becky Sharp*. A finger pointing dramatically toward hitherto unrealized possibilities in the motion-picture art." —*The Post*.

"It is safe to say that when it is perfected further and if used with well-written stories, it will be of great help to the cinema. If not it will always remain a novelty. But if it is skillfully blended with story, acting, direction and dialogue, it can bring a tempo and an excitement to films that are missing in black and white photography." —*The World-Telegram*.

"Color photography is still in the experimental stage, but *Becky Sharp* shows the strides that have been made in the Technicolor laboratories." —*The Daily News*.

"The picture, as drama, is both helped and hindered by color. Color photography, of course, will some day be taken for granted.

That day does not seem to be yet upon us. Hollywood, cautiously watching the opening of *Becky Sharp*, need not hysterically throw away its reliable black-and-white cameras." —*The Sun.*

"This department enthusiastically contributes its vote to the assured success of *Becky Sharp*. Further, it predicts that it will be henceforth as important to the cinema as *The Jazz Singer.* —*The American.*

"A handsome production that, technically, is a great improvement over the earlier experiments in color photography. But color is still a novelty, and it is still too early to say whether, as its sponsors hope, it can replace the black and white of the screen." —*The Evening Journal.*

"The color is exquisite. Subtle olive greens, turquoises, flames, pearls are captured by the camera with accurate fidelity. No previous color picture compares with *Becky Sharp*." —*The Daily Mirror.*

Here we discover enthusiasm, uncertainty and confusion among the town's professional film-goers. Although many brief scenes in *Becky Sharp* have been pigmented with extraordinary cunning and beauty, it seems to me that the problem which faces us is that of using color not as a novelty or as an extra-curricular thrill, but as a constructive and integral element in film-making. The answer, I think, may be found in Rouben Mamoulian's magnificent employment of color, emotionally and dramatically, in the British ball in Brussels when the merry-makers are thrown into confusion and terror by the rumble of Napoleon's cannon in the distance. Here Mr. Mamoulian uses his colors, not as a merely decorative scheme, but as an authentic element in building the scene to its crisis, the hues mounting in excitement in great waves of color emotion and achieving an overwhelming climax in the angry blues and scarlets of the British officers as they rush to their posts.

The major hazard is that this precious new element may fall into the hands of the unlettered and cause such a rape of the laws of harmony and contrast, such a blare of outrageous pigmentations, that only the color-blind will consider it safe to venture inside a motion-picture theater. While men possessed of the artistic conscience of Rouben Mamoulian and Robert Edmond Jones are engaged in charting the unknown for the future use of color on the screen, we can feel reasonably safe. All of us can recall the aural bombardment which plagued us when the screen learned to talk. *Becky Sharp*, coloristically, is further advanced in this fascinating new domain than the early talkies were in their grasp of the principles of sound on film.

Becky Sharp, experimentally, is of enormous interest. Perhaps it was because of its experimental usefulness that this particular story was selected in the first place. As a testing ground for the new process, with its great variety of color blends, the early nineteenth century no doubt impressed the Technicolor sponsors as ideal in its opportunities for symphonic arrangements of brilliant colorings.

The next step, if it is to be an advance over *Becky Sharp*, must be to repress color deliberately to the needs of our modern literature and to recite films in grays and pastels and the subdued colorings of the life which we live in these 1930's. The color in *Becky Sharp* was not natural in any sense except the obvious one that it was an accurate representation of the colorings arranged by Mr. Mamoulian and Mr. Jones for the settings and characters of this particular film. On that basis it would be safe to say that color in its present stage of development is almost ideally suited to the production of screen fantasy and highly sentimental romance. But I believe it is fated to be more than that. The next great step forward must be in the direction of realism.

Meanwhile, we can thrill to *Becky Sharp* as another momentous advance in an art form which has progressed at unbelievable speed during the last thirty years. Perhaps Aldous Huxley was not jesting when he predicted that the cinema would ultimately progress beyond the talkies and become feelies and smellies.

The New York Times, June 23, 1955.

1 9 4 0 - 1 9 6 0

"The notion that a motion picture cannot be a unified work of art because it is the work of many hands is absurd. The work of a single man may lack unity if he is a poor craftsman; the work of a multitude may have magnificent unity if, as in the case of a gothic cathedral, they are unified in the spirit of creation."

MORTIMER ADLER

TUESDAY BROWN

Meyer Levin

Rarely does a new candidate appear for that select category of
motion pictures: creators who may be said to have opened new
ways for their art, the circle that includes Griffith, Chaplin,
von Stroheim, Eisenstein, Rene Clair, Pare Lorenz. Carl Lakewood is not yet known in the film world. But he has made a motion picture that will be remembered when the last billion dollars worth of Hollywood product is forgotten. He made it in De-
troit, Michigan, during the last two years, in his free time, while
holding a job as draftsman in an automobile factory.

What he has created is the epic of the life of an ordinary man,
in terms that are purely cinematic, fresh and vital with the force
of true feeling, and therefor original. *Tuesday Brown* could and
should be to filmdom what Joyce's *Ulysses* was to the literary
world a generation ago. Not that *Tuesday Brown* is "like" *Ulysses*, for it is characteristic of works of art that, while each is related
in many ways to many masterpieces, it has no precise parallel,
either in form or in spirit, among them. *Tuesday Brown* is not
highbrow cinema, as *Ulysses* was intellectual literature; it is muscular, direct, simple in total meaning. Though some of the cine-

matic methods employed by Lakewood will give added pleasure to experts, no special knowledge is needed to get the full force of their effect. There is this similarity, however: Lakewood, like Joyce, attempts to create a total relationship of man to the world he lives in: a psychic as well as a physical relationship; and Lakewood, like Joyce, uses every historic means of his medium, and invents new means in order to achieve his objective.

Pare Lorenz, the documentary poet of American life, Von Stroheim, the first great realist, Rene Clair the satirist, Eisenstein the realist symbolist, von Sternberg the imagist, even Cocteau the surrealist—all have contributed to the nevertheless individual art of Carl Lakewood. He has drawn from literary sources, and from painters too, for there are times when his scenes compose like the giant industrial frescoes of Diego Rivera; but what the film achieves, beyond form, is a sense of life itself.

From the first smoke-enhanced sunrise over the city, when the men coming off nightshift collect down the factory avenues, uniting toward the main gate, and then spreading from it like hourglass sand, diverging into the various streets of the city, there is a sense of actuality that I can remember only in one other film: a film, also, that was made outside of established studios. A dozen years ago, at the Vieux Colombier theater in Paris, I saw a German picture called *Menschen Am Sonntag*: it dealt quite nakedly with an ordinary Sunday in the lives of a few young people of Berlin. The story was of a girl going over from one man to another, during a country excursion. There was a good deal of hidden-camera street photography; and the style throughout was so utterly casual that one could have taken the entire film for a record of actual life.

That Lakewood was influenced by this film is evident, even in his title; but *Tuesday Brown* is far more than a record of casual incident. It deals, not with a cross-current created by a chance meeting, but with the organic relationship that exists in a family; it rises above the cult for the ordinary that has engendered a tendency to reduce folk to the least common denominator of thought and behavior. *Tuesday Brown*, in the manner of a Thomas Wolfe epic, exalts man himself, discovers the common

man again as an individual, without violating the idea of Brown
as representative.

It is no grain of dust that is picked up out of the flow from the
factory gates. It is Luke Brown, a highly complex character, with
passions and suppression, with elements of fine and gross; we
learn the conditionings of his character; the granite streaks that
go back through the hill-folk racial strains in him, the rounded
places where he has adjusted to his wife, the deep-echo caverns of
distant folk-lores and far historic strains. Luke Brown is representative in the sense that any other man picked out of the crowd
could have revealed as great a complexity, within the larger pattern of their place in society.

Luke pauses with his friend Matty for the afterwork drink,
a shot of corn in a tavern where baseball returns are chalked on
the wall, under a nude-girl calendar. Lakewood catches the whole
feeling of man-life in that little period between work and home,
when men try to stretch out their time together, while knowing
they must head different ways to their families. Here, too, Lakewood introduces a brilliant innovation. Doubled upon the scene
is a fleeting succession of thought-exposures, picturing the fluc-
tuation of Luke's mood. When the conversation touches upon
wives, there is an instant flow of images: the girl on the calendar,
over several wife-images: a woman placing a dish upon a table;
a woman in the beautiful instant of combing her child's hair;
a woman, mouth open, snoring in a rumpled bed; the woman
emerging, body-flushed, from a hot bath; a woman and children,
Sunday-dressed, waiting to go somewhere. All this, while Luke
Brown grouses about the foreman keeping him on nightshift. "My
old lady can't get used to it."

This touches off the objective, introduces the series of delicate
and uproarious and near-tragic, the trivial and grand maneuvers
by which Luke Brown is going to get himself back on the day
shift. The problem opens out to reveal a factory world of high
complexity, with morals of its own; while Luke and his cronies
are shown, not as people with numb, limited minds, but as wise
and nimble experts among the crags of that vast region.

The argument about how to handle the foreman continues in
Matty's car, during the shared ride home, four men clubbing to-

gether to save gas. Their talk is pure Americana, with its atmosphere both derisive and respectful of family life, with wisecracks about each man's personal situation as he drops off at his home. Most striking, though, is the unpolitical way of thought in these men, the brushing aside of great public questions, the fatalistic irony with which they regard society.

Lakewood's portrait is strangely pessimistic in this regard. These men, these citizens, he says, have lost faith; they think everything is spinach, and the only difference is the label on the can. Yet when taken in entirety the film declares faith in the common man; indeed, it exudes a Whitmanesque love of mankind.

In the awakening sequences of Luke Brown's wife, Grace, Lakewood provides another brilliant passage of psychological intimacy. His thought-images capture fully what only a few experimentalist films of the late 20's dared attempt: the relationship of dream to reality. Through a growth of street and housesounds, accented as they are to a person emerging from sleep, Grace snatches at the fleeting remnant of her dream of swimming with Luke, watching another Luke high-dive; she hears Matty's car stop, and dream-visualizes Luke entering the house; her dream-Luke pendulums between handsome and brutal, but slowly fixes into the image of the real Luke.

The few scenes of sexual transport in *Ecstasy* are only a feeble, romantic introduction to the completely natural transcription of the married relationship which Lakewood has filmed. Grace goes to the bathroom; she hesitates whether to prepare her contraceptive. There has been a series of misunderstandings, the couple's mutual time of wanting being upset by Luke's night schedule; the reticent modesties by which the marriage act is still held in respect have added to their confusion. Grace isn't sure whether he comes home tired, or whether he has stopped wanting her. Some dawns, she has been pretending to sleep through his coming home.

Now she goes out to sit with him while he eats. Luke is uncertain whether she blames him for breaking her sleep; in his hairtrigger temper, founded upon a man's sense of being bound to irksome work by family obligation, there is even an undercurrent fear that she doubts his potency. The delicacy of this scene, the breadth and depth of its sociological and psychological base, is immeasurable. Luke's careless undressing, his moment of waiting, inspecting his veins, his speculative glances at his wife, and then the early waking of the child occurring through their approaches toward each other—all these details are presented with a compassion that utterly eliminates the danger of vulgarity in such material. The numbness of the couple, the frustration between them, as they lie with their separate hungers, with the resolution so simple and yet so impossible for them, contains a pathos and a beauty almost painful to endure.

The film omits nothing. Lakewood has worked as a pure artist, with no thought of eventualities. It is conceivable that some sections of *Tuesday Brown* could be cut for public showing without impairing the vitality and drama of the whole; but the question will probably never arise since commercial distributors are unlikely to become interested in a work so purely conceived.

While Luke falls into an unpeaceful sleep, his wife, starting the children to school, rehears her unsatisfactions in her mind. Suicide thoughts, murder-fantasies are not excluded; the woman is goaded by economy-tasks, by unfulfilled desires, by the myriad irritations that exist for people who never quite have security and comfort. The compromises made with cheer, in a time of marital adjustment, are now irksome, infuriating.

Through ensuing days, the jarred family relationships break further apart. The suppressed sexual antagonism becomes overt in money-bickering, in Grace's harping upon Luke's hillbilly origin, finally in insults before others. And yet there are moments when common problems draw them together, or when vacation dreams bind them. All these home-scenes are expressed in a style closely akin to the terse poetic dialogue used by Pare Lorenz in *The Fight for Life*. As the films must have been made at about the same time, the double finding of this mode of expression emphasizes its fittingness to the material of modern life.

All of Luke Brown's ambitions now center on getting back to daywork; happily, Lakewood avoids stress on the apparent symbol of coming out of night into day. In the rabelaisian dialogue of the factory sequences, as the worker craftily pursues his end, the human core of industrial life is revealed as never before. Brown's respect for the machine and for workers more specially skilled than

himself, even when one of them is a Negro, the rhythm of the
factory and the pleasure the men take in it when things are going
right—all these concepts are expressed with amazing camera ease,
amidst industrial compositions of dynamic beauty. Avoiding the
arty montages and machine abstractions that characterize the advertising documentaries of heavy industry, such as the Ford film
shown at the World's Fair, Lakewood presents the machine in its
relationship to its operator, but with a draftsman-designer's perception of utility in form.

Luke Brown feels himself slipping, makes work-errors, fears
losing his job. His sex-worried inferiority, nurtured in the general
insecurity of his background, mounts, finds expression in suspi-
cion of his wife. Ashamedly, awkwardly, he begins to spy on her.
There is a touching bit where the Browns attend a movie, and
everybody except Luke laughs at a keyhole scene.

The solution which Lakewood finds for Luke Brown has a human warmth and folk-simplicity equal to that of *The Baker's
Wife*. In Pagnol's film the community entered into and solved
the baker's most intimate problem, when he was too miserable to
bake their bread. In *Tuesday Brown*, the same idea is expressed
paradoxically through the very loneliness and isolation of the
American type. It is only when this frozen individualism is
broken into that happiness can return for Luke Brown.

Luke's mates on the job, sensing his troubles, decide to help
him get "what he needs." That cruel yet indelible moment in
The Baker's Wife when the cuckold is presented with a set of
horns is the only comparable moment in films to the stag session
at which Luke's pals,with terrible intuition, burlesque his marital
life. Carl Lakewood, brilliantly ironic, uses an empty bottle as
the theme-symbol here.

When it dawns on Brown that he is not the only one who is
suffering from the maladjustment of work-pattern to home-pat-
tern, the point of the film evolves. The grotesque, ribald, collective plea which the men address to the distant factory, whose
smokestacks form a gargantuan reiteration of the bottle-symbol,
is classic.

The factory, the men find, can very well adjust itself to rotat-
ing their night-duty. It is not a trivial issue that has been solved,
for Luke Brown has learned that his life is not really out of his

control; since he and the boys can fix a thing of this sort, they need not despair of greater problems.

If *Tuesday Brown* has a point to make, it is in this optimistic view of man's eventual power. But actually this is no message-film. It is a film that transmits man's life-experience. The cumulative scene in which Luke and his wife get together, having purposefully—with a shyness utterly touching in long married folk —sent the children to a double-feature, is a poem of carnal humanity. All elements are balanced and resolved. The instant of coition is a complete synthesis for Grace and Luke Brown; the motion of engine pistons, the upspringing of trees, the calendar girl, the hills, the doors of tenements, the smokestacks, the furnaces, the child's eyes closing, all, all find inclusion. But Lakewood does not forget reality. As Luke turns away into sleep, his wife sets the alarm clock, so he'll wake in time for work.

How Lakewood, without studio, without funds except what he could save from his salary, made this film is an epic in itself. He had to limit himself to 16mm. film; an electrical engineer helped him with sound apparatus. The result, however, cannot be called amateur, for it is far beyond the talent and skill of many professionals who are earning vast salaries in Hollywood.

The cinema is not adapted to the individual artist: he is dependent on the cooperation of so many others: actors, musicians, technicians of every sort. Because of this, and because of the expense of the medium, *Tuesday Brown* has many flaws: Lakewood is the first to admit them. The sound effects occasionally seem crude; the musical score, ingeniously pieced together from orchestral recordings, is uneven; the film begs for an original musical setting by Copland or Gruenberg. One of the miracles of *Tuesday Brown* is the quality of non-acting achieved by the players. The intimate attention given the life of Luke and Grace makes the film dependent upon the playing of these roles. Lakewood, who showed his masterpiece to a small group of critics while taking his vacation in Hollywood, confided that the Browns were played by relatives of his, who were equally interested in recording the truth of their lives. Most of the street and factory scenes were made with hidden camera.

What can be the effect of such a film, since general exhibition is not to be contemplated? Undoubtedly, the better directors and writers in Hollywood will draw from it, for many of Lakewood's innovations are adaptable to commercial films. Whether Carl Lakewood should attempt a professional career in motion pictures is debatable. Certainly a man with the patience, the intelligence, the craftsmanship that went into the making of *Tuesday Brown* could adapt himself to any set of restrictions. But the record of great innovators in Hollywood is disheartening. For *Greed*, which has outlived all the pictures of its time, and become a permanent classic, von Stroheim was broken professionally. Rene Clair's work watered down as soon as he left his own studios in France. Von Sternberg, at the height of his creative powers, is doing nothing. The studios are not crying for Pare Lorenz, from whom they have borrowed more than from any other director in the last few years. Hollywood alone is not always to blame. Some great art, like Chaplin's, fortunately exists on the popular level. Some, like Joyce's, does not.

Lakewood's work seems to me to have a dynamic appeal that would hold any audience. Yet it can be predicted with almost complete certainty that *Tuesday Brown* never will be given a chance to reach a general audience. It is not only because the film contains some frank sexual scenes that Lakewood will be neglected. If anything, these scenes, or what a censor would leave of them, would draw attention to the picture. Lakewood will be neglected because his film deals with life, because it treats the whole relationship of man to his work and his home, because it dares to suggest that the common life of the common man is the worthiest of all cinema material, because it dares to show a group of men acting together in a democratic way toward the solution of their problems. This is too strange for filmdom.

All Carl Lakewood wants is a little more time, and a little more money, for making his kind of pictures. Whether he does it entirely his own way, or partially in Hollywood's way, will not alter the fact that he has already enlarged the motion picture medium. If he does nothing more, Carl Lakewood can be certain that, in *Tuesday Brown*, he has produced a permanent work of art.

The Clipper, 1940.

ORSON WELLES'
CITIZEN KANE

Cedric Belfrage

Apparently *Citizen Kane* is not, after all, destined to go down in history as the great Hollywood myth. The press has seen it, with highballs, caviar, canapes and soft music to follow—and never were these traditional cushioners of a flop's fall so superfluous. It is not difficult to imagine the tremendous forces that have been at grips behind the scenes to decide whether it should be shown or shelved. On the one hand, a picture which the people of America will pay millions of dollars to see. On the other, the might and majesty and profits of dark yellow journalism—exposed by *Kane* so effectively, because so humanly and with such inspired craftsmanship.

There has never—and I speak as one who has attended thousands of them—been a more exciting press show. For on that screen the slaves, the houris and the camp-followers of the press lords saw some of the truth told about what enslaves, degrades and makes prostitutes of them. And at the same time they saw the whole spangled pyramid of Hollywood movie conventions, which they have had to support with their bodies in their advertisement-controlled "criticism," toppled over and left in ruins by the heroic Orson Welles and his Mercury Theater nobodies.

Heaven knows what lies or evasions many of them had to go back to their offices and write about the picture's theme— for it is very much one of those assignments in which, as we delicately phrase it, "questions of policy" are involved. But never mind. The people are going to see *Citizen Kane*, and not one of them will *be quite the same person after seeing it as he was before*. It is as profoundly moving an experience as only this extraordinary and hitherto unexplored medium of sound-cinema can afford in two hours. You leave it with regret, wishing you could see it all through again, feeling all of your old belief in the medium restored, all of your shattered illusions made whole. You become dizzy trying to recall all the good things in it, the excellencies of different kinds—lighting, composition, direction, dialogue, acting, make up, music and sound, editing and construction—which are present simultaneously at almost any moment in the picture. You realize how rusty your faculties for apprehending all the qualities of a motion picture have become, through long experience of striving to find even one good quality at a time.

Certainly it represents a revolution, and a major one, in Hollywood's approach to cinema. Trying to find in my critical memories any Hollywood celluloid that gave me a comparative emotional and artistic experience, I could only think of Chaplin's *Woman of Paris*. One recalls how the techniques used in that picture turned the studios upside down and inside out. Remember Edna Purviance waiting for the train which was to take her away from her home and her lover to Paris. She stood quite still, filling the screen, looking straight ahead of her just over the camera. The train was never shown except by shadows from its lights which passed, gradually slowing to a halt, over her face—then she walked toward the camera and out of the picture. Remember how the fact that she was being kept by Menjou in the Paris flat was shown simply by Menjou going to a drawer and taking a handkerchief—then a close-up of a collar dropping out. Simple and obvious, perhaps—but something nobody had ever done before; as exciting as the cross-cut simultaneous-action chase was in its day, and for the same reason, it was a use of the medium in an authentic way, giving it the dignity of being a medium different from the stage or any other, able to do things the others cannot do. Only the movie could in a few seconds emphasize that collar and what it meant, and so tell a whole story with it.

Since then sound has come. And one can fairly say that, if possibly there are a hundred uses of sound authentic and appropriate to the sound-film medium, at most one or two have been exploited by Hollywood. Perhaps of all the delectable flavors that linger on the palate after seeing *Kane*, the use of sound is strongest. Welles brings to the movie studio a mastery of sound technique in the radio medium, yet that mastery is such that it adapts itself to cinema with effortlessness and discrimination. The scene that everyone will be speaking about—that will be to sound-film what Chaplin's train scene was to silent-film—is the breakfast-table sequence between Kane and his first wife. The whole story of that marriage is told while they sit at the table. There are perhaps five or six lapses of time during the sequences, each one necessitating a change of costume, make-up and position by the two characters. But the dialogue runs straight on without a break, from the first scene where Kane speaks lovingly to his wife, to the last where the wife silently picks up and is hidden behind a copy of the rival paper to Kane's.

Without seeing the picture again it is only possible to touch on what it has. In sound invention Welles seems inexhaustible. He varies it constantly and shatters at every turn the complacency of the critical hack, who never quite recovers from the effect of the first two or three minutes: the main title in silence, then the use of music with the death scene of Kane, then the sudden plunge into gaudy newsreel tempo as accompaniment to the 'March of Time' film-within-a-film showing the legendary Kane's life in headlines. An essay or two could be written about the 'March of Time' sequence alone. The scenes of Kane's earlier life are scratched as if the film were taken from newsreel archives, and a camera of early days has presumably been used, exposing fewer frames to the second than the cameras of today. The effect of the 'real thing' is quite startling.

But the script, the approach to and treatment of the material, is a revolution in itself. It does everything that cannot, must not

be done according to Hollywood's dreary 'box-office' conventions. The story of a man's life begins with his death: he
speaks a single word which all by itself gives every foot that
follows pace and suspense. His story is unfolded through the
efforts of a 'March of Time' scout to discover the significance of
this deathbed word: the strange word "Rosebud." You cannot possibly guess the answer, and the investigator never finds it, though
Welles gives it to the audience in the final scene of all. The
worst 'crime' of the script—its most fascinating and praiseworthy
feature—is that it not only darts about in time from Kane's boy-
hood to his old age, back to his heyday as a newspaper publisher,
back again to his first day on his first paper, on again suddenly
to his political and personal decay; not only that, but that it
shows the same events several times over. But as each time they
are seen through the eyes of a different person, the repetitions
do more to build the whole structure of the character and his
environment than new scenes could do. Here we are really in
the cinema medium, in that and nothing else. What other
mediums could show so forcefully that truth is not merely objective, but subjective also and at the same time? Not even the
novel.

And what all this does is to make Kane the most three-
dimensional human being who ever walked and talked on the
screen—I would almost say the only one. Welles does not merely
show us one aspect of the man and pound on it. He comes not
to praise nor to indict Kane, but to reveal him, as he is and as others
see him. The result is that profound pity is stirred up in the audience, and the indictment is not of a man but of environ-
ments and social and economic factors which make him what
he becomes. The Hollywood axiom that men are born good or
bad, and that wrongs and tragedies occur because Mr. Bad temporarily triumphs over Mr. Good, is shown up for the infantile
and completely shopworn thing it is.

The implications of *Citizen Kane* for Hollywood and its future
products can hardly be estimated at this time. A big man in the
studios who was among those privileged to see *Kane* soon after
it was finished, is said to have declared that not Hearst, but the
top writers and sound men and cameramen and other experts
had reason to be scared silly by what the picture revealed. He

meant that *Kane* showed them all up as incompetents who need to go back to school to learn the first principles of the medium.

I do not share his concern for these people. Certainly, Hollywood has an extra-large quota of those phonies in high places who infest every sphere from politics to waterproof roofing. Anything in the way of showing them up and kicking them around that *Kane* can do will be a service to art and mankind. But by no means all of the craftsmen who have not been doing the things *Kane* does are 'shown up' by *Kane*. The reason they have not done these things is not that they cannot do them but that they have not been allowed to do them.

Imagine, just for example, a regular Hollywood writer of even the most eminent class daring to submit to his producer a script like *Kane*'s! Imagine a make-up man daring to allow real sweat and agony to disorder the hair and face of the heroine as she comes out of a stupor after taking poison! Imagine a set designer putting the characters under real ceilings only a foot or two above their heads! Imagine a cameraman placing his lights so that almost half the time the faces are in shadow! Preposterous! Throw them out!

Yet does any film-goer really think that only Orson Welles and his staff are *capable* of such things? He need not think so. To say that there are in Hollywood a score of cameramen, a score of writers, a score of sound experts, a score of make-up artists—all equal to Orson's men in their own field—is probably to underestimate. For years they have been hoping and trying for a chance to show their skill and originality, but always the film salesman, speaking through the producer, has had the last word; and the film salesman is one trained in not seeing the wood for the trees. Those who are honest in Hollywood know that the regular craftsman, who earns his salary in studios year in and year out, is not allowed to show originality save within the tiny limits that the box-office tradition has laid down. Only when it is a best-selling novel does Hollywood make a *Grapes of Wrath*. And only an Orson Welles or a Chaplin, whose names cast a spell of magic even over the sales force and who are quite independent financially, can break the spells that bind the rank and file to formula. The slaves and houris of Hollywood are like the slaves and houris of Kane's empire, except that the chains of some of them are made of platinum. Yet when a Welles does come along and break the spell, and the box-office tune changes, the effect is like the big scene in *The Sleeping Beauty*. Suddenly tongues begin to talk, brains to operate, everything to move again.

It is just about certain that we shall now see another of Hollywood's copy-cat orgies, with whole films in which nobody's face is ever seen at all, time sequence is mixed up like a Christmas pudding, and every time lapse is shown by continuous dialogue over changing pictures of the same people. But with that, there will also be the release of a whole storehouse of original invention and craft skill which has been bottled up.

None of this is intended as any detraction from the stature of Orson Welles. Hollywood has no score, no dozen, of Welles'. Probably it has only one. He is bigger than any of them, or he could not have put *Citizen Kane* across. He would, I believe, be the first to admit that the things that seem miraculous in *Kane* could, taken individually, have been equalled by many other craftsmen in the departments concerned. But the unique quality he has is the ability to lead and to coordinate the skilled work of others. He does not try to tell the specialists on his staff how to play their own game, but recognizes the skill of each, and gives it full expression within a disciplined and ordered framework which can display it at its best. That, at least, is the impression *Kane* gives me. It is the work of many artists and yet, with and above that, the work of one, as great works of art in any medium have always been up to now. It is correctly described as "By Orson Welles"—not "produced" or "directed" or "from a story" by Welles, but *by* him. And because it is all *by* him, because of his conception and coordination of the work, his collaborators on camera and art direction and sound and all the rest shine more brightly.

He is the biggest man in Hollywood today. And he is the Prince Charming whose bold, smacking kiss on the brow of a bewitched art puts us all in his debt.

The Clipper, May, 1941.

CINEMA AS AN ART FORM

Maya Deren

Even the most cursory observation of film production reveals that the entire field is dominated by two main approaches: the fiction-entertainment film, promoted internationally by commercial interests; and the documentary-educational film, promoted by individuals and organizations interested in social reform, visual education and cultural dissemination. What is conspicuously lacking is the development of cinema as an art form—concerned with the type of perception which characterizes all other art forms such as poetry, painting, etc., and devoted to the development of a formal idiom as independent of other art forms as they are of each other.

The seriousness of this gap in our cultural development is in no way lessened by the utilitarian validity of the camera as an instrument for recording and infinitely reproducing imaginative or factual material which would otherwise be accessible to a very limited audience. Nor should this lack of cinematic form be obscured by the growing body of sometimes sensational film techniques which are developed and exploited in the interest of a more effective rendition of the subject matter.

However, the most serious aspect of the entire situation is the passive acceptance and casual neglect of this state of the cinema by those whose active, compulsive interest and devotion is responsible for the varying but constant vitality of their art forms. This passivity on the part of those who should, presumably, be the most actively interested, is the more serious since it derives not from an innocent ignorance of cinematic possibilities, but constitutes a reaction to the apparent failure of the film avant-garde of France and other countries. It is true that, out of the flurry of cinematic experiments which marked the twenties and early thirties, only a few emerge as art expressions of lasting, intrinsic value. The great majority of them are of interest as period-pieces, symptomatic of a given stage of film history. But it is false to deduce from this, and from the dwindling away of the movement as a whole, that there is something in the very nature of film-making which precludes the possibility of its development as an art form.

It is true that an anlysis of the failure of the first film-avant-garde would seem to indicate certain formidable and paralyzing conclusions. First among these is that since the production of films is necessarily expensive (much more so than the production of a poem or a painting) they must appeal to large audiences in order to meet their expenses—those very audiences who daily indicate their approval of the present Hollywood product. Second, but no less important, it seems that the machinery, the enormous personnel of assistant directors, cameramen, lighting men, actors and producers, represents a kind of collective monster who, standing between the artist and the realization of his vision, is bound to mangle any delicate or sensitive impulse. This is an obstacle which the poet, in his direct control over words, and the painter in his direct relationship to the canvas, does not confront. Finally, the use of the camera as a utilitarian instrument for recording remains such a fertile field of activity that a completely creative use of it will remain, both to potential producers and to potential audience, a rather superfluous excursion.

The basic fallacy in this entire line of argument lies in the fact that those who advance it have (unconsciously, to be sure) been the victims of elaborate propaganda. The cosmic production figures which Hollywood takes great care in making public, represent a typically grandiose conceit. In Hollywood let no one be guilty of achieving something with less expense, less fanfare and less trouble than can possibly be employed, for in that glittering system of values, economy of any kind constitutes a debasement. In Hollywood logic, this is sound enough, for if a film is dependent upon the recording of reality, or rather its *papier-mâché* stand-in, then all possible lavish care must be taken in the construction of that reality—from the star (with her background of publicity, make-up men, etc.) to the real mink-lined dress in which she will dance. If, however, a film were itself, through camera and cutting, to create a reality, the star salaries, the set-builders, the costumers, the full orchestrations, the million-dollar gag writers, the fantastic hierarchy of executives and overhead would disappear. A film can be treated on 16mm. for varying sums of from $500 to $10,000. Once this is achieved, the problem of the mass audience vanishes, for the audience which supports (in modest style, to be sure) the other art forms, is also sufficient to return such relatively modest production costs.

Moreover, the monstrous division of labor which characterizes the industry and makes of a film an assembly line product—passing from idea-man to writer to screen-play writer to shooting-script writer to actor (while the electricians and the cameramen are engaged in another section of it), and so on until the dismal end—this is not only unnecessary, but completely destructive to the idiom. Intrinsic integrity is possible only when the individual who conceives the work remains its prime mover until the end, with purely technical assistance where necessary.

It is true that even with these simplifications, the magnitude of the purely practical problems of film-making is rather unique; but it is also true that, whatever they are, these remain problems of execution only, and should not be confused with the creative and esthetic problems of conception. Nor do they excuse films from incorporating those values which we expect to be present in other works of art.

When we agree that a work of art is, first of all, creative, we actually mean that it creates a reality and itself constitutes an experience. The antithesis of such a creative work is the merely communicative expression whose purpose it is to register, through description an existent reality or an experience. When the created reality differs from the existent reality only by subtle variations, or when great skill and accuracy are brought to the description of an extra-ordinary reality, the distinction between the products seems almost obliterated. It resolves itself into a question of form, which I shall discuss later.

What is important, however, is that the descriptive expression approaches the creative expression when (as in all creative expression) it is devoted to the experience of reality rather than reality itself. It is revealing that the best use of cinematic form (camera, editing, etc.) appears in those commercial films which seek to describe an abnormal state of mind and its abnormal perception of reality.

The consistent popularity of horror films, on one level, and of "psychological" films, on another, testifies to the seductive quality of experiential reality as subject matter for cinema, since cinema is uniquely capable of presenting the unbelievable with a show-it-to-me convincingness. It is significant that Hollywood conceives intense experience to be the particular attribute of abnormality either in the environment (horror films) or in the individual "psyche" (psychological films). The implication is, that non-objectively-real, imaginative force (and here the subconscious appears as a manifestation of the supernatural) may be interesting, but that they are essentially malevolent. In the end, the imagination as a way of life does not pay. The imaginative individual is represented either as a psychic criminal who will receive his just deserts at the hands of a society determined to re-establish the same way of life; or as a psychically diseased organism which should be restored to a normal condition.

Thus, the imaginative experience which is for the artist a desired normality, is for the motion picture industry a dangerous, psychic illegality. As producer of a "mass art," the industry assumes a social responsibility. Accepting a predisposition towards evil in even the most innocent, it provides them with catharsis through the vicarious experience of its seductive aspects. At the same time it threatens them with dire consequences should they replace the vicarious experience with the direct.

In devoting at least some attention to the powerful potentialities of the imaginative experience, the industry has been more acute than that considerable body of theoreticians who hold that a "mass art" should concern itself with the common problems of a common, objective reality in terms of a common denominator of perception. Actually the distilled, experiential emotion of an incident is more universal and timeless than the incident itself. Fear, for example, as a subjective experience is universal as the incidents of reality in which it arises are singular. Yet these critics claim that a work of the imagination is an esoteric object, accessible to the comprehension only of a select few.

It is therefore relevant to underline here the fact that the appreciation of a work based on experiential, or inner, realities consists not in a laborious analysis based on the logic of a reality which a 'prepared' spectator brings to the work. It consists, rather, in an abandonment of all previously conceived realities. It depends upon an attitude of innocent receptivity which permits the perception and the experience of the new reality. Once this reality has been perceived and experienced, its logic may be deduced if one wishes. Such a deduction is not necessary to the perception and can only follow it as a secondary activity, much as an analysis of love, for example, can only follow upon the experience but can never induce it.

The audience for art is limited not by ignorance nor by an inability to analyze, but by a lack of innocent receptivity. The defensism which is responsible for this reluctance to surrender one's own reality, at least temporarily, in order to experience another, is symptomatic of a social condition for which the artist is not responsible. It is based on the fact that if one concedes validity to contemporary realities other than one's own, the self-righteous convictions—those "absolute" truths—upon which social organization is based, are undermined. To this the average social being is instinctively and traditionally opposed.

At the opposite pole to the objective realists stand the psycho-socio-analysts, a movement which has gained impetus from the self-conscious alignment of the surrealists with Freudian and political theory. Here, any expression is regarded as a compulsive confessional, and a comprehension of it is considered dependent upon an analysis of the relationship of the images to the psyche of their source.

The most interesting results of this method occur in the work of a few highly intelligent, sophisticated film-critics who regard commercial films as the somnambulistic confessionals of modern society. They proceed on the assumption that the significant meanings are not so much incorporated in the intended statement (which is the case with a work of art) but are concealed in its decorative periphery and in the relationships between the statement and its source.

The psycho-analytical approach is also rewarding in a comprehension of fantasy. In Hollywood films the significant meanings are derived from an analysis of the morally-determined (both conscious and unconscious) censorships which give form, through limitation, to the work. In fantasy such censorships are presumably absent and the organizational integrity (hence the significant meaning) of these completely compulsive projections of psychic imagery, resides forever in its particular psychic source.

But if the psycho-analytical approach is brought to a truly creative, imaginative work of art, it yields a distorted interpretation. For such a work, although it is also based (like fantasy) on the personal psyche, is a process in which the raw materials of fantasy are assorted, selected and integrated in terms of a dominant idea or emotion. The energies of the artist are devoted to so mating his psychic images with the art instrument that the resultant product is imbued with a vitality independent of its source. Thus it is conceived, shaped, fed and formed towards the day of its emergence from the parent body as an independent, organized form. As such, its reality and meaning are contained within itself and in the dynamics of the interrelationships of its component parts; even though the nature of that reality and dynamic is determined by the conceptual sources from which it derives.

Art is distinguished from other human activities and expression by this organic function of form in the projection of imaginative experience into reality. This function of form is characterized by two essential qualities: first, that it incorporates in itself the philosophy and emotions which relate to the experience which is being projected; and second, that it derives from the instrument by which that projection is accomplished.

While the relationship of form to content has been given much consideration and recognition, the role of the instrument, in the case of cinema particularly, deserves special attention. The relationship of the instrument to the form—the oneness between them—is clear enough in painting, where the form of painting is one with paint and brush; or in poetry, where the form is one with words. Here the conception of technique is expressed in the somewhat idealized notion that the brush of a painter should act, almost, as an organic extension of the hand. But to think of the mechanism of the cinema as an extension of human faculties, is to deny the advantage of the machine. The entire excitement of working with a machine as a creative instrument rests, on the contrary, in the recognition of its capacity for a qualitatively different dimension of projection. That is why, in cinema, the instrument (and by this I mean both the camera and the cutting of the film) becomes not a passive, adjustable conveyor or formal decisions, but an active, contributing formative factor.

The mechanical similarity between the lens and the eye is largely responsible for the use of the camera as a recording, rather than as a creative, instrument, for the function of the eye is to register. However, it is in the mind behind the eye that the registered material achieves meaning and impact. In cinema this extension has been ignored. The meaning of the incident or experience is here made an attribute of the reality in front of the lens rather than a creative act on the part of the mechanism (including the human being) behind the lens.

In keeping with this theory of the camera as a registering eye, there is a substantial school of thought which holds that the documentary film, by exploiting the capacity of the camera to record reality, constitutes the cinematic art form. Certain sequences from *Fighting Lady* (a war documentary), in which enemy planes are engaged in combat and are strafed at close quarters, are advanced as an example of great cinematic achievement. Actually, these sequences were achieved as follows: the camera shutter was connected to the gun in such a way that it was automatically released when the gun was fired. These sequences are, then, the result of the automatic functioning of a brainless mechanism which operated in synchronization with another mechanism, a gun, which was operated because of the desire to kill. This, as a motivation, has obviously little in common with the motivation of art.

When the camera is used to register (for infinite reproduction) either theater, or a picturization of fiction, or a so-called 'objective' reality, there is no more oneness between form and instrument than there is between the poem and the typewriter. But whereas the typewriter can hardly be considered capable of creative action, the camera is, potentially, a highly creative instrument.

We are, however, in a period in which the reporter, the international correspondent, stands as a Man of Letters in the public mind. All who have read fine poetry could not confuse even the finest reportorial account with a poem. Documentaries are the visual counterparts of reportorial dispatches, and bear the same relationship to cinema art as the dispatches do to poetry. If, particularly, in film, the flowering of the documentary has almost obscured all else save the 'entertainment' film, it is because the events and accidents of reality are, today, more monstrous, more shocking, than the human imagination is capable of inventing. The war gives rise to incidents which are not only beyond the inventive power of the human imagination, but also beyond its capacity, almost, to believe. In this period, where we are concerned with the unbelievableness of incidents, we require a reportage and a proof of their reality. But the great art expressions will come later, as they always have; and they will be dedicated, again, to the agony and the experience rather than the incident.

What has been most responsible for the lack of development of the cinematic idiom is the emphatic literacy of our age. So accustomed are we to thinking in terms of the continuity-logic of the literary narrative that the narrative pattern has come to completely dominate cinematic expression in spite of the fact that it is, basically, a visual form. We overlook the fact that painting, for instance, is organized in visual logics, or that music is organized in tonal-rhythmic logics, that there are visual and auditory experiences which have nothing to do with the descriptive narrative.

Once we arrive at an independent cinematic idiom, the present subservience of cinema to the literary story will appear unbelievably primitive. It will seem comparable to those early days when the airplanes flew above and along the highway and railroad routes. The fact that they moved by air—a dustless, faster, pleasanter method than railroad or automobile—does not negate the fact that they traveled by earth, not by air. It is also true that, before one could travel really by air, many instruments, techniques, etc., had to be developed. But the fact is that if these efforts to discover the element air—as contrasted to the elements earth and water—had not been made, airplane travel would have remained a merely minor, quantitative improvement over earthly locomotion and would never have so qualitatively affected our concepts of time and space and our relationship to them.

There are also those who, riding in an airplane, turn their attention to recognizing earth landmarks and who complain for the lack of bird songs and flower perfumes. In their fixation upon the familiar and the recognizable, they fail to enlarge their experience. As long as we seek for literature in cinema, whose peculiar beauty and creative potentialities have hardly been touched, it will be denied development.

The fact that an individual may find walking in the country more satisfying than swimming in the ocean or flying through the air is a question of his own personal preference; but it is only in terms of personal disposition that preferential comparisons can be made between experiences which differ qualitatively. Moreover, ideally, such personal preferences and predispositions should not be permitted to minimize the value of an experience which differs, qualitatively, from that towards which the individual may be predisposed.

I hope therefore that it is clear that, in my repeated references to literature and other art forms, in my insistence upon the independence of cinema from them, and in my suggestion that, as an art form, cinema seems especially appropriate to some of the central problems of our time, I am not implying a comparative value judgment. On the contrary, by insisting upon its independence from other art forms, I strike at the very heart of the growing tendency to think of motion pictures as a somehow superior method of communicating literary or theatrical experience. (Dance, for example, which, of all art forms would seem to profit most by cinematic treatment, actually suffers miserably. The more successful it is as a theatrical expression, conceived in terms of a stable, stage-front audience, the more its carefully wrought choreographic patterns suffer from the restiveness of a camera which bobs about in the wings, on-stage for a close-up, etc. . . . There is a potential filmic dance form, in which the choreography and movements would be designed, precisely, for the mobility and other attributes of the camera, but this, too, requires an independence from theatrical dance conceptions.)

The development of cinematic form has suffered not only because the camera has been used almost exclusively to pictorialize literature and to document reality, but also because it came into a world in which other art forms had already been firmly established for centuries. Painters, for instance, inspired by the possibilities of this new medium, brought to it the traditions of the idiom with which they were first preoccupied. Consequently, in many abstract films, the film frame has been used as an animated canvas. But these are developments in painting rather than in film. In most cases the creative energy of the artists who came from other fields was dedicated first of all, to the arrangement of objects in front of the lens rather than the manner of manipulating the mechanism behind the lens.

Nor does the direction of cinematic form consist in a wide-eyed game with the camera as if it were a new toy in the hands of a curious, clever child. It does not consist in making things appear or disappear, go fast or slow, backwards or forwards, just because a camera can do that. This results merely in a sensationalist, virtuoso exercise of skills and techniques. Cinematic form is more profound than that. It is a concept of the integration of techniques, a search for the meaning of a skill.

Cinema—and by this is understood the entire body of technique including camera, lighting, acting, editing, etc.—is a time-space art with a unique capacity for creating new temporal-spatial relationships and projecting them with an incontrovertible impact of reality—the reality of show-it-to-me. It emerges in a period marked, simultaneously, by the development of radio in communication, the airplane and the rocket-ship in transportation, and the theory of relativity in physics. To ignore the implications of this simultaneity, or to consider it a historical coincidence, would constitute not only a failure to understand the basic nature of these contributions to our civilization; it would also make us guilty of an even more profound failure, that of recognizing the relationships of human ideology to material development.

The nazi concept of racial integrity, for instance, belongs to that period in which a mountain between two valleys served to localize the tribes of each. In such primitive civilization, subjects to all sorts of natural disasters, rigidly localized by geographical and material restrictions, a philosophy which placed the unity of the tribe above all else was appropriate. The isolation gave reason to an absolutistic philosophy of time and space. The need for tribal unity gave reason to the concept of absolute authority in the state, religion and mores in general.

Today the airplane and the radio have created, in fact, a relativistic reality of time and space. They have introduced into our immediate reality a dimension which functions not as an added spatial location but which, being both temporal and spatial, relates to all the other dimensions with which we are familiar. There is not an object which does not require relocation in terms of this new frame of reference, and not least among these is the individual.

Imperceptibly, almost, this sense of relativism has begun to influence our thinking. In spatial terms, for example, the absolutistic differentiation between here and there loses meaning as here and there, being so mutually accessible, become, in effect, almost identical. In terms of time, the chronology of the past, present and future has also increasingly lost its meaning as we have come to understand the continuity of the past with the future—and, prodded on by the actual acceleration of historical processes, to deal with the present moment as an extension of the past into the future rather than as an independent temporal period.

Moreover, because of the quality of this new referential frame, validity is no longer a function of the object itself. It has become, instead, a function of the position of that object in the constellation of which it is part. The concept of absolute intrinsic values, whose stability must be maintained, gives way to the concept of relationships which ceaselessly are created, dissolved and re-created and which bestow value upon the part according to its functional relation to the whole. We face the problem of discovering the dynamics of maintaining an unstable equilibrium.

The individual, deprived of the absolutisms which molded the moral pattern of his life, is faced with a critical, desperate need to discover in himself an integrity at once constant enough to constitute an identity and adjustable enough to relate to an apparently anarchic universe whose gravities, revolutions and constellations operate according to a logic which he has yet to discover. The solution does not rest in the infinite adjustments and revisions of a Ptolmeaic system of description.

Cinema, with its capacity to manipulate time and space seems eminently appropriate as an art form in which such problems can find expression. By manipulation of time and space I do not mean such established filmic techniques as flash-backs, condensation of time, parallel actions, etc. . . . these affect not the action itself, but the method of revealing it. In a flash-back there is no implication that the usual chronological integrity of the action itself is in any way affected by the process, however disrupted, of memory. The turning of spring into winter by one swift dissolve is a condensation of the presentation of the seasons, but does not affect the implication of customary seasonal rhythms. Parallel actions—as in a sequence when we see, alternately, the hero who rushes to the rescue and the heroine, whose situation becomes increasingly critical—is an omnipresence on the part of the camera as a witness of action, not as a creator of it.

When dislocations of reality occur in commercial films, they are inevitably presented as a quality, not of the reality itself, but of a distorted view of it. But the dislocations of modern life—are, precisely, dislocations of reality itself. And it is conceivable that an individual should be incapable of a distortion of vision which, designed to compliment and "correct" these dislocations of reality, results in an apparent 'adjustment.'

The external universe which we once considered, at least in our immediate locality, as the passive recipient of the manifestations of the individual will—the stage upon which the conflict of human wills was dramatically enacted—has been revealed as an active creative force. And again, cinema, with its capacity for animating the ostensibly inanimate, for re-relating the ostensibly immobile, is especially equipped to deal with such experiences.

The potentialities of cinema are rich and unexplored. It can relate two unrelated geographies by the continuous unity of an uninterrupted movement begun in one and concluded in the other. It can project as simultaneities, chronologically distant events. Slow motion, and the agony of its analysis, reveals in the most casual incident, a cosmic constellation. Yet no verbal description can convey the sense of a medium which is basically visual.

And here we return to the first considerations of this article, for such potentialities as the cinema contains for giving expression to these problems, will be developed only when the cinema is treated as an independent art form, rather than as an instrument for the illustration of literary narrative. How little that is understood is evidenced by a recent article by the film critic of the *New York Times*. In a review of the "Best Film Plays of 1943-44" he applauds the fact that "the plays are presented—uncomplicated by the numerous camera directions which used to be the bane of the reader." When the day comes that the camera—the visual element—ceases to be thought of as an annoying complication by 'film' writers who concern themselves with cinema not out of an appreciation of it as a medium, but because the film industry provides the most lucrative employment for 'writers,' cinema as an art form will begin to come of age.

New Directions, #9, 1946.

DEATH OF A CRITIC

Dudley Nichols

The report of his death the other day, coffined in a lonely
paragraph and buried humbly in the depths of pages of advertising, brought to my mind the memory of my first meeting with
Henley James. I recall that at first I did not wish to see him.
Contrary to the general impression, when one is engaged in film
production and faced by its multitude of harassing decisions there
is no time to talk with anyone who is not directly concerned in
the job at hand. Fortunately Henley James bore a letter from
Hermine Rich Isaacs of *Theatre Arts* and that was the open
sesame. Had I been a little less preoccupied I should have remembered his name in connection with several brilliant pieces of
film criticism which I had read in obscure journals.

He entered, an ordinary enough man until his eyes caught
your own. Then you realized you were looking into knowledge
and imagination, into a source of light that tolerantly evaluated
you and everything it glanced upon.

As I came to know him I marveled at his visual power. He
derived more joy from his eyesight than any man I have ever
known. Perhaps painters and astronomers—and great film-mak-

ers—share that faculty. He had a fresh and unprejudiced way of seeing things. I felt embarrassed when he would casually point out something that had been under my very eyes—the meaning and implications of the human scene.

Everything is before us, he would say—the universe and all its secrets, man and all his mystery, his tears and laughter—and yet we neglect to see them. Don't make a dead-set at seeing, he would say. Don't use will power. The will is destructive in the realm of feeling and imagination. Only desire can open the doors of the heart and mind. Love seeing and you will gradually begin to see. And love what is seen. But be careful how you point your visions out to others, they won't thank you for it. Men, he said, really don't want to see anything new, just as they loathe experiencing anything new. You will really be disliked, said James, if you offer men a new experience. That is why the way is always hard for pioneers and innovators in the arts, for art of course offers us new emotional experiences.

Yes, he was intensely eye-minded. He cared little for the sound of words, only for their color and images, and he confessed this was a shortcoming. For one thing it had made the study of music difficult for him. He finally knew a great deal about music, learned it doggedly, for he felt it was essential to the knowledge of film—that great film was in itself a sort of visual music. It was this principal defect, he held, that had kept him from becoming a film-maker himself. But I believe the real reason was that he was a born critic, a discerner of values, loving the whole of architecture too much to play with blocks. Perhaps a perception of values can be more important than creation.

His whole life had become a search for values and he concentrated this search in the field of cinema. He called himself a moralist and said it was absurd for anyone not a moralist to be interested in the theater, for the eternal subject-matter of the drama is the conflict of good and evil. Of course, he would add, there are large moralists and small moralists. The small moralist is insufferable because he believes man is born good and that evil is something baleful outside him, from which he must be protected as a child learning to walk must be protected from bumping into chairs or tripping over rugs. He trusts neither himself nor humanity and so in mortal fear goes through life disclaiming the evil that is in himself by accusing it in others. The large moralist faces his own guilt without fear and thus armors his own portion of goodness and strengthens it in others.

But though a moralist for man and his works, James held no ethical view of the universe. He liked to quote Conrad's paragraph on the aim of Creation being, perhaps, purely spectacular . . . "In this view there is room for every religion except for the inverted creed of impiety, the mask and cloak of arid despair; for every joy and every sorrow, for every fair dream, for every charitable hope. The great aim is to remain true to the emotions called out of the deep encircled by the firmament of stars, whose infinite numbers and awful distances may move us to laughter or tears . . . or again, to a properly steeled heart, may matter nothing at all."

"Man," said Henley James, "is God's creation. Art is Man's. A knowledge of the first is essential to the second creation—but let no artist or critic confuse the two. Nature is the miraculous tree and art—man's work—is the flowering that makes the mystery and wonder of the tree manifest. Art—or, to make myself clearer, that poetic faculty which is the animating spirit of all the arts— is always that which renders the invisible visible and the intangible tangible. Music, for example, is that which makes Time audible. Sculpture makes Space visible. Literature strives to make life intelligible.

"An artist," he said once, "is a born liar who uses his lies to tell the truth of his time. A critic has the harder task of telling the truth without the liar's gift."

Clearly Henly James was born to be a critic, but why not a critic of the drama, or of literature, or of music or painting? He was gifted to go in any direction. The answer is that he loved the cinema. Love is a mystery. A man loves a woman and forever after her face is stamped on every dream. A man falls in love with archaeology, say, and spends the rest of his days digging in desolate places for the remains of ancient man until perhaps he himself is caught in some cave-in and sealed away until another lover of his mistress—some future archaeologist thousands of years hence—shall dig up his bones and rejoice over the remains of another ancient man. James made no attempt to explain his passion for film. He scorned any critic who did not love his chosen medium. It is hard to believe that a man will practice film criticism if he does not love the cinema or book reviewing if he does not love books, yet there are some. Only more insufferable to him than the film critic who secretly dislikes all films was the critic who secretly likes any film. Discrimination and the perception of values were his religion. He quoted G. B. Shaw, in his memorial essay on William Archer, defining the essence of genius as the "perception of values."

James, who could have been a fine literary critic, was derided by some of his bookish friends for devoting his talents to the cinema. He retorted that in his opinion the cinema was the most important art form of the twentieth century and that it could and should integrate all the arts. He also said that film criticism was the most difficult career a man could choose, not only because it demanded a knowledge of all the arts but for the reason that there were so few films worth criticizing. Besides, the film-makers feared true criticism. Every film is launched like a squid in an obscuring cloud of spectacular publicity. No critical appraisal is wanted. No sound evaluation is possible.

I frequently heard James despair of finding intelligent editors with any respect for the cinema. Reviews and magazines of standing have their heads in the cultural clouds, forgetting that every culture is rooted in the people whose dreams are shaped in no small degree by the glut of movies they get, overlooking the plain fact that what happens on the land masses below ultimately affects even the highest-sailing clouds. Such publications either hold snobbishly aloof from so mundane a thing as the movies or they assign a staff member who writes intelligently, literately and entertainingly—but is, alas, in no way equipped to practice film criticism.

James would not review films as they came along in their endless bulk because he practiced discrimination in his subject-matter. He pointed out that the literary critic, as distinguished from the book reviewer, did just this. The presses of publishers whir at an appalling rate, just as do the cameras of film-makers around the world. Does the literary critic report on every issue of *Red Book* or *The Saturday Evening Post*, on mystery novels and detective fiction and true confession pulps? He respects these phenomena for what they are and, keeping one eye on the great literature of the past, directs his attention on what is important in new production.

Yet James had no exclusive or snobbish attitude towards the cinema. He said that the medium by its very nature was not for the few but for the many. He wanted films to be better so that the many could have greater enjoyment. Most Hollywood films were bad, he held, not because Hollywood wished to make poor films but because it did not know how to make them better. Hollywood workers did not understand their own medium and its unimaginable possibilities. They were not entirely to blame. They lacked penetrating criticism which would aid them to understand what they had done. And how can we have penetrating and informed criticism when there is no one to encourage or publish or support the critic?

First-rate criticism has always been a thankless task in any department of the arts. Those who for the sake of entertainment and success exploit their wit and personalities until their own gifts are exalted above their subject-matter stultify their profession. The true critic, who must combine the heart of a poet with the intellect of a scholar, must find his reward in his work, in his sense of growth and discovery, in winning the respect of a few people whom he respects. It is strange that gifted people should ever choose the career of criticism. Perhaps it chooses them and they have no escape save in the suicide of going against their bent, as is the case with every true artist. Yet the artist has it easier. His are the rainbows, however wretched his life may appear to himself.

The compulsive artist, who pours his dreams and passions into various forms which reflect the realities hidden behind the appearances of things, thus releasing us from the blindness and chaos in which we eternally walk, such a man may make not only his fortune but his name a household word; though often his fortune is only for his heirs and his fame for the obituary columns. But the equally compelled critic, a man no less devoted to high and passionate aims, who spends his mature life in service to the great realities of art, sorting out and examining the abundance of man's and not God's creations, evaluating and integrating achievements so that a culture may keep on growing and continue on its path and climb mountains, such a man may live and die and yet be known with honor to very few.

Yet these few have shaped and will continue to shape every-thing that makes life worthwhile. Nothing is completed, no caught dream can be secure, no work of art or letters be certain of itself, until these few in every generation have stamped its value and arranged its place, have traced its pedigree and clari-fied its features, have rendered clear its meaning and related it to life as well as to art. And the process is continuous in the sum of the generations as long as culture is developing. When it fails or falters you may be sure the culture is dying.

"There is nothing peculiar," said James, "in the fact that the artist is not always sure of where he is going or why. If he stopped to ask he might never do it—so dangerous is the critical faculty, which must always keep one eye open, so to speak, to the creative faculty which sees best when both eyes are closed —for only then are imagination and intuition fully awake. Nat-urally artists at times work blindly and compulsively. The poet tracing the hidden truth of some experience or following the footprints of some savage dream is Kit Carson in the wilderness of his own heart.

"The artist desperately needs the critic because he cannot con-tain him. And the people need him just as urgently because nei-ther can they contain him. They are blind to values without him. They can in fact more easily contain the artist because the poetic faculty is instinctual in mankind whereas the critical mind is based on knowledge and must be consciously trained and de-veloped."

"My function?" he said one day when I had asked him. "I'm a middleman. A window-cleaner for the mass, a mirror-polisher for the film-makers. It's all the same glass, but there are two ways of looking at it, depending on where you stand. For the public I scrub and squeegee with all my wits and say, 'Look, a new constellation is in the sky. Look, that dim little star you thought was a speck of dust on the windowpane is going to grow brighter than Aldebaran and will change the horoscope of our time. Look, those bright lights you see are not the sun, moon and stars but a neon sign down on the corner advertising another gaudy lie.'

"For the artist I give the glass an extra rub and he either breaks the mirror in a rage or lifts up his heart and turns encouraged to another piece of work; for the mirror reflects not only what the artist has done but what he really is, and once he has looked he cannot stand upon a pile of dollars or a heap of dung—or even on a mountain of publicity—and pretend he is strutting on Olympus."

James had great enthusiasm for the film library of the Museum of Modern Art and for the critical writings of Iris Barry about that growing collection of films. "In the early days," he said, "film criticism was possible because the critic had direct knowledge of all that had been accomplished in the medium. Today the young critic would be ignorant of the past, he could gain no historical perspective, if he had no access to this library of world films."

The last time I saw James he admitted the cinema had got itself into a blind alley but he had no doubt of its eventual emergence.

"The medium is more powerful," he said, "than those who work in it. It will always force its way ahead. From the beginning people have confused it with the stage but in the early days there was less confusion because film did not talk. It was pure dream and the dream compelled the invention of its technical devices—the dissolve, the fading out and in, cutting to successive images, camera movement, the long shot and the close-up. This silent film attained a higher artistic development than sound film has approached because it was not confused with the stage, and because the mechanism of its creation was simpler. The less machinery the artist has to deal with, the purer will be his art. Sound film complicated and multiplied the mechanism. The present-day film-maker is still too aware of his machinery. He must learn all there is to know about it and then forget it. This will come in time. Today it accounts for the slick professional products that pass for film.

"And the confusion with stage continues. At first the cinema began to dominate the theater—though those who are wedded to the stage will hardly admit it. But the loosening-up of stage techniques, revolving or sliding stages, cutting to quick successive scenes by means of lighting effects, expressionism itself was a result of the influence of cinema. Now the influence is the other way and the stage begins to dominate the cinema. I suspect you will find the stage in the next decade returning to its classic form and the cinema regressing from its own classic form until it suddenly realizes its mistake and discovers again its pure direction. I have no objection to the photographed play, when it is done with cinematic skill, but it is not true cinema."

After that visit ended, I never saw Henley James again . . . yes, he is dead. He is dead of course because he never lived. I wish he had . . . And if you are annoyed by this deception let me plead that I knew of no other way to describe the kind of film critics we need—and he would have starved to death before this time anyway!

Theatre Arts, April, 1947.

RASHOMON

Henry Hart

In *Rashomon* the Japanese have provided the West with a major emotional experience. Also with an esthetic delight, intellectual stimulation, and a memorable example of what the motion picture can be.

I shall begin with the story. It has a timeless theme: human beings describe things the way they want them to appear. This poignant axiom is the core of a tale about a murder in ninth century Japan.

The picture opens with a heavy summer rain falling upon the

Rashomon gate of the city of Kyoto. Three men are sheltering
beneath its broken and decaying timbers. One is a gatherer of
firewood; the second is a servant; and the third is a Buddhist priest.

The woodman is oppressed by a murder that had just occurred
in a nearby forest. He had discovered the body and he tells his
companions about it. The murdered man was a merchant who
had been traveling through the woods with his wife. A bandit
attacked him, bound him to a tree, violated his wife before his
eyes. Then he released the husband, gave him his sword, and
fought him to death. When he turned to find the woman, she
was gone. All this the bandit confessed to the police.

But the woman had also been arrested, and had told a different story, which the woodman had heard while at the police sta-
tion. The woman testified that after the bandit's attack he
laughed at her, and made off. She went up to her husband to
release him and saw in his eyes implacable hatred—of herself.
She begged her husband not to stare at her with such loathing,
cut the rope that bound him and beseeched him to kill her. He
continued to stare. She started toward him—and fainted. When
she regained consciousness she found her dagger in her husband's
breast.

The priest then spoke and said that a medium had told the
police a still different version. The murdered merchant, speaking
through the medium, declared that after the violation of his wife
the bandit had wooed her and that there had come upon her face
a radiance which he, her husband, had never evoked. He said his
wife had begged the bandit to take her with him and had then
urged him to kill her husband. Whereupon the bandit had kicked
the woman to the ground and asked the husband: "Shall we kill
her?" The wife ran and the bandit started after her. The husband
worked himself free of his bonds, and finding his wife's dagger
on the ground, escaped from his dishonor by stabbing himself.

Whereupon the wood gatherer confessed that he had witnessed
the actual murder.

After the bandit attacked the woman, the woodman declared,
the bandit was contrite, and asked the woman to marry him
and said he would abandon his evil ways. Her reply was that
she was only a woman, and hence unable to decide between the
desires of men. Thereupon the bandit released the husband and

gave him back his sword. But the husband cried out that he would not risk his life for the sake of a harlot. The woman was infuriated, and incited the two men to kill each other by calling her husband a coward and the bandit a fool. In the ensuing duel the bandit killed the husband.

As the wood gatherer concludes this fourth version of the murder, the wail of a baby is heard. The three men search for and find it. The servant seizes some of its outer garments, and when the wood gatherer rebukes him, the servant laughs with scorn and asks: "Do you think I don't know you stole the woman's pearl-handled dagger?" The woodman is humiliated, and goes to the baby and picks it up. The priest thinks he intends to strip it of its remaining clothes and remonstrates. But the woodman replies: "I have six others at home. One more won't make any difference." The priest is moved, and says: "I think you have restored my faith in humanity."

It will be observed that the different versions of the events in the forest aggrandize or protect the egos of the persons who related them.

The bandit wanted people to believe he had given the husband his sword and had killed him fairly in a duel.

The woman wanted society to believe she had been blameless, and that her husband had rejected her unjustly.

The husband wanted it known that the wife he had never completely possessed was inherently faithless.

And the woodman, who stole the woman's dagger, wanted everyone connected with his theft to be blackened. The bandit was a murderer, thief and rapist; the husband was mean and cowardly; the woman was a destroyer, exulting when she had set man against man in mortal combat. Stealing from such people wasn't really theft.

What of the baby?

It is a symbol for one of the most important facts about human beings: within us, along with thieving, murder, rape, and deceit, there is also compassion.

Were *Rashomon* distinguished only by the insights into the human heart that put Western psychologizing to the blush, it would be an unusual picture. But this is only half its merit.

The other half is the astonishing art with which the film itself was made. I think I do not exaggerate when I say that almost every camera shot—long, middle, close and panoramic—was composed as a painter composes. That the subtleties of costume, acting, direction and photography are breath-taking. That the shots of the woman dressed in white, riding on a white horse, concealed by a white veil hung from the brim of an enormous hat, was so instantaneous an emotional evocation of medieval Japan as to be sheer cinema magic.

There were innumerable other magical moments: the camera panning through sunlit woods (as it did in the German film *Siegfried*, only much more inventively); the sequence with the medium, in which wind, lightning, drum, chant and make-up conspire to suspend disbelief in the supernatural; the fall of the dagger from the woman's hand *into* the ground when desire came upon her during the bandit's attack; the primitive ferocity of the sword duels; the music that blends the scales and harmonics of West and East (Ravel's "Bolero" was Easternized) . . .

But I must stop, or there will be no room to conclude with a few words about the allegories people find in *Rashomon*.

Some find an analogy to the present international situation. The basic contention is that the Japanese are saying to the world: who knows who is guilty, who, in terrible truth, is without guilt?

Others find analogies to the domestic condition of Japan.

A Japanese journalist told me that this ninth century tale was filmed at this particular time because the moral decay that entered Japanese life after Japan's defeat resembles the immorality that engulfed the Japanese people 1200 years ago.

Films in Review, Jan., 1952.

The Impossible Voyage (1904) GEORGE MELIES

The Great Train Robbery (1903) EDWIN S. PORTER

D. W. Griffith *(under camera)* Directing a Scene in 1910

The Birth of a Nation (1915) D. W. GRIFFITH

The Birth of a Nation (1915) D. W. GRIFFITH

Intolerance (1916) D. W. GRIFFITH

Blind Husbands (1919) ERICH VON STROHEIM

Greed (1923) ERICH VON STROHEIM

The Cabinet of Dr. Caligari (1919) ROBERT WIENE

Metropolis (1926) FRITZ LANG

The Golem (1919) PAUL WEGENER

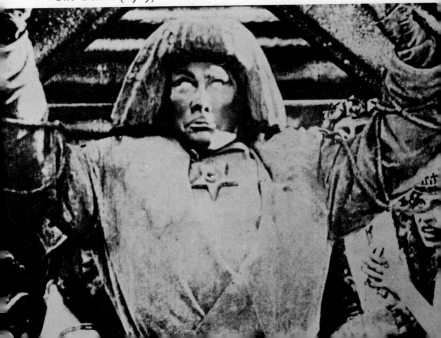

Variety (1925) E. A. DUPONT

The Last Laugh (1925) FRED MURNAU

Sunrise (1927) FRED MURNAU

Potemkin (1926) SERGEI EISENSTEIN

Ten Days That Shook the World (1927) SERGEI EISENSTEIN

The End of St. Petersburg (1927) V. I. PUDOVKIN

Soil (1930) ALEXANDER DOVZHENKO

The Crowd (1927) KING VIDOR

The Passion of Joan of Arc (1927) CARL DREYER

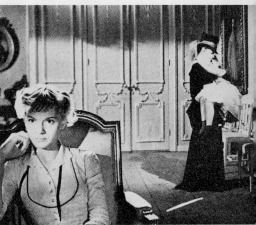

Miss Julie (1951) ALF SJOBERG

The Italian Straw Hat (1928) RENE CLAIR

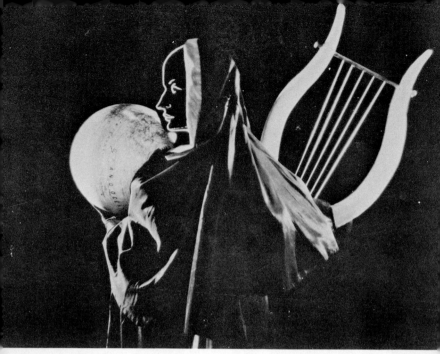

Blood of a Poet (1930) JEAN COCTEAU

The Informer (1935) JOHN FORD

Citizen Kane (1941) ORSON WELLES

Rashomon (1951) AKIRA KUROSAWA

The Seventh Seal (1957) INGMAR BERGMAN

THE ONLY DYNAMIC ART

James E. Davis

After thirty years as a painter and sculptor I have come to the conclusion that the only recording medium with which a visual artist can express the ideas of our time adequately is motion picture film.

My own experience, and observation of the work of contemporary painters and sculptors, have convinced me that the traditional media of painting and sculpture are too limited for the full, or even satisfactory, depiction of the complexities of the twentieth century. I believe the artist who clings to these old tools dooms himself to repetition of ideas better expressed in previous cultures, or to regression into the primitive, or to being so subjective he ceases to communicate with anyone but himself.

I have therefore abandoned painting and sculpture and adopted the film medium.

In the motion picture camera the artist has a tool that enables him to communicate to his fellow men all that is new and progressive in contemporary existence and thought. The motion picture camera opens up a vast new subject matter—the unexplored world of visual movement. Now, for the first time in history, an artist can express reality dynamically instead of statically. In the artist's increasing perception of the role of motion in nature and the universe (and man's life) future historians will discern our day's major contribution to the development of the visual arts.

Because motion picture film is a dynamic medium, the artist, by means of it, can depict and deploy concepts of modern science that have hitherto defied representation. Current scientific dogma describes reality statistically, not statically, as a never ending flux, a continuous process of becoming. Even the man on the street now speaks of time as the fourth dimension, however ignorant he may be of what physicists imply by a space-time continuum. As our minds become accustomed to the notion of time as the fourth dimension, to the relativism implicit in the space-time concept, and to electronically revealed glimpses of the microscopic and the magroscopic, our thoughts, and our dreams, alter. With what, if not with these alterations, should the genuine artists be concerned? And with what but the motion picture camera can the artist express these new perceptions and intuitions?

When the artists of the Renaissance abandoned the flat, two-dimensional painting of the primitives for the then revolutionary three-dimensional kind, they also abandoned tempera, mosaic, stained glass, etc., for the newly invented medium of oil painting. Similarly, the artist who has abandoned the static concepts of the nineteenth century for the more inclusive space-time ones of today, must abandon oil painting for something more dynamic. What else is there but motion picture film?

So-called modern art is static and is a regression to the two-dimensional perceptions of the primitive, or the child, or to three-dimensional concepts of the last five centuries. I agree with that large section of the public which says: "If this is art, give me the movies." For implicit in the public's preference is an instinctive sense of the universal fact that nothing is static and that the only changeless thing we know is change (i.e., motion).

In the past artists have used forms of color to represent—or imitate—the forms of familiar objects in nature. Whenever the artist did not imitate nature, and used non-representational, or invented, forms, he did so merely for decorative purposes. Not so the architect. To solve his problems he has evolved shapes and forms that have no counterparts in nature. So must the artist who is aware of the miracles that occur in our body's cells and in the all-pervasive ramifications of light, and in those workings of the atom that are so prescient of the future.

Invented forms are abstractions and the serious artist uses them to suggest the causative processes of nature, not the concrete objects which are their results. These processes of nature are dynamic, and to be expressed adequately must be shown in motion. Abstract painting and sculpture, of course, are static, and thereby invalid. Without motion abstract forms and patterns are meaningless. At best, they are mere decoration. At worst, they are esthetic and psychological obfuscation.

The artist who uses film adds, to the problem of how to organize space, the element of time. Other arts have been concerned with time, most notably music, and the abstract film is more closely related to music than to traditional painting, which has predominantly been concerned with the literary, and only recently with the abstract.

Just as the musician organizes rhythms of sound in order to stimulate imagination and produce an emotional response, so I organize visual rhythms of moving forms of color. Also like the musician, who doesn't use the sounds of nature but invented sounds, produced by various instruments, I use invented forms of color which I produce artificially with brightly colored transparent plastics. I set them in motion, play light upon them, and film what happens. Obviously, I am not trying to present facts or to tell a story. I am trying to stir the creative imagination of my fellow men.

When watching my films it is a mistake to search for hidden meanings, or to try to identify shapes with familiar concrete objects. I do not know what these invented forms signify, or adumbrate. Nor does anyone else—yet. I only know they have the power to elicit emotional, imaginative, and intellectual, responses, which vary with each individual. Their meaning is of the future, and may lie in the realm of kinetics, or in that of optics. Their meaning may ultimately be nuclear. But my purpose is to stimulate interest in hitherto unperceived aspects of the physical universe, in hitherto unrecognized potentialities in the human imagination, and not to explain them.

But I do not deal in fantasy. My invented forms should not

be confused with distortions of natural objects irrationally produced. I work rationally toward nature, not away from it into psychological unreality. Let us remember that though mathematical symbols are abstractions, they elucidate the workings of nature, and that although when Reimann invented his tensors he did not know of any application for them, Einstein supplied one.

Although I am interested in suggesting analogies to science, I am more interested in the analogies in my films to music. I deem music the most abstract, as well as the most human, of all the arts, and the art that comes closest to expressing the truth.

I also consciously suggest relations to the dance, for the art of gesture is a basic ingredient of moving pictures.

Film also has the power to express subjective ideas, and it is with these that the artist is temperamentally most concerned.

I personally prefer fact to fiction, for I believe there to be more poetry in the former, and that human beings ought, as W. D. Howells said, to have "due regard for the poetry which exists in facts and which resides nowhere else." It is, of course, as all artists know, possible to organize facts in a manner more related to poetry than to fiction. In the films I have photographed from nature I have preferred not to use visual facts for documentation, but for the creation of subjective moods and the suggestion of ideas. This is a personal predilection.

In photographing nature I have concentrated upon aspects of it which are so obvious and commonplace they are usually unnoticed. As, for example, the reflection and refraction of light from and in moving objects.

The artist who concerns himself with nature's unperceived natural phenomena need not travel to faraway places. All he needs is an open eye and a certain serenity, a freedom from his own concerns, and, above all, release from the anthropomorphic compulsion. He also needs light, and a motion picture camera.

So incredible are the forms and movements of nature that, when they are shown on the screen, they are often confused with the inventions of the abstract artist. Needless to say, they should not be.

In addition to recording unnoticed aspects of uncontrolled nature, I also make abstract films. But these derive from my nature films. For I am at some pains to study the principles underlying those phenomena of nature which visually can be so astonishing, and after I have mastered these scientific principles, I try to apply them when I create wholly invented forms and movements.

For example: I recently made a motion picture of the astonishing images produced by the reflections of houses, trees, clouds, etc., on the surface of moving water. Later, I made a film of equally surprising images produced by the reflections of invented objects on the moving surfaces of sheets of highly polished plastics. It may be asked: what do these photographed reflections of invented objects connote? Do they appertain to the nature of light, or are they psycho-physiological phenomena? I think much about these things, and believe the philosophic concept of "becoming" has relevance here.

Abstract films do refer to reality, be it chemical, electrical, physical, or psycho-physiological, be the reference ever so remote. But films of fantasy do not. They refer to unreality—the unreality of the dream, or of the subconscious mind. Fantasy arises not from objective fact, or from invention, but from distortion of fact. Now when distortions of fact are set in motion the effect is surprisingly powerful. Need I say that it is film, not painting or sculpture, which makes even the unreal world of fantasy seem more "real"?

I recently made a film that is pure fantasy. In it I did not record nature accurately, nor present new, invented forms and movements. Instead, I distorted nature's forms. Specifically, I distorted the forms of the human body to such a degree that they are almost unrecognizable. The effect is quite nightmarish. In making this film I did exactly what the surrealist and other modern painters do—i.e., I irrationally distorted nature's forms in accordance with the dictates of the whims, obsessions, rationalizations, delusions and compulsions of my subconscious mind.

Unfortunately, the subjective fantasies and distortions of reality in present day painting and sculpture are accepted as reality by a great many people who ought to know better (most of whom profess a disdain for the movies). Even Picasso's absurd "I detest nature" is taken seriously. Because it is taken seriously it is a far graver threat to culture than Grade B movies. For they, at least, do not lead to a rejection of nature and of the life of our period as well. Modern art is not revolutionary, and presents nothing that is new. It merely distorts the old and the familiar.

Today, the artist who prefers reality to fantasy, and his own period in history to that of the past, will find there are few things the old tools of painting and sculpture can do that film can not do better, and many things film can do the older media cannot do at all. Clinging to the old tools obliges the artist to reject the new ideas of today simply because they cannot be expressed in the old media. Thus, by clinging to painting and sculpture the artist impedes the development of a new culture.

William James said that history "is nothing but the record of man's struggle to find the ever more inclusive order." Today we live in a dynamic, scientific, industrial and democratic order, not in a static, religious, agricultural and socially exclusive order. The old hand tools are as inadequate in the arts as in the crafts. It has been said that "everyone sides with the priests or with the prophets." As an artist I side with the prophets rather than with the high priests of art.

Therefore I have no choice, I must adopt this new medium of the motion picture film.

Films in Review, Dec., 1953.

THE FILM AS AN
ORIGINAL ART FORM

Hans Richter

The main aesthetic problem in the movies, which were invented for reproduction (of movement) is, paradoxically, the overcoming of reproduction. In other words the question is: to what de-

gree is the camera (film, color, sound, etc.) developed and used
to reproduce (any object which appears before the lens) or to
produce (sensations not possible in any other art medium)?

This question is by no means a purely technical or mechanical
one. The technical liberation of the camera is intimately inter-
related with psychological, social, economic and aesthetic problems. They all play a role in deciding to what use technique is
put and how much it is liberated. Before this fundamental matter with its manifold implications, is sufficiently cleared up it is
impossible to speak of the film as an independent art form, even
as an art form at all, whatever its promises might be. In the
words of Pudovkin: What is a work of art before it comes in front
of the camera, such as acting, staging or the novel is not a work
of art on the screen.

Even to the sincere lover of the film in its present form it must
seem that the film is overwhelmingly used for keeping records
of creative achievements: of plays, actors, novels or just plain
nature, and proportionately less for the creation of original filmic
sensations. It is true that the commercial entertainment film uses
many of the liberating elements, discovered since 1895 by Melies,
Griffith, Eisenstein and others, leading towards an original cinematic form. But the general tendency of the film industry, as an
economic institution, is the distribution of each film to a maximum number of people. This institution has to avoid it to move
away from the traditional forms of story-telling to which the maximum number of people are conditioned: the theater, with the
supremacy of the actor—and the novel or the play, with the
writer. Both traditions weigh heavily upon the film and prevent
it from coming into its own.

David Wark Griffith forced the stage actor, as early as 1909,
into mosaic-acting, and broke up, in that way, the uninterrupted
scene—acting of the stage actor into hundreds of separately acted
scenes which assumed continuity only in the cutting room. His
innovation of the close-up and the crosscutting of simultaneous
events were revolutionary steps towards a filmic style. But when
he broke with theater-acting he gave, involuntarily, an overwhelming influence back to the actor in the creation of the star.
As Star the actor immortalized reproduction and dominated the
film form once again.

The novel on the other hand has adapted itself in the last 50 years to the film. It has become increasingly image-minded. But its technique of psychological character-development, its style of story-telling, traditional property of literature, dominates the film and makes it also, from this side, reproduction (of literary works, which were original art before they were produced in Hollywood, London, Paris and Rome).

It does not concern us here that in spite of dependency upon other art forms, and in spite of the greater or smaller degree of reproduction, many films have shown exceptional qualities. It is known that the film industry has produced fascinating works, full of inventiveness, inspiration and human values. The problem with which we are dealing here is the film as an original art form. Good or bad have no meaning as long as it is not clear upon what aesthetic fundamentals the film is supposed to be built.

The uncertainty of whether film as such (i.e. the entertainment film) is essentially theatrical, literary, or fine-art, ends with the doubt in the minds of many sincere film historians and critics as to whether the film is, or ever will be, an original art at all! There is also another school of thought which defies the present form of the film altogether, in spite of its overwhelming success and powerful influence, rejects its values as social compensator in offering paradises, complete with gods and godesses (sic), and sees in it a grandiose perversion of the medium.

Between the two schools I would prefer to say that the fictional film in its present form is a reproduction of several art forms mixed with original cinematographic elements. But the fact is that there are at least two film forms besides the fictional film, which, less spectacular than Hollywood, are more cinematographic in the proper sense of the word.

Several times in the history of the movies a revolt has temporarily broken the hold of the two traditional arts over the entertainment film. To state the two most important revolts: the post-revolutionary silent Russion film (*Potemkin*), and after the liberation of Italy from Fascism the post-war Italian film (*Paisan*). In both cases the fictional film has turned from fiction to history and from theater style to documentary style in the use of natural setting, people not actors, and real events.

With the documentary approach the film gets back to its fundamentals. Here it has a solid aesthetic basis: in the free use of nature, including man, as raw material. By selection, elimination and coordination of natural elements, a film form evolves which is original and not bound by theatrical or literary tradition. That goes of course, as much for the semi-documentary fictional film (*Potemkin, Paisan*), as for the documentary film itself. These elements might obtain a social, economic, political, general human meaning according to their selection and coordination. But this meaning does not exist *a priori* in the facts, nor is it a reproduction (as in an actor's performance). It is created in the camera and the cutting room. The documentary film is an original art form. It has come to grips with facts—on its own original level. It covers the rational side of our lives, from the scientific experiment to the poetic landscape-study, but never moves away from the factual. Its scope is wide. Nevertheless, it is an original art form only as far as it keeps strictly to the use of natural raw material in rational interpretation. The modern, more convenient techniques of re-enacting factual scenes and events is sometimes not without setbacks, as it might easily introduce reproduction through the back door again in reproducing enacted scenes.

The influence of the documentary film is growing but its contribution to a filmic art is, by nature, limited. It is limited by the same token by which it has overcome the influence of the two old arts. Since its elements are facts, it can be original art only in the limits of this factuality. Any free use of the magic, poetic, irrational qualities to which the film medium might offer itself would have to be excluded *a priori* (as nonfactual). But just these qualities are essentially cinematographic, are characteristic of the film and are, esthetically, the ones which promise future development. That is where the second of the original film-forms has its place: the experimental film.

There is a short chapter in the history of the movies which dealt especially with this side of the film. It was made by individuals concerned essentially with the film medium. They were neither prejudiced by production cliches, nor by necessity of rational interpretation, nor by financial obligations. The story of these individual artists, at the beginning of the twenties, under the name of avant-garde, can be properly read as a history of the conscious attempt to overcome reproduction and to arrive at the

free use of the means of cinematographic expression. This movement spread over Europe and was sustained for the greatest part
by modern painters who, in their own field had broken away from
the conventional: Eggeling, Leger, Duchamp, Man Ray, Picabia,
Ruttman, Brugiere, Len Lye, Cocteau, myself and others.

The fact that it was nearly exclusively modern artists who represented this movement gives a hint of the direction in which the
liberation of the film was sought. Already, in the 1910's Canudo
and Delluc in France spoke of photogenic as the new plastic
quality of the film medium. Rene Clair went further and declared
film as a visual medium *per se:* "A blind man in a regular theater
and a deaf mute in a movie theater should still get the essentials
from the performance." The spoken word for the stage, the silent
image for the film—those are the elements!

These artists discovered that film as a visual medium fitted
into the tradition of the art without violation of its fundamentals.
It was there that it could develop freely: "The film should
positively avoid any connection with the historical, educational,
romantic, moral, or immoral, geographic or documentary subjects. The film should become, step by step, finally exclusively
cinematography, that means that it should use exclusively photogenic elements" (Jean Epstein, 1923). Problems in modern art
lead directly into the film. Organization and orchestration of
form, color, the dynamics of motion, simultaneity, were problems with which Cézanne, the cubists, and the futurists had to
deal. Eggeling and I came directly out of the structual problems of abstract art, *nolens-volens* into the film medium. The
connection to theater and literature was, completely, severed.
Cubism, expressionism, dadaism, abstract art, surrealism found
not only their expression in films but a new fulfillment on a new
level.

The tradition of modern art grew on a large front, logically,
together with and into the film: the orchestration of motion in
visual rhythms—the plastic expression of an object in motion
under varying light conditions, "to create the rhythm of common
objects in space and time, to present them in their plastic beauty,
this seemed to me worthwhile" (Leger)—the distortion and
dissection of a movement, an object or a form and its reconstruction in cinematic terms (just as the cubists dissected and rebuilt

in pictorial terms)—the denaturalization of the object in any form to recreate it cinematographically with light—light with its transparency and airiness as a poetic, dramatic, constructive material—the use of the magic qualities of the film to create the original state of the dream—the complete liberation from the conventional story and its chronology in dadaist and surrealist developments in which the object is taken out of its conventional context and is put into new relationships, creating in that way a new content altogether. "The external object has broken away from its habitual environment. Its component parts had liberated themselves from the object in such a way that they could set up entirely new relationships with other elements."—Andre Breton (about Max Ernst).

The external object was used, as in the documentary film, as raw material, but instead of employing it for a rational theme of social, economic, scientific nature, it has broken away from its habitual environment and was used as material to express irrational visions. Films like *Ballet Mecanique, Entr'acte, Emak Bakia, Ghosts Before Breakfast, Andalusian Dog, Diagonal Symphony, Anaemic Cinema, Blood of a Poet, Dreams that Money Can Buy* and many others were not repeatable in any other medium and are essentially cinematic.

It is still too early to speak of a tradition, or of a style, comparable to those in older arts. The movement is still too young. There are, nevertheless, general traceable directions which cover a great deal of these efforts: abstract art and surrealism. Here in the U. S. is the work of the Whitney brothers and Francis Lee, the most characteristic of the one; the films of Curtis Harrington, Maya Deren, and Frank Stauffacher are examples of the other. There are many serious attempts but also many followers who use and abuse the sensations easily obtainable in this medium. Especially surrealism seems to offer a welcome excuse for the exhibition of a whole menu of inhibitions.

In England, France, Denmark, Holland, Belgium, experimental film groups of individual artists, mostly painters, have taken up the work begun by the avant garde of the twenties. They are following the only realistic line which an artist can follow: artistic integrity. In that way a tradition, temporarily interrupted by the stormy political events in Europe has been taken up by a young generation, here and abroad. It is obvious today that this tradition will not be eradicated again but will grow. As small or as big as this movement might become, it has opened a new road to film as an art-form and has, as such, more than mere historical significance.

The stronger and more independent the documentary and the experimental film become and the more the general audience has occasion to see them, the more they will adapt themselves to a screen-style instead of a theater-style. Only after such a transformation of the general audience has taken place, the entertainment film can and will follow. At such golden times film entertainment and film-art might become identical.

Film Culture, Jan., 1955.

TOWARD TRUE CINEMA

Slavko Vorkapich

1. Two Aspects of the Motion Picture: Recording and Creative

The name *motion picture* may stand merely for the technical process which consists in a rapid succession of pictures projected on a screen, or for any kind of popular entertainment produced and presented in such a way, or, among other things, for a truly creative use of a rapid succession of pictures projected on a screen. The name is a general one and a general name is expected to cover a variety of things. But a special meaning of a general name like *painting* becomes immediately apparent when it is placed in a simple context, for example, in "Teaching Painting at a University." Obviously here the sense of creative use of the tools of painting is intended, and not house- or furniture-painting and other similar uses of brush and paint. It may be worth noting that in the case of *painting* the general name is reserved for the creative use of the medium, while other uses have to be qualified.

Now, with the word *creative*, especially in connection with motion pictures, one can get into real semantic and philosophic difficulties if one tries to prove as true one's assumptions about it.

One of my claims is that most of the films made so far are examples not of creative use of motion picture devices and techniques, but examples of their use as recording instruments and processes only. There are extremely few motion pictures that may be cited as instances of creative use of the medium, and from these only fragments and short passages may be compared to the best achievements in other arts.

Often, when a specific example, like the lunch hour sequence in the documentary *The City*, is mentioned, a number of listeners would come up with some such question: "You mean a series of quick cuts?"—"Do you think it is possible to make a whole picture like that?"—If I mention McLaren's *Fiddle-Dee-Dee*: "Oh, you mean abstract shapes dancing to music?"—If I describe passages from Cocteau's *Beauty and the Beast*, some jump at the conclusion that I mean fantasy and symbolism, and if, with some hesitation, I mention some of my own work I can almost hear a few of them thinking: "Now we know! You mean camera tricks! You mean montage: the Hollywood kind, not the Eisenstein kind! You mean flip-flops and wipes and zooms and the camera on the flying trapeze!"

Perhaps the right answer would be: Yes, all of these things and much more. But first let me try to explain what may *not* be considered as the creative use of the medium, what may be called the *recording* use only, or an *extension* of some other medium of communication or expression.

The technical nature of the film medium is such that it may very easily and profitably be utilized as such an extension. In this sense it may be compared to various uses of printing of words; to various uses of still photography: reporting, keeping records of events, people, things, etc.; to uses of drawing and painting for scientific exposition such as diagrams, charts, and illustrations in books on biology, botany, medicine, etc.; or it may be compared to various uses of the sound recording devices for preserving speeches, lectures, memorable performances of music or for making transcriptions of radio shows. In fact, the film medium *is* used mostly as an extension of each of the various media mentioned. And it is natural that the chief value in such films should lie in that which is recorded: the event, the performance, the person, or the object photographed and the verbal and sound accompaniment that usually goes with it. Rarely is it required that the value consist in a unique filmic structure about the subject.

The fact that some of these recordings have been so effective and at times emotionally very moving may have led many people into believing that this efficient power came from the medium itself. Now, no one would call a *phonograph record* of a master conductor's interpretation of a great composer's composition—no one would call that record a musical masterpiece, no matter how technically perfect it was. But, quite often, technically polished *visual* and sound recordings of great performances in various fields have been hailed as great films. This applies, equally, to most dramatic or story films. Let me illustrate this with a hypothetical example.

Suppose, we take a piece of creative writing, e.g., the famous soliloquy from Hamlet, and, suppose, we photograph with a motion picture camera that passage just as it is printed on the page in a book. Or, for this particular shot, we may have had the monologue printed on parchment in some fancy type designed by a creative typographer, and we may, for extra embellishment, use some real "mood" lighting, like throwing a faint shadow of "a bare bodkin" upon the page. Now would this, in a "rapid succession of pictures projected on a screen," give us a motion picture? Technically, yes. But what creative contribution was achieved by the use of the motion picture camera, apart from giving us another *record of Shakespeare's* creative work? Obviously, none.

Suppose we elaborate a little more on our shooting of the monologue and we get a creative actor and we dress him in a costume designed by a creative designer and put him in a setting designed by a creative art director and we light him with lights full of mood and photograph him with a motion picture camera and register on film all his expressive actions and gestures and movements of his lips and tongue and cheeks and record his voice on the best sound system available. What do we get this time? A performance really worth preserving and showing all over the world. *But what have we as makers of the picture created except making an embellished record of an actor's acting of a writer's writing?* Again the answer is: obviously nothing. No matter how "amazingly lifelike" the picture may seem, strictly speaking, this is what was actually achieved: from a living creative performance a shadow was abstracted by mechanical means. This applies also to complete photoplays. *Photo plays*, how precisely descriptive that name is!

At this point the thought of the close-up as a real filmic contribution usually comes up. The close view is not something specifically filmic, if it is taken in the sense of something brought closer or magnified for closer scrutiny only. Long before the advent of the film, the close-up was to be found in all except stage arts and music. Portraits and still lives in painting, sculpture, and still photography; descriptive detail in literature.

There is a controversy about who "invented" the close-up. Probably the inventor got the idea from observing someone in the audience of a theater—a *legitimate* theater, of course—who was using a pair of binoculars to see an actor's or an actress's face at close range. And it is mainly in this telescopic sense that the close-up is still used. No doubt that it adds dramatic emphasis to a photoplay and thus makes up for some of the loss of the performers' living presence. Still we are talking in terms of the theater, and still we are using the medium to record bits of that other art, the actor's creative acting. Let me at this point make clear that I am not opposed to the use of the film medium as an extension of the theater, I only object to calling such extension creative use of the unique characteristics inherent in cinematography.

Considered filmically or creatively, the close-up has two main functions: visual-dynamic and associative. Close-up here means close view of anything relatively small. We react bodily, kinesthetically to any visual change. As a rule the bigger the change the stronger the reaction. For example, in a sudden cut from a long view of an object to a very close view of it there is, always, an inevitable optical and kinesthetic impact, an explosive magnification, a sudden leap forward. If the object is in motion, the close-up intensifies this motion; as a rule, the greater the area of the screen in motion the greater the intensity. This seems obvious. And thinking in these terms, one should, obviously, be led into thinking of *degrees* of change, impact, and intensity, and how important—if one hopes to use film creatively—the relative organization of these factors must be. To use a visual medium artistically is to make the visual parts "go well together." Problems of duration, harmony, contrast, proportion, and rhythm, are involved in this sort of visual-dynamic organization, i.e., cutting, which is quite different from editing a sequence of long shots, medium shots, and close-ups according to literary-dramatic requirements only. And a little more thinking in this direction leads one to deeper fundamental differences, through proper shooting for that sort of cutting, down to the original conception, to the problem of how to express a theme filmically. And that is a long way from the stage.

In a close-up an object appears somehow dissociated from its context. It is thus more or less liberated and made available for new combinations, both in respect of its visual values and meaning connotations. The latter are called "association-fields" by Gyorgy Kepes in his remarkable book *Language of Vision*. (Although primarily a study of visual principles operative in static graphic arts, this book is full of fruitful suggestions applicable to motion pictures.) In certain combinations with other fields an object acquires a quality that may be compared to that of a poetic image, but this similarity should not be taken too literally. Each different aspect of the same object has a unique quality and thus it differs from a word, which is more readily variable in a different context. The possibilities of creative organization of filmic imagery are so little known and explored (to some extent by Cocteau) that it seems like an insolence to compare our crude gropings with masterpieces of other arts.

It is clear that the emphasis here is on visual values. But this means more than striking photography, unusual camera angles, and ingenious dolly and boom shots. It is not a question of artistically composed tableaux. It is a problem of composing visually, but in time. Individual shots may be incomplete, as individual musical tones are incomplete in themselves, but they must be

"Just right and go well together" with other shots, as tones must with other tones, to make complete and esthetically satisfying units. Beautiful photography is only surface embellishment, while *cinematography* is the gathering of visual-dynamic-meaningful elements, which creative cutting combines into living entities.

The emphasis, then, is on the development of a visual dynamic language, independent of literature and theatrical traditions. The emphasis on the visual aspect does not exclude creative use of sound. It is, however, somewhat amusing to read a chapter on "counterpoint between sound and image" when no one can claim to have mastered the fundamental organization of the factors spoken of in connection with the close-up.

No doubt, the film medium is related, in some ways, to other arts. But relation does not imply imitation. It may learn from other media, but, if it is to be dignified with the name of art, it must not merely copy. In art "speaking likeness" is not a criterion of value.

2. A Method of Teaching the Creative Use of the Medium

In essential ways the motion picture medium is unique. And to the study of the possibilities inherent in the medium a method has to be worked out. I can give here only a rough idea of certain aspects of such a method, based on my own experiences teaching film at the Department of Cinema at the University of Southern California.

The teaching should be based on a literal interpretation of the name of the medium: *motion pictures*. *Pictures* should be taken in the sense of *images*. The goal is integration of motion, image, meaning, and sound, but at the beginning the emphasis should be laid on the first part of the name: *motion*.

An effort should be made to dissociate the meaning of the word from certain undesirable connotations. It does not stand merely for stage action, nor a certain type of agitation now so popular with film directors. This may be exemplified by the "movements" of a star, who, during the span of a brief dialogue moves from the couch to the fireplace and to the window, where with a toss she turns her back to her lover and comes to rest, staring out of the window. Nor does it stand merely for a perpetual agitation of the camera, also very popular with the movie directors, who treat the camera like an infant who is not satisfied until it is perambulated or dollied about. The students are asked to make a fresh mental start, if they can, by forgetting, for a while, the daily film fare they have seen. It is then explained that a whole new world is open to them for exploration: the world of motion.

The invention of the cinematic tools has not only given us the means to make "amazingly lifelike" recordings, it has also extended, immensely, the possibility of a heightened perceptual grasp of reality.

In static visual arts students are trained in a sensitive perception of the shape of things, while here they are directed toward a keener perception of the *shapes of the motions* that things generate. At first they are required to observe simple motions. An example of a simple motion would be a segment of space as it is cut out by a door opening or closing, a complex motion would be one traced by a newspaper dancing high in the wind. The emphasis is on object motion, because of the geometric simplicity of such motions. The students are requested to observe, analyze, compare, classify, and describe these motions.

The human perceptive mechanism is such that it may interpret as motion certain phenomena where no actual motion occurs. This was thoroughly investigated by Gestalt psychologists and is called phi-phenomenon or apparent movement. "Under appropriate conditions successive presentation of two lights at two points not too distant from each other results in an experience of movement from the first to the second." (Koehler). Our experiments show that there is a sensation of displacement or a visual leap in a cut between any two sufficiently different shots. This may be demonstrated very vividly if short strips of the shots, approximately ten frames each, are rapidly alternated. In certain cases a clear transformation of one shape into another may be experienced. By making their own selections of shots or designs and intercutting them in various ways students become aware of a new purely filmic force: more or less intense visual impact that occurs at each cut.

The project following these exercises consists in a thorough observation of a complete simple activity or occupation where a limited variety of motions is involved. Again the emphasis is on the motions of objects, for example in the wrapping of a package, preparing food, loading of a truck, etc. The complete action is broken down into as many simple motions as possible and each is shot from a great variety of angles. This kind of analysis, or over-analysis, is different from recording previously discussed. Here the motion picture camera is in its natural element. This process is really a filmic liberation of bits of dynamic visual energies, extracted from a simple event in reality. Each angle is selected to take hold of a single clear visual note. None is intended for an individual display as a "best shot" in the picture, not any more than a note is intended to be the best in a melody. In the re-creation of the event in cutting, each filmic facet acquires value only by its place in the total filmic structure. And the student's sense for structure grows out of these exercises in analysis.

Sometimes, in cutting, the movements are slightly overlapped, i.e., each new fragment begins a little back of the point already reached by the preceding fragment; in other words, in each new strip a small fraction of the preceding movement is repeated. Often surprisingly beautiful effects result. A sort of rhythmical time-stretching occurs. There are several striking instances of this effect in Eisenstein's earlier films.

Most students soon will become aware that very simple every-day actions may be made exciting by means of filmic analysis, and that there is a new kind of visual beauty to be found in the ordinary world around them. One can say that where there is physical action there is visual poetry.

The next stage in the student's work should consist in exploring the associative possibilities between images. Students should be asked to make simple statements entirely by visual means. Some may become capable of expressing truly poetic moods; those with vivid imaginations may bring in surprisingly effective free combinations of images, while others may succeed in making simple documentaries interesting and visually exciting.

The work done this way may be compared to the creation of simple melodies. Once the student has mastered this elementary process, he should be prepared to orchestrate several movements within a shot and to achieve a more complex organization of images for themes of greater complexity, so that perhaps, some day, he may learn how to make, not *photoplays*, but dramatic *motion pictures*.

Film Culture, March, 1959.

THE OTHER BERGMAN

Hollis Alpert

Although *Smiles of a Summer Night*, and *The Seventh Seal* have attracted a certain amount of attention from those who regularly patronize their local art cinemas, the name of Ingmar Bergman is not so well known as it ought to be, and probably will be. Bergman is a forty-year-old Swedish director who has written most of the twenty movies he has made—a peculiarly fortunate combination of abilities that allows his films to express exactly what almost all other movies, with their multiplicity of craftsmen and egos, lack—a sense of personal vision. In Paris and other European centers, Bergman has already been taken up as an important cultural and artistic phenomenon (five of his films recently played simultaneously in Paris), and the film festivals at Cannes, Berlin and Venice have duly recognized his worth with plaques and statuettes of varying inscriptions and metals. *Wild Strawberries*, the most recent of his movies to be seen here, will help focus more attention on Bergman in this country, although judging by the reception of the other films of his in American release, it is not likely to be popular, nor to attain very wide distribution.

I hesitate to say that Bergman's films are for the connoisseur, for that implies that their appeal is snobbish and even esoteric. It's already possible to determine whether someone is middlebrow or upperbrow, depending on whether the word Bergman suggests Ingmar or Ingrid. There is no real reason why reasonably large audiences shouldn't find his movies stimulating. They have enormous visual appeal, are excellently acted, and his themes are universal rather than national or regional. They often do have the dark, gloomy preoccupations that Swedish films, not to mention Strindberg's plays, have exhibited in the past, but the modern movie can probably use a good dose of gloom about man's spiritual condition. Yet, even the delightful, wickedly erotic *Smiles of a Summer Night* crept in and out of art houses without causing much fanfare, except among an appreciative few. The heavier, allegorical *The Seventh Seal* was more difficult, and I suppose required more from audiences in the way of intellectual response. Nevertheless, the small company that arranges for the American distribution of Bergman's films is singularly hesitant about publicizing him. He is not nearly so well known, or often heard of, as Fellini, the only other film-maker in the world today who approaches Bergman in stature, if not productivity.

Smiles of a Summer Night (shown here last year) was reminiscent of a Rene Clair grown more introspective and ironic. Its marital infidelities and amorous intrigues in a turn of the century Swedish setting were beautifully and deftly acted, although a contretemps occurred in the American showing. During a passage in the film when a young wife and her maid are discussing indecorous matters the sound track continues in Swedish, while the subtitles disappear. The Swedish-speaking members of the audience (very few, naturally) laughed at the dialogue; the rest of the audience laughed at the censors. *The Seventh Seal* was opened here with such secrecy—one might have thought, for instance, that the Paris Theatre in New York was showing contraband goods—that it took word-of-mouth and Bosley Crowther's appreciative review to get it any audience at all. A member of the releasing organization explained that it was the policy of Bergman to avoid publicity, to let him "catch on" slowly. *How*, one might ask, if no one hears about him?

The rather uncapitalized Swedish film industry, of course, hardly has the resources for widespread publicity efforts in behalf of its films abroad. Bergman himself has resisted coming here, and even more wisely has resisted Hollywood's offers. The average Swedish movie costs about $100,000, less than the price of a cheap American monster movie, and about one-third of the sum Ingrid Bergman gets for one screen appearance. This irony aside, the other Bergman has shown that he isn't the least hampered by a need for rigid economy. He tends to use the same group of actors for most of his films; an actor who takes a large role in one may be given a small role in the next. In *Wild Strawberries* the photography is not only impeccably professional, it is exquisite, worth seeing even if the story failed to interest—something hard to imagine. The most precious commodity in the movie is what Bergman brings; there's no way of pricing it.

The framework for *Wild Strawberries* is deceptively simple: it is a tale of one day in the life of an elderly professor of medicine, who is being honored for fifty years of service. But within the frame are fascinating complexities, minglings of dream and reality, of past and present. The time shifts and backflashes, although on occasion cumbersome, are achieved with lucidity. The professor is played by Victor Sjostrom, once a famed director of silent films who returned to acting after a frustrating Hollywood career and who is now Sweden's most eminent actor. His performance is remarkably subtle and sensitive, as he lives through a dream-like day and a past that is nostalgic and painful.

Even more painful are the nightmares he must endure throughout the day. The first takes place just before he awakes. The dream is of his own funeral, and before the day has ended the starkly visual symbols of the dream recur in distorted form, as though the events of the day were foreshadowed. In other dreams and reveries he is led back to his past life (particularly to that turn of the century period on which Bergman evidently likes to dwell in his own imagination). The vignettes and cameos recall a lost love, an unfaithful wife, an idyllic glimpse of his parents. The old man, we discover, has been living in a shell of isolation, avoiding intimate human contact because it might result in pain. Here we encounter another prevalent Bergman theme. The ending he has chosen for the old man's day is a relatively peaceful one, but not before he puts him through the worst nightmare of all, one in which his medical qualifications are seemingly reviewed. It turns out, however, to be an examination of another kind. He is put on trial for what amounts to his humanity.

In this same hallucination the professor catches his palm on a nail, and as he holds up his hand we see for a moment a wound resembling a stigmata, meaning perhaps, that his day is a kind of Passion for him. Bergman's father was a preacher, and because Bergman's work includes the personal element these religious symbols tend to recur in his stories, sometimes adding to their obscurity. His preoccupation with the symbolic detail makes all that he does interesting, even haunting, but probably detracts from the popular appeal of his movies. Nevertheless, he is not so obsessed with his personal message that he fails to communicate, even to entertain. There isn't much doubt that Bergman has, almost single-handed, brought back the Swedish film to its once high eminence. As more of his pictures are shown here, evaluations of his meanings and importance will grow more precise. Meanwhile it is time to know him. *Wild Strawberries* makes a fine acquaintance.

Saturday Review, March 21, 1959.

NOTES ON THE

CONTRIBUTORS

HOLLIS ALPERT is a film reviewer for *The Saturday Review*.

ALEXANDER BAKSHY was the film critic for *The Nation* from 1927 to 1933.

LE COMTE DE BEAUMONT was a patron of avant-garde filmmakers in Paris in the twenties.

CEDRIC BELFRAGE, former novelist and screenwriter, is at present in England writing criticism.

RALPH BLOCK, a former contributor to *The Dial* and *Vanity Fair*, is now in government service.

KIRK BOND has been engaged in film criticism for many years. At present he is editor of *The Film Courier*.

JAMES E. DAVIS, a former painter, is now making motion pictures.

MAYA DEREN is an avant-garde filmmaker who has lectured and written widely on film esthetics.

SERGEI EISENSTEIN, teacher, theorist and motion picture director, died in 1948.

EVELYN GERSTEIN wrote motion picture criticism for *The New Republic* and other periodicals in the thirties.

PAUL GOODMAN, essayist and novelist, is the author of *The Empire City* (Bobbs-Merrill, 1959).

JAMES SHELLEY HAMILTON was the editor of the *National Board of Review Magazine* in the thirties.

HENRY HART, novelist and critic, is editor of *Films in Review*.

DOROTHY JONES has been associated with several Rockefeller and Carnegie Foundation studies in the field of film content.

SIEGFRIED KRACAUER was the film critic of the *Frankfurter Zeitung* from 1920 to 1933. He is the author of *From Caligari to Hitler*.

FERNAND LÉGER was the renowned modern painter.

MEYER LEVIN has written novels, plays, screenplays and film criticism. He is the author of the best selling novel *Compulsion*.

ANDRE LEVISON wrote numerous articles on film esthetics in France in the twenties.

JAY LEYDA is the translator and editor of the two Eisenstein books: *Film Sense* and *Film Form*. He has just completed a history of the Soviet Cinema.

VACHEL LINDSAY, widely known as a poet and reader of his own poems, wrote one of the first important books on movies: *The Art of the Moving Picture* (Macmillan Co., 1915).

DWIGHT MACDONALD, critic of life and letters is at present on the staff of *The New Yorker*.

KENNETH MACGOWAN, former play and movie producer is the author of several books on theater craft and anthropology.

HENRY MACMAHON was a feature writer for *The New York Times* in 1915.

DUDLEY NICHOLS is the outstanding screenwriter of *Stagecoach*, *The Informer*, etc.

HARRY ALAN POTAMKIN died in 1934. He contributed film criticism to *Close Up*, *New Masses*, *Hound and Horn*, etc.

HANS RICHTER is one of the old masters in the field of avant-garde movies.

HERMAN G. SCHEFFAUER was a correspondent for *The New York Times* in the twenties.

GILBERT SELDES is the author of numerous books on movies. At present he is director of The Annenberg School of Communications, at the University of Pennsylvania.

ANDRE SENNWALD was the motion picture editor of *The New York Times* in the mid-thirties.

SEYMOUR STERN, authorized biographer of D. W. Griffith, is the author of *The Griffith Index*, *The Screen's Creative Victory Over the Stage*, and many essays on Griffith and the movies; taught Motion Picture History and Film Technique at USC and UCLA, 1945-1955.

JAMES JOHNSON SWEENEY is director of The Solomon R. Guggenheim Museum in New York City.

SLAVKO VORKAPICH, formerly famed in Hollywood for his "montage effects" is at present making independent motion pictures.

RICHARD WATTS JR., is the drama editor of *The New York Post*.

HERMAN WEINBERG has written many articles on motion pictures for periodicals in America and Europe.